ANCIENT & MODERN

STEPHEN MUECKE holds a Chair in Cultural Studies at the University of Technology, Sydney, and is a Fellow of the Australian Academy of the Humanities. His books include (with Paddy Roe and Krim Benterrak) *Reading the Country: Introduction to Nomadology* (1984, 1996), *Textual Spaces: Aboriginality and Cultural Studies* (1992), the fictocritical *No Road (bitumen all the way)*, a translation of José Gil's *Metamorphoses of the Body* (1998) and the children's story *About this little devil and this little fella* edited for Albert Barunga (1999). He recently edited (with Adam Shoemaker) David Unaipon's *Legendary Tales of the Australian Aborigines* (2001). He is co-editor of *The Cultural Studies Review.*

ANCIENT & MODERN

TIME, CULTURE AND INDIGENOUS PHILOSOPHY

Stephen Muecke

UNSW PRESS

For my father

A UNSW Press book

Published by
University of New South Wales Press Ltd
University of New South Wales
Sydney NSW 2052
AUSTRALIA
www.unswpress.com.au

First published 2004

National Library of Australia
Cataloguing-in-Publication entry

Muecke, Stephen, 1951- .
Ancient & modern : time, culture and indigenous philosophy.
Includes index.
ISBN 0 86840 786 0.
1. Indigenous peoples - Philosophy. I. Title.

149

Cover design Di Quick
Text design Dana Lundmark
Cover image *Sexy and Dangerous,* © Brook Andrew, 1996, Licensed by VISCOPY, Australia 2004.
Printed and bound by CPI Group (UK) Ltd, Croydon, CR0 4YY

CONTENTS

Acknowledgements *vii*

Section One TIME 1

1 'Once I knew how the world worked' 3
2 When, or where, did modern Australian culture begin? 5
3 Why I am not a historian 8
4 The return to place 13
5 History's poison blanket 23
6 Performing life 29
7 Morning coffee with Clarrie 41
8 Devastation 43

Section Two COUNTRY 57

1 How do you get to Alice Springs? 59
2 '... a burly Salt Water woman of about my own age' 61
3 Towards the Centre 67
4 'OK if we camp here again?' 69
5 Landscape and country 71
6 Back to Rottnest 80
7 A character called '62 Pontiac Parisienne' 82
8 A space for ethics 91

Section Three TECHNOLOGY 95

1 'He thinks, he desires' 97
2 Indigenous capitalism 102
3 Travelling the subterranean river of blood 106

4 Life, abundant life 109
5 Boxer deconstructionist 120
6 Indigenous modernities 132
7 The religion of technology 140
8 'I don't think they invented the wheel': New Right assimilationism 142

Section Four PHILOSOPHY 153
1 Philosophy of the Other continent 155
2 Philosophical magic 159
3 Nomads 162
4 Secret English 163
5 Language as singular or general 169
6 Feelings of power 170
7 The Other continent 172
8 Philosophy from afar 173

Notes *179*

Selected Bibliography *191*

Index *194*

ACKNOWLEDGEMENTS

This essay (in four sections and eight subsections) has the modest aim of opening a door onto the possibility of indigenous philosophy as an area of study and experiment. To do this it plays tricks with time, and juxtaposes anecdotes and concepts. This is no journey towards any indigenous philosophy that might be out there somewhere in the bush, as if your narrator were just another whitefella on the quest for something to be discovered. So, in order to avoid coming back with *that* same old story, this philosophy will have to start here, in the middle of things.

As for you indigenous communities whose struggles for justice I am at all times mindful of, I am neither borrowing from you nor trying to give you anything, except in dialogue when I quote the words of your scholars and offer my own. In the end it will be up to the readers to make their own assemblages, just as I have, for here there can be no final word. Paddy Roe was the first mentor for me, a great and wise teller of tales.

I have spoken to quite a few people along the way who have offered their help or encouragement: Jeremy Beckett, Andrew Benjamin, Dipesh Chakrabarty, Gillian Cowlishaw, John W Durack, Gary Foley, Stephen Gapps, Devleena Ghosh, Liz Jacka, Brian Massumi, Fiona Probyn, Debbie Bird Rose, Noel Sanders, Katrina Schlunke, Adam Shoemaker and Mick Taussig. I am especially indebted to Gillian Cowlishaw, Angelique Edmonds and my father Doug Muecke for their thoughtful reading of the manuscript.

Philip Morrissey generously offered to be my ***kurdungurlu*** and co-author at one stage, and Angelique Edmonds worked as a research assistant in the summer of 2002–03. To her feisty arguments

I owe in particular the abandonment of the fragmentary and the adoption of situatedness and continuity; some of her words are in the text. Thanks also to Stephanie Bishop for research assistance, the Transforming Cultures Centre at UTS, a small grant from the Australian Research Council, the delegates at *Frontier Australia*, Darwin, 23 and 24 September (ANU/NARU) and the ANU Visiting Scholars program *Biophilosophy and the Politics of Life* and *Towards an Ecology of Practices* in July–August 2003. Many sections of the book have been published in earlier versions elsewhere.

Albert Namatjira, *Haast's Bluff* (c. 1956), with thanks to Legend Press. David Mowaljarlai's drawing, *Body of Australia*, from David Mowaljarlai and Jutta Malnic, *Yorro Yorro: Everything Standing up Alive, Spirit of the Kimberley*, Magabala Books, Broome, 1993, reproduced with permission.

Thanks to Shaun Wilson for permission to reproduce (on p. x) his video still from *Searching*, 2002–4.

Thanks to Gordon Bennett and Sutton Gallery, Melbourne, for permission to reproduce *Black Swan of Trespass*, from the *Home Decor* [Preston + de Stijl=Citizen] series, 1996.

All reasonable efforts were made to obtain permission to use copyright material reproduced in this book, but in some cases copyright holders could not be traced. The author welcomes information in this regard.

The Master Narrative of the US proclaims that there were no 'Indians' in the country, simply wilderness. Then, that the 'Indians' were savages in need of the US. Then, that the 'Indians' all died, unfortunately. Then, that the 'Indians' today are (a) basically happy with the situation, and (b) not the real 'Indians'.

Jimmie Durham, quoted in Laura Turney,
'Ceci n'est pas Jimmie Durham',
Critique of Anthropology, *vol. 19 (4), 1999, pp. 430–31.*

These outlaws, these peoples without a history, are frequently delivered to history by being marched through the defiles of a secular modernity. When they arrive at the signposts of progress, they are shorn of their stories and traditions; they are no longer hidden from history, but they have turned into spectral figures, transparent testimonies to the world triumph of a secular capitalist modernity.

Homi K. Bhabha, 'Foreword', in Dipesh Chakrabarty,
Habitations of Modernity: Essays in the wake of subaltern studies,
University of Chicago Press, 2002, p. xi.

Is an asphalt road modern? If a traditional peddler is walking on a modern road, does the road become more traditional or the peddler more modern? Both, either, neither?

Renato Rosaldo, 'Foreword', in Néstor García Canclini,
Hybrid Cultures: Strategies for entering and leaving modernity,
Minneapolis: University of Minnesota Press, 1995, p. xv.

Shaun Wilson, from *Searching*, <wilsonsp@postoffice.utas.edu.au>

SECTION 1

TIME

1

'ONCE I KNEW HOW THE WORLD WORKED'

In Rachel Perkins's remarkable film, *One Night the Moon*, Paul Kelly sings about not knowing how the world works any more:

> Once I knew what was wrong and right
> God was good, black was never white
> Once I knew what I was living for
> Now I don't know anything any more.[1]

Not knowing anything is a good place to start my little book about knowledge, a book that will attempt to build an architecture of thought incorporating the ancient and the modern. This architecture will have less tangible feelings in it as well as some kind of solid logic, just as the real architect knows that the people who will come to live in a new house will want to feel good in this space that will accommodate their bodies in movement. The house will thus reproduce a kind of culture, something that is by nature expansive rather than restrictive. The house will tell them stories as they move in from the cold weather outside and wander around, sit down, eat or go to bed.

There are expressions of the abstract that have concrete effects. When the architect thinks about the plans of the house, will he or she have to think about the transcendent, the 'up there', or elevation as a persistent idea immanent to Western cultures? This idea is a part of Bruno Latour's modernist idiom, which refers to the 'settlement between science, politics, ethics, and theology', a settlement 'built up' after the Enlightenment. Its conceptual architecture consists of

> [first] ... a world outside untouched by human hands and impervious to human history; second, a mind isolated inside its own mind striving to gain access to an absolute certainty about the laws of the world outside; third, a political world down there, clearly distinct from the world outside and from the mind inside, which is agitated by fads and passions, flares of violence and eruptions of desires, collective phenomena which can be quieted down only by bringing in the universal laws of science ...; and fourth, a sort of position 'up there' that serves as a warrant for the clear separation of the three spheres above, a view from nowhere occupied by either the God of ancient religions ... or the physicist-God [who makes] sure that there are always enough laws of physics to stop humans from behaving irrationally.[2]

My Australian ancient/modern world looks more like this: first, as seeing *country* so full of traces of life that nature is second nature and history is transformative potential (*a range of hills is always becoming a woman lying down is always becoming a blue-tongue lizard*);[3] second, as having a feeling of the immanence of life in and through worlds that fold in and through each other again and across time, life being movement and growth; third, as developing a generative and contingent politics gathering energy by multiple branching; and fourth, as installing the rule of the attractive concept,[4] empirically tested and problem-solving.

2

WHEN, OR WHERE, DID MODERN AUSTRALIAN CULTURE BEGIN?

Modernity must have come from the East, surely? When Captain James Cook, in his early modern conveyances, sailed out of the Pacific into Botany Bay in 1770 he was the bearer of new technology, ideas of progress and all-powerful science and reason. Modernity *must* have begun in Australia at this point, it must have flowed one-way from Europe, for the 'stone-age' inhabitants observing, laughing and resisting had nothing to offer in this encounter, at least that is what the wisdom of 220 years of colonisation has determined. They seemed to lack that philosophical, political, economic and industrial complex that was European modernity in full development at the time. In fact, they were seen, as were many other indigenous peoples, precisely as a primitive counterpoint to that modernity, defining it by contrast and confirming the Europeans' advantage. In this book I want to suggest that indigenous modernity is indeed possible, not as a full-blown political–industrial complex, but as a predisposition to (both) resistance and adaptation to the rapid changes introduced by invasion and colonisation. This modernity is quite distinct from European modernisation processes since it developed its own forms, later including modernist and postmodernist aesthetics.

Was there not a hint of disappointment when Cook writes '... they seem'd to set no value upon any thing we gave them, nor would they ever part with anything of their own for any one article we could offer them'? By definition indigenous people cannot be modern because they refuse to participate in the economy whose logic would have them, in the end, assimilating. We are careful now, in our relativistic way, not to designate the whole of European civilization as superior to the one it would largely displace, but we are happy to allow one of its minor but key concepts – the modern – to continue on a search-and-destroy mission. The indigenous Australians were not modern and are still not, as far as one of the protagonists in the following debate is concerned.

Under the banner 'KURNELL'S EUROPEAN SYMBOLS FACING AXE', we find a Sydney evening tabloid reporting on the plan from the National Parks and Wildlife Service to redesign the site where Cook landed.[5] The plan, *From Middens to Monuments*, will include the removal of trees such as Norfolk Island pines (they have a 'European look') to 'return the land to its original vegetation'. A new walkway will be built that better explains the foreshore monuments commemorating various figures on the Cook voyage and it will continue into the bush, telling stories of Aboriginal culture.

Malcolm Kerr, conservative MP for Cronulla, reacted in the press report by saying that these changes would be 'an example of "political correctness" ... I think they are downgrading Cook, and there should be a bit of equity in relation to history'. Then Mr Kerr added: 'Let's have more credit for Cook's achievements in a place that is the birthplace of modern Australian culture.'

In that historical event that was the encounter between two vastly different cultures, was the flow of ideas really all one way? No one has said that the indigenous peoples were passively accepting of the new arrivals, nor that they failed in their attempts to communicate. On the contrary, it seems they were very active from the start (if not very successful) in trying to teach, influence and assimilate the newcomers. They could only do this with a capacity for adaptation and change that was already in place at Kurnell. Maybe they were already modern in ways whitefellas still don't have words for. Cook's party offered items for trade (beads, mirrors, axes) and some magically modern items, such as astrolabes and guns, were in evidence. These were the artefacts of an emerging European modernity, one that was supposed to take over the world. It seems that the seeds of this modern culture have germinated and flourished in many places, but only bloom if the savage and foreign species in their way are regularly cleared to make way for the new ones. The victors continue to write history, which is why they cannot see that the 'others' may already have been as inventive as they were. Maybe they were just as modern and, when it comes to living in the world and drawing on its natural resources in a sustainable fashion, maybe indigenous ideas still have a lot to offer the newcomers.

3

WHY I AM NOT A HISTORIAN

Historian Dipesh Chakrabarty has recently asked: 'Can the designation of something or some group as *non-* or *premodern* ever be anything but a gesture of the powerful?'[6] He goes on to elaborate the specific forms this question might take for the history of a country such as India. I take up a similar task for Australia, hoping that what I say will be pertinent for indigenous peoples around the world and for the specific relationships of ancient and modern ways of living in the contemporary world. I aim to try things out rather than write down the truth because I think this is the only way to proceed honestly,[7] which means to proceed with a strong awareness of events around us and of how we can participate in them ethically.

I shall begin by trying to do without the mediation of historical thinking, this being a mode of thought elaborated largely by Western traditions, in which past and present are linked within the rhetoric of an illusory continuity, but which excludes most of the peoples of the world from participation. In the process it often puts these others in a position of weakness or lack and in an historical catch-up position. Thinking of cultures synchronically, rather than in terms of competitive historical progress, means one has to consider how co-existing cultures, in the same country, are related to each other strucutrally and how their values are ordered.

Like the historians, I too shall work with continuity, but this continuity is something I associate more with the category of place than time. Why? Because Australians (and perhaps other colonials) feel less allegiance to any imperial history emerging from Europe, because we have seen specific histories emerge only though listening to the local guides (they tell us you must go to the place first; how else can you know?) and because thinking about place-based continuity seems more sustainable in its key ecological and ethical perceptions. In short, one lives in a place more than in a time (I feel it is more vital to my sense of self to live in Sydney, for example, than it is to live in 2004, or even 'now').

Australia will be my most important focus because I write from here and because of a curious contingency: the European settlement of Australia occurred at precisely the time in history when the European Enlightenment in the late eighteenth century created a new temporality via a major philosophical rupture to usher in an age of European modernity and scientific rationalism that would put all 'primitive' superstition behind it.[8] As explorers and scientists, armed with this new theory, arrived in Australia they discovered here a nature and a culture that they were constrained to see as ancient because of the conventions of their own emergent modernity. So while the European enlightenment staged the first debate to be called a 'quarrel between Ancients and Moderns', it is still with us in a new form, I maintain, as the more global struggle between indigenous and late capitalist philosophies.

So Europe was in the birth throes of what it came to call its modern culture just as it began to disseminate it as civilisation to Australia, a nation that now stands as a key example of the discontinuity between ancient and modern ways of being in the world. The indigenous peoples of Australia are ambivalently representative of the most ancient the world has to offer, while the whitefellas who took their lands like to think of themselves, like whites in India or Africa did, and still do, as bearers of an unambiguous modernity. I shall argue that this modernity is actually, by definition, contradictory and partial, and always incorporates forms of antiquity in ways suggested by Walter Benjamin's slogan, 'Modernity possesses antiquity like a nightmare that creeps over it.' I suggest that this incorporation or possession is not traumatic, but rather essential to, and productive of, all forms of lived culture.

An old wagon wheel decorates the front garden of a suburban home. This bygone object has an aura of antiquity and emblematically installs a historical dimension to an otherwise everyday modern setting. It is a counterpoint. Uluru has a similar function on a national level, powerfully shimmering in its ambivalence, both natural and cultural, and claimed by indigenous owners, the tourist industry and The Nation. The ceremonies that regularly take place at its foot unify the nation, not in the name of the modernity epitomised by the big cities, but in the name of the ancient, the unchanging and the natural, which we can all know in the same way. Except for the lore of *kuniya* and *liru*, which remains obscure to most people: the oldest stories about the place that would rupture that superficial national consensus.

Our antiquities, which are still with us, not only give us the impression of profundity in culture, but can also deliver great vitality to the present. Likewise our modernity is not a smooth existence, but is punctuated by events (temporal nodes) that knot and bind our energies in rituals that are still structured as the most primitive ceremonies. Michel Serres, that 'troubadour of knowledge', says, 'every historical era is … simultaneously drawing from the obsolete, the contemporary, and the futuristic. An object, a circumstance, is thus polychronic, multitemporal, and reveals a time that is gathered together with multiple pleats.'[9]

The question is: What kind of antiquity is Australia's modernity incorporating? This is the question that defines the very nature of Australian culture, for, if in the early years of national consciousness 'our' antiquity was clearly European, this is no longer the case. For many reasons indigenous antiquity can now make a valid counterclaim. We are at a time of transition in this respect; now, the quarrel over national identity is as forceful as it will perhaps ever be. If I ask what distinguishes indigenous and non-indigenous orientations to the world, it is not to keep them apart, it is to ask what modes of relatedness between them are possible in a country such as Australia. While the anthropological vision generally labours to clarify the differences between the two sets of cultures and to describe each culture separately, I want to set up a mode of relating that can, rather, go to and fro on equal terms.

This will involve asking questions about the *milieu*, a useful French word (much exploited in the philosophy of Gilles Deleuze and Félix Guattari) because it means 'middle', 'surroundings' and 'medium' (as in artistic media). So I want to ask questions about the potential space of the in between, the (external) conditions for the emergence of things and the nature of the cultures in which things and beings are 'grown'.[10]

Where might a whitefella understanding of an Aboriginal way of Being in the World begin? If we called it 'Aboriginal philosophy', would the name itself – a combination of words of Latin and Greek origin – indicate that it acknowledges being a whitefella discourse, or would it simply look like another foreign and culturally inappropriate category? For this project I have my own philosophical prejudices. I am not interested in finding systems of thought in Aboriginal philosophy, or cosmologies, or sequences of logical propositions. My prejudice tends more towards the pragmatic and ethical, towards 'philosophy as a way of life'.[11] Looking at various texts that give accounts of indigenous cultures, I will not be trying to boil them down to foundational principles, trying to establish models or methodologies for an indigenous philosophy, but rather to see in a series of events, sometimes, the many aspects and expressions of the indigenous or concrete exercises in Aboriginal becoming, or indigenous ways of being in the world or ways of conducting oneself as an indigenous person. These are things I should brush lightly by, without pronouncing upon. It is not the place of the outsider to do that; it is insulting to those who want to retain the power of their cultures. But in the *milieus* I can forestall efforts (for instance, in the name of assimilation) to suppress cultural discontinuities or differences and, conversely, resist the relativist temptation to celebrate difference for its own sake or compel respect for differences as 'interesting' curiosities or as witnesses of bygone days.

For a moment I want to forget about the determining content and disciplinary allegiances of anthropology, history or literature and say that there are only specific situations, events, objects and bodies of texts and treat them pragmatically as things that inspire action as well as 'contain meaning'.[12] This involves a collapsing of subject and object, observer and observed, so that they mutually transform in the immanence of fields of the present.[13] I want to leave behind the distant shores that would give us 'objective' views on 'reality', even though, it seems, in arriving in our here and now, the Western theory, which has given us so many good ideas, is still there with us, like an old friend with whom you can still have a good laugh.

While in Australia there is a surface debate about the meaning of history, deeper narratives seem to obey an atemporal logic, behaving more like natural phenomena, slowly, like climactic change, or powerfully, like sudden storms. Greg Dening, an historian of the imagination rather than a collector of facts or factoids, says that

> Some of the things we have to imagine are the deep narratives that engulf our cultural experience. Sometimes deep narratives are mistaken for the Unconscious, but the Unconscious is too much a creation of model-makers to be real. Deep narratives are not unconscious. Deep narratives are consciously present to us, but always in transformed ways. That is why it takes imagination to see them.[14]

Our renewed historical imagination can go wide as well as deep. I am thinking also of a collective and polyphonic history, as described by Jean Starobinski:

> The possibility of a polyphony in which the virtually infinite interlacing of destinies, actions, thoughts and reminiscences would rest on a bass line that chimed the hours of the terrestrial day, and marked the position that used to be (and could still be) occupied there by ancient ritual.[15]

'Deep narrative' and 'ancient ritual'. It seems to me our complex being-in-the-world is – if you will excuse such preposterous philosophising – composed (like music) of layerings of ancient forms and imaginative inventions. It oscillates between the ancient and the modern. And in a country such as Australia you have to ask: Whose ancient forms? Whose modern inventions? It is a challenge to express both at the same time. What goes into writing the narratives of culture and of history so that this writing might, in some mysterious way, take on proportions and swell in volume to express a poetic force? Simple truth is not enough to answer to power; something more like creative events are needed to answer back to the blunt force – the primitivism – of the singular fundamentalism that tends to assert that 'we' are ahead of the Others. These questions are about the resurgence of the ancient in our dreams, like images from an epic poem. If this poem still sings to us of our humanity and of our virtues, it is one that may retune our listening in such a way that a certain type of continuity may be recovered through the recognition that modern societies are always also quite ancient.

4

THE RETURN TO PLACE

Time and space are axiomatic philosophical concepts, possibly in any philosophy. Different definitions, values and ideologies can be attached to them. But even to the extent that humans have made them into mathematically universal concepts, they are not habitable as such. We live in places and times (places more than times, as I contend) and certainly not spaces. Living in a space would literally be like living in a triangle or a cube. In recent years place has made a comeback in Western thought and Edward Casey's work, *Getting Back Into Place*, presents a strong argument for this. Places are ontologically singular: the world is replete with places, from the strongly settled, such as cities, to the more ephemeral places that shimmer into being as they are created by a dividing line, a wall or a hollow in the ground where a kangaroo might have spent the night. Gaston Bachelard, in his classic phenomenological study, *The Poetics of Space*, almost universalises one kind of place, the house, as fundamental to the psyche, but it is a particular culture being elevated here, as there is no doubt about the love and personal history going into his descriptions of French village and city dwellings.[16]

A world without places is unthinkable. The horror of the void can be experienced personally – when one is lost – and what is threatened is a loss of identity and direction. Migrants and refugees experience the trauma of placelessness to different degrees, buoyed only by the hope of eventually being able to come and go as they please in their own place. At a more collective level we find all cultures emplaced according to their own patterns and, in Australia, the so-called nomadic culture of the Aboriginal tribes was not one the British colonisers knew how to recognise. The British invented the designation of *terra nullius*, empty land, 'nowhere', to justify their occupation, effacing in the process the specific modes of emplacement of Aboriginal cultures, which is tantamount to effacing the people themselves: if they are nowhere, where are they dwelling?

European occupation proceeded with spatial technologies, metrical instruments of surveying and measuring. These could be considered a kind of ritual of occupation if one thought for a moment about sciences too being certain kinds of cultures; this is what whitefellas did to consecrate places as their own. Out of a scientific knowledge of space they thus created places. What they thought they were doing was letting science encounter nature without the mediation of any kind of culture (least of all indigenous ones). In this disembodied act a new modern life was conjured into being: 'Through the mediation of scientific objectivity, technical efficiency and economic profitability, anybody could join this fatherland without ancestors, this ethnic group without rituals, this country without borders; this country of reason …'[17]

But let us retain the idea that ritual connects people to place and that this happens not only with traditional ceremonies, but also modern ones. Let us also retain the idea that, while the concepts of space and time are somewhat abstract and universal, places are specific and contiguous to their human inhabitants who make them meaningful through ritual. Pause for a moment on 'human'. The English were right, the Aborigines were not quite human. In the philosophical sense of being a people without an intellectual discourse of humanism that was used to putting Man at the centre of the world and above Nature. But if it is true that place has a renewed significance in Western thought, it may be because this complex body of thought, without borders, has finally become aware of the survival of so-called traditional societies and that it is these very societies that have insisted, in arguments to Western powers, that their sustainability depends on retaining their places. Suddenly, we find place elevated to more universal significance, especially in a powerful combination with global indigenous and ecological movements.

In indigenous Australian country, where such sustainability has existed for thousands of years, time has none of the urgency of the imperial power seeking to improve quickly its capacity to exploit nature. Could it have been that the displacement that characterised imperial expansion brought with it an intensification of the sense of linear time, as well as a codification, in the books of History, of what would eventually be called 'historical consciousness'?

Tony Swain, working in studies of religion and setting up an opposition between Western Time and Aboriginal Place, sees the origin of linear time as a fall from place. In support of this he offers a seminal historical example:

> History, associated quintessentially with the Hebrews, was something which intervened when the Israelites had lost their place. The covenant, God's promise, was to reinstate place, but this was only feasible by the Godhead entering a world given over to time. From the moment God said to Abraham, 'Leave your country', instead of their place the Hebrews had history and a promise of a land ...[18]

The thesis of Swain's book is that, through the relationships with strange visitors, Aboriginal peoples have adapted their way of being to accommodate different versions of strangeness and that these changes, by and large, have involved the incorporation of cumulative time.

For instance, he argues that the treatment of the dead in places where place seems less influenced by imported versions of time, there are rituals that return the focus of death to place, where death would otherwise 'logically' mark the passage of time (as well as, like birth from a human mother, privileging corporeal individuality):

> Desert traditions oppose 'lineage' by eradicating the social memory of the dead with extensive taboos against referring to their past existence. Generations are therefore not amassed and thus in turn cannot (no more than uncounted seasons or other natural rhythms) constitute the measured units of time. To the North, however, where memorials are made to celebrate the dead, we hear the whisper of time ...[19]

Here identity and being do not emphasise genealogy (identity stretching back through parents or grandparents), but tend more towards maintaining the relationship to the deceased through their country, connecting country in a web of relatedness overlapping with the structure of kinship:

> The basic tenet ... as Nancy Munn has perceptively shown, is that something came out of, moved across, and went into the earth. Graphically, Desert societies render this by employing two basic iconic elements: the concentric circle representing sites and lines standing for tracks between sites. In the boldest of terms, Aboriginal ontology rests upon the maxim that a place-being emerged, moved, and established an abode ...[20]

Aboriginal people in the desert, specifically the Warlpiri who Munn speaks of, believe human lives follow this path. Children are born from the ancestor's spirit emerging from the ground, relating a person with their place of birth (and incurring the responsibilities of care for that country) and that, upon their physical, corporeal death, their spirit returns to that place. This is why, upon death, the emphasis is shifted away from the body and towards place as the enduring location of their spirit. Their name is replaced by the term *kumanjayi* as a speech restriction, enacted so as not to contain the deceased in their last physical location, but to allow an unhindered return journey of their spirit back to their place of origin from whence their spirit emerged. The safe return of their spirit is imperative to the wellbeing of the place so that it may continue as an enduring life source and again be the site from where life will continue to emerge.

Now, movement is more important to Aboriginal modes of being than territoriality, and lines (or pathways of movement) more than boundaries, as I have argued before on the basis of 'nomadic' rather than settled civic life.[21] But Swain gives further reasons. 'Why must place move? There seem to be two facets to the answer to this question. The first is intentionality. Place itself is stretched by conscious action.'[22] The Ancestor moves, for example, in order to transform into something else. Ancestor travels, either real or projected, link these places one to another, whereas human manifestations of spirit most often emerge from and return at the same place with various trips in the course of one's life. What maintains the relationships between places is the maintenance of kinship, the interconnected web of kin and country and the roles of custodianship (*kirda* [owner] and *kurdungurlu* [manager]).

> The second reason why place must move is to relate sites ... the Ancestors do not move *from* one place *to* another but rather they link sites by common intentionality of place ... the Aranda person 'believes in the simultaneous presence of the Ancestor at each of the many scenes which once witnessed the fullness of his supernatural powers. [Strehlow][23]

The Aranda (now spelled Arrernte) understanding of the simultaneous presence of an Ancestor in many places is indicative of the absence of cumulative time and an understanding that presence can be held in place, enduring. Since country endures, is always already there, place becomes the horizon of temporality against which human finitude finds a rhythm. Country can hold several moments simultaneously, just as an Ancestor may be present at many places simultaneously. So indigenous Australian time, while not metrical, was periodised nonetheless and enacted in rituals that brought out Ancestral power in ever-tightening rhythms, from the slowest cycle of the ancient dreaming, to the cycle of generations, to the life of one custodian, to the seasonal ritual cycle to the song cycle itself and its repeated phrasings and stamping of feet into the earth. Deborah Bird Rose adds intensification and life to her perception of Yarralin time:

> Time, rather than being rendered static or absent, becomes experientially and overwhelmingly focussed, present and shared. The person flips from being an actor in time to becoming a heartbeat of time, and the whole on-going systole and diastole of life/time pours into and through persons, places and other living things. Perhaps time itself is a sound, a wave, a call that is pulled into specific places ...[24]

Swain is tempted to call such rituals Abiding Events, in which 'there was no fashioning of time, linear or cyclical, but rather a sophisticated patterning of events in accordance with their rhythms'.[25]

Time is not opening out into an unknown future, but is intensifying onto the present moment down through concentric circles of forces and meanings. The song and dance happening now have their reference in the place, the dreaming, the kin group and so on. So, as with naturalist Aldo Leopold's 'land ethic', as explored by Deborah Bird Rose,[26] 'the humans who are of a land's stuff do not, and cannot, exclusively control that site. The immediate result is relationship',[27] relationships to things, animate and inanimate, in the kinship system. And the other result is that war in the form of territorial conquest is impossible in this logic for, as people embody country, it is impossible to appropriate another person's being. Being and belonging have not yet been prised loose from country in such a way that would both permit those sorts of appropriations of country (in representation, for example) *and* allow for survival of individuals' identity where homelands are lost: 'Structured locative interdependence means to consume other people/lands is to destroy the world-pattern upon which one depends.'[28]

What Swain then goes on to look at in following chapters is the effect of strangers upon an ontology of place in its individual, social and cosmological levels. It must be cautioned that 'cosmology' is a non-Aboriginal term that encapsulates a European enlightenment thrust to systematically explain cultures as totalities from a reflective distance, positioning the speaker as outside of and thus able to see the (conceptual) whole. But cultures are not lived as totalities; they are better conceived of as partially acquired skills and attributes. The indigenous emphasis on participation and a world lived-in means an absence of the reflective distance that allows terms such as 'cosmos' and 'cosmology' to describe, in a singular term, the relatedness of all that is. The discussion of Aboriginal 'cosmos' is an imposition that continues with Swain: 'Cosmologically, the continuum starts to shift from the uncompromisingly locative Abiding place to the temporalised Utopian vision.'[29]

However, the forms that time starts to take through contact with various strangers such as Macassans, Torres Strait islanders, Timorese and, of course, Europeans, involves, as Swain sees it, a dangerous dislocation from place and reorientation of being in time. This is shown in the performance of various new ceremonial cults or even, simply, the invention of a single god, for instance *baiami*, around the most colonised parts of southeastern Australia:

> For a people who had lost much of their lands and most of their kinfolk, the High God's elevation from the land was simultaneously a rise beyond localised affiliations and a politico–religious premise which theoretically could, and in other hands has, embraced or conquered worlds.[30]

Baiami was modern, not by virtue of when he appeared, but because we can see from the description that he is clearly a highly inventive syncretic figure; it is harder to tell that about earlier aspects of culture we have become used to calling traditional or classical. We learn from Swain's source that he 'dwells in heaven on a throne of transparent crystal surrounded by beautifully carved pillars from which emanate the colours of the rainbow'.

Swain's politico–religious figure, which conflates the Christian God and colonialist expansion, is uncompromising in this instance and could be tempered by descriptions of local and more benign and humanist Christian traditions associated with village life and pastoral care. Nevertheless, he helps develop a description of the power of a representation that is portable (therefore not a fixed representation at all in that sense) in a way also suggested by new historicist Stephen Greenblatt describing the bringing of crucifixion images to the New World.

Greenblatt captures the dreadful beauty of Christianity: 'a religious ideology centred on the endlessly proliferated representation of a tortured and murdered god of love.'[31] Columbus and company, bearing flags and crosses, were literally armed with these representations, along with an immense confidence in the centrality (yet speed of expansion) of their own culture. And let's not forget that one of the holiest mysteries of the Christian church of Rome, the Eucharist, is the symbolic cannibalism of this 'god of love'; it was this strange concept that was imposed by force on incredulous 'savages', their death often marking the end of one era and the beginning of another. As the Christians continue the ancient chant that He gave His life so that you may live, the life promised is, of course, eternal, individual, Father-oriented (Oedipal) and an *after* life, a paradise on which you would hesitate to put a down-payment with any real estate agent.

Millenarian cults were modern inventions in Aboriginal Australia in the late nineteenth century. They unravelled concentric circle time to give it an endpoint, which involved inventing new hybrid rituals. We find, according to Swain's sources, the emergence of cults that were frightening for their participants. For instance, the *Mulunga* seems to be based on the shooting of Aborigines; the dancers, who carry forked sticks like rifles, are 'destroyed' by the cult hero. The imperative to participate in this ceremony as it spreads around the countryside is compelling; it is announced that everyone who hasn't seen the ceremony (including all the whites) will die. Yet, as a ceremony not based at a specific site, its power to spread could have the effect of displacing more traditional ceremonies, which are essentially locative. Swain further speculates that the genesis of *Mulunga* lies in the 1884 massacre of the *Kalkatungu* at Battle Mountain. Here, supposedly, war took place in which hundreds of warriors died. As the survivors regrouped their strength, they invented a powerful modern response, the travelling cult. But is this confirmatory historical 'truth' really necessary? Does it provide comfort for whitefella ways of seeing the world by returning the phenomenon in question to the available documentary sources?

Another example, that of the cult called *Djulurru*, sees

> ceremonies begin with the women distant from the main camp. The men huddle to consult a piece of paper, *mili* [mail], which when opened reveals a drawing of a dancer and the words

> '8 o'clock'. The women receive a similar letter, and thus the Business starts with a White message form announcing an onset symbolically co-ordinated by clock time.[32]

As philosophical exemplars these Europeans of the frontier can present only the most rudimentary rituals and languages, a kind of 'white trash' (there was no Opera House in the Kimberley all those years ago, no education to speak of), but the Aboriginal cult seems to be able to produce a fascinating transformation of it:

> *Djulurru* dresses in white in the style of a cowboy, complete with hat and pistols. He variously rides his white steed or his motorbike, and he consumes vast amounts of alcohol ... While his ceremonies are being performed, *Djulurru* travels in adjacent areas recruiting those who have avoided his conscripting tradition and playing havoc with European technology. On the one hand he is something of a saviour, for if an initiates car runs out of oil or petrol, the Father will come to their rescue. On the other hand ... a pearl shell ... could be used to cause cars to crash when drivers failed to offer the person who carried it a lift. The shell was kept in company with another said to depict serpents and aeroplane propellers.[33]

These cults will be important in the examination of Aboriginal philosophy because of the way in which certain practices or exercises are incorporated as ways of being Aboriginal in connection with European ways. These cults are not primitive representations of European ways, rather, they mobilise all the transformative force of the mimetic, as described by Taussig in *Mimesis and Alterity*.[34] The event generates its own kind of ritualistic magic, where 'mimetic excess' mobilises 'human capacit[ies]', and where the participants are 'neither subject nor object of history but as both, at one and the same time'.

The *djulurru* 'participants' are just that: they are living and animating the experiences. But a phrase like 'onerous trials of deprivation' in the text below gives the ceremony a Christian asceticism:

> neophytes are referred to as 'prisoners' and those thus captured are kept in a shelter referred to as the 'prison'. In the days before the singing and dancing begins, the inmates are put through a series of onerous trials of deprivation, including spending extensive periods lying immobile (hence 'Sleeping Business') under the watchful eye of the 'policemen'.[35]

The functionalist residue of this language ('referred to'; the scare quotes) makes the ritual sound as if it is not real, that it is a mere construction invented for some purpose other than its own, a purpose that 'we', with anthropological or historical knowledge, are moving towards, as if we were free of the obscured vision that primitives participating in ritual must have.

This participation is, however, the expression of the necessary process that all human beings are involved in as they are involved in the world, as neither subject nor object, but mutually implicated. Mary Graham, as we have seen, usefully strips the word 'culture' of metaphor and reminds us that it is all about growing things. We make things grow in the country so that we can live off them, and Aboriginal English vernacular also speaks of 'growing up' children, an active verb expressing the responsibility of educators. Children, plants, animals and things must all be made to 'grow up' in country.

Dreaming stories, ritual acts and experiences are the forms of expression of indigenous Australian philosophies. By 'expression' I do not mean the representation or construction of some pre-given content or essence, I mean the expressions are the dreaming. 'This is my country,' an artist will say with pride in front of her canvas, and there is a crucial sense in which she does not mean this is a representation of my country, she means that this very object – the painting – carries some of that country's vitality (power-to-grow) with it always.

Vitalism, in early biological thinking, was the idea that there was some indefinable essence in living things which made them grow, and it gave way eventually to a more mechanistic and scientific idea that an explanation of the operation of all the parts would explain the life of plants. Scientists are yet to succeed in the process of putting all those parts together to explain 'life'. In the meantime I borrow the idea of vitalism to stress the process of living as experiential and experimental. Vitalism is the surprise of the new concept that animates thought, just as the hunter is alert to, yet surprised by, the animal suddenly 'standing up' in the scrub. This then is a philosophy of process in attendance to a complex, networked world of living beings and inanimate things. It has no universal principles of judgement, nor any atomistic indivisible parts that everything can be analysed down into. It looks not to the transcendental heavens for the higher concept (for concepts, like things, are of this world) nor to future or past ideals. Is it possible that a vitalistic philosophy (bringing together both scientific and humanistic thought) could both precede and supersede both objectivist science and the reaction to it that was literary romanticism?

The indigenous Australian creation stories – just like the ceremonial songs which are chanted as one travels the country, encountering sacred sites – keep a multiple sense of being in flux. People can be sure about their belonging in places; historical time becomes far less important. The power that created the world resides in these physical locations. When an Aboriginal man or woman travels to one of these sacred places they put their bodies in the locus of creation and of continuity, and thus the power that resides there not only recognises them but also inspires them to act.

5

HISTORY'S POISON BLANKET

Australian history is a non-event, relatively speaking, Australian history, that is, conceived of as the spinning out of a narrative of settlement and progress beginning in 1788. A couple of hundred years out of how many millennia of human civilisation here?

Once that history is pushed back beyond and across the frontiers of the original and often lawless violence that founded the state, it crumbles and disintegrates; it cannot be the same kind of history. There is, for a start, a polyphony of untranslated languages and there are layerings of legends and myths. Some historians, most famously Henry Reynolds, are enlightened by a change of perception as they start to glimpse what an 'Aboriginal point of view' looking across those frontiers might have been like. As we have found time after time a change of perception can create a new paradigm in history writing (otherwise no labour history, no feminist history could have emerged). Others find new sources in the documentary evidence to complement this change of perception. Reactionary historians come along and try to debunk both the change of perception and the new evidence.[36] It all seems so ephemeral: all we are left with, really, are the bones in the dry rocky hills of the country. These are the signs of an ancient world, which we see from the shores of our modernity, whose 'sinister glamour' can rub off so easily as indigenous Australians reinvent themselves in all sorts of ways, some quite shocking, as Ross Gibson sees the Native Police:

> On the frontier, the Native Police imbibed whatever they wanted: grog, black women, the astonishing extension of power poised to spring from a loaded gun, the ravenous brigandry of rogue male companionship. For a brief time they were supermen, distance-consuming, machine-strong with

> personal armament, transcendent of the laws constraining most people (blacks and whites), and therefore they felt unrestrained, beyond good and evil. In short, they were singular modernists, with no allegiance to the past and no responsibility in the present.[37]

That such an image of Aborigines as 'singular modernists' could emerge after only three decades of the study of Aboriginal History shows the diversity and richness of the field today, but was it such a gift to Aboriginal peoples that initially their history was brought into being as a prehistory to European settlement? Or that, in the early 1980s, '20 000 years' became a mantra of truth? Nevertheless, Captain Cook histories of exploration and discovery have been displaced and, with that triumphalism deflated, history, anthropology and the law combined in a powerful way to create the conditions whereby the 1992 Mabo judgment could become a reality and *terra nullius* denied.[38]

From the beginning, history has been wielded against Aboriginal peoples as something they, along with other non-Western peoples, lacked. And much more recently too as something they and their sympathetic historians failed to get right.[39] The Hegelian assertion excluding non-Europeans from history needs to be qualified. There was no traditional indigenous history in the sense of a set of texts setting out a linear chronology of events. But as we have seen there certainly was, and is, a radically different sense of time in its graphic, oral and ceremonial forms, which are ways of connecting past events to ones taking place in the here and now. This historical attitude is not just produced as a set of texts, oral or written, it is produced, rather, more ritually or ceremonially.

So Aboriginal peoples and the colonisers had radically different philosophical orientations. Let us hazard that, while Aboriginal peoples were anchored by place, the Europeans were busy marking time. There were technological and philosophical aspects to the Europeans' activity. The technological includes the need for the invention of chronometers to make the fixing of longitude possible in navigation; it also includes timetabling of the working day, calendars and so on. The philosophical includes the positioning of imperial activity at the endpoint of a linear forward-thrusting history. The philosopher Giorgio Agamben would call these technological and philosophical positions an 'experience of time':

> Every culture is first and foremost a particular experience of time, and no new culture is possible without an alteration of this experience. The original task of a genuine revolution, therefore, is never merely to 'change the world', but also – and above all – to 'change time'.[40]

Revolution – genuine or not, good or bad – certainly has the effect of marking an event that periodises. Henceforth, things will not be the same as they were and, with typical idealism, the future will be brighter. But this 'revolutionary' effect is an unfortunate feature of modernity to the extent that any powerful figure can attempt to erase (or idealise) the past as they create their own arrival as a turning point. The modern future is one that is pure and full of light and its past, by contrast, is replete with superstition, outdatedness or error. The genocides and totalitarian regimes of the twentieth century provided some motivation for this forgetful aspect of modern temporality. As it moved to the postwar disillusion in the narratives of progress and a mistrust of history itself, temporalities became juxtaposed in a debate that took us back to the turn of the eighteenth century and the crisis of human consciousness, which was the quarrel between the Ancients and the Moderns.[41]

The early 1980s in Australia saw such a revolutionary change in time. For some people this experience was ephemeral, for others it was deeply felt, but in any case the germ of a new Australian culture was born. It began in 1968 with the discovery of an ancient human cremation at Lake Mungo; by 1982, with the publication of *The Other Side of the Frontier*, Henry Reynolds had pioneered a new history. 'Twenty thousand years' became an activist slogan that had the effect of stretching national time back into the distant past, crossing an intellectual frontier (just as the real 'bush' one was disappearing), indigenising history and creating new beginnings for the national story. This process of changing Australia's time by awakening a past has not gone all the way to completion; further steps could be taken, steps that broaden and consolidate the process and, in some ways, make it less the business of historians and more the business of philosophers, for it is not just a question of extending a timeline or uncovering a new archive. This new time is tied in with questions of justice (sovereignty), meaning, ceremony and nationhood.

Chakrabarty speaks philosophically, yet as a historian, when he listens to complex voices in subaltern pasts, murmuring in the background, as Marxist historians take a peasant revolt of the Santal people in nineteenth century Bengal to be an instance of a modern revolutionary consciousness at work. Flip to the archival documents and here are the peasants' words, clearly insisting that they were acting under the inspiration of their god Thakur. Their actions and their history have a supernatural dimension, which we moderns can nevertheless understand because 'we have a pre-theoretical, everyday understanding [of this dimension] because the supernatural, or the divine, as principles, have not disappeared from the life of the modern'.[42] In other words, as Bruno Latour says, 'we moderns' (who 'have never been modern') have a continuity with the premoderns; it is just that our historicism keeps us busy drawing and redrawing the boundaries between nature and culture. As Jane Bennett, drawing on Latour, says,

> Modernity, an inconsistent and paradoxical combination of claims about nature and culture, passes itself off as the clean, enlightened alternative to a messy, primitivistic cosmology that confuses the natural with the cultural, mixes the animal with the human, mistakes the animate for the inanimate, and contaminates the moral with the prudential.[43]

Latour reminds us that modernity too is a kind of cosmology, as cited earlier in this book as the 'modernist settlement'. Latour and Bennett use the morphing of hybrid beings as evidence for the messy complexity of both the modern and ancient worlds. I prefer to stress the spatiotemporal complexity of processes, such as rituals that condense and intensify moments of (total) primitivity or disperse into that pluralisation that marks modern social inventions such as democracy.

Chakrabarty argues for the complexity of time to be written into historians' accounts and for the peculiar contemporaneity of Others to become part of understandings giving rise to 'forms of democracy that we cannot yet either completely understand or envisage'.[44] One kind of polity is not the destiny for all moderns; our times are complex because we find the slow cycles of sacred time juxtaposed with the rapidity of commodity time coexisting. Indian democracy is accented by such differing temporalities, which is understood in the lived experience of the people as well as by the cultural analyst. But white Australia still tends to hold indigenous time at arm's length as it imagines for itself a uniform and dominant modernity.

The production of cross-cultural historical knowledge is not just an epistemological problem concerning the foundations for knowledge (principles we can settle on in order to work from them), but it is also an evolving temporal one occurring in rituals such writing an historical essay. It is therefore crucial continually to contrast accounts of ways in which other peoples come to know things with ways in which Europeans' institutions organise knowledge rituals; this is one of the strategies of this book. For instance, about 50 years ago linguist TGH Strehlow reported an account of a promising pupil of Arrernte knowledge:

> The old men took me apart from the other young men of my own age at an early date. They showed me many gurra ceremonies which they withheld from the other members of my bandicoot clan because they were still too young. I remember their teachings well. I often had my veins opened to supply blood for the ceremonies. I dutifully paid large meat-offerings for the instruction that I had received. Some of the ceremonies were too secret to be shown even to ordinary men of the bandicoot clan ... My elders kept repeating these ceremonies time and again in my presence: they were afraid that I might forget them.[45]

Now, while university students don't come to seminars with large meat-offerings or open their veins (rather, the state bleeds them with tuition fees), it is more significant that the exhortation here is to remember the sacred text exactly through mimeticism and the practice of constant and creative repetition. In university seminars students are urged to put the text in their own words, to contribute, eventually, to the endless proliferation of commentary, which is the European way of sacralising texts, to renovate the classic text by making it 'mean something' in the contemporary context, coordinating the responses of other commentators, finding a new relevance for a theory by attaching it to a new object, in other words: dis*place*ment. So what is interesting for me in both cases is not core knowledge as such, but ways of practising knowledge repetitively, keeping it alive. If I were to risk a generalisation I would say Aboriginal philosophy is all about keeping things alive in their place.

We could therefore ask a question of ways of knowing something like 'Australian history'. Which is more important: the existence of major historical texts on library shelves or the way in which they get activated as social memory through rituals such as annual final year school examinations as rites of passage?[46] Or, indeed, does the Gallipoli episode get reinforced as an Australian foundation myth more through the annual ritual of the ANZAC Day dawn services and the march or through the books, films and school excursions?

6

PERFORMING LIFE

Lloyd Robson's *History of Tasmania,* despite its two volumes, omits any reference to the Hobart Carnival of 1910.[47] It is, however, of significance in the research into the life and writings of David Unaipon, a South Australian I have been researching for a few years with my colleagues Adam Shoemaker and Harold Kropinyeri. There are two reasons for our interest. One is that Unaipon's visit to the Carnival is another brief and scantily documented episode in his peripatetic life. The other will cause us to reflect on processes of historical representation. It seems that Unaipon was not supposed to appear there as himself, so to speak. He, along with the 11 other Ngarindjerri, who travelled across Bass Strait in the late summer of 1910 on the S.S. *Manuka*, were invited to perform semi-theatrically in the carnival as representatives of their race and thus to be an indigenous presence in a state that had failed to have the foresight to retain a few representatives of its own 'full-blood' population for exhibition purposes.

Who was Unaipon? When he 'dressed up' for performance purposes, in a white surplice to preach or, for everyday purposes, in a three-piece suit, what did the Others think? How complex were his motives? Here is another possibility: 'In times past the shamans warded off danger by means of images imitating that danger,' says Michael Taussig.[48]

At a high point of the carnival, there was a historic pageant, documented on film[49] and which represented the history of Tasmania beginning with the seventeenth century exploration of Abel Tasman. Professional actors and many local amateurs dressed up to represent, first, the history of the Dutch at Batavia, including an elaborate display of Javanese ballet, then the various episodes of Tasmanian history, represented in discrete scenes, which included 'large models of the Dutch ships *Heemskerk* and *Zeehaen* pass[ing] along the stage by means of an ingenious mechanical contrivance'.[50] The *Mercury* of 12 February 1910 reported that the Historic Pageant was

> the first thing of the kind ever undertaken in Tasmania, and, on a large scale, in Australia. In the Old Country historical pageants are common, as it has been found that they possess great educational influences. They are, in fact, looked on as a connecting link between the church and the stage, and sometimes they are carried out on a magnificent scale ... Australian scenery, as a rule, does not lend itself to displays of this nature as we lack the sylvan beauties of England.

Historical pageantry had emerged in England by 1905, with Louis Napoleon Parker's pageant at Sherbourne, a revival of medieval and renaissance imagery inspired by the arts and craft movement. In 1902 May Morris, daughter of the famous socialist and craftsman William, publicly advocated such a revival.[51] Pageantry then became something of a craze, spreading to America at a time when public officials were looking for a means of raising moral and civic consciousness and establishing a collective sense of history in towns where there were ethnically diverse local populations subject to rapid social changes. David Glassberg's history of American pageantry describes how the pageant developed as

> a responsibly led common civic culture [that] ... would combine the customary patriotic and religious themes of the historical oration, revised for an age of mass spectacle, with a growing interest in the past as a source of communal traditions that could offer an emotional respite from the consequences of modern progress.[52]

A major pageant in Hobart as early as 1910 was a significant event, occurring only two years after America's first historical pageant in Philadelphia. Its omission from Robson's *History of Tasmania*, which strikes me as quite serious, could conceivably be put down to a bias against popular historical representations in mainstream historical accounts, as if an event designed to shape a certain historical consciousness in the minds of the people is not as important as other events of more concrete political–historical connection. The importation of the 12 Ngarindjerri was also significant, possibly the first return of the repressed since the genocide. I take the fact that they were reported as enjoying the trip immensely[53] (despite patronising attitudes and racist framings of their talents and of 'their' place in

Tasmanian history) as evidence for the argument I wish to advance: that the pageant represented an opportunity for them to integrate their own style of public moral persuasion and performance into this new format. Its outdoor, public and popular nature made it a perfect vehicle for them.

The *Mercury* confirms that the figures in the film are the South Australians, as it describes: 'Four horses, covered with red trappings, then appeared, each led by a genuine aboriginal, clad in furs.' One of these people was probably Unaipon. As they took their place in this march through Tasmanian history they were participating in a history that demanded their presence as a primitive counterpoint to the aspirations of commercial progress, which the Tasmanian Tourist Association was keen to sponsor with this carnival. This was a presence that was elided in the representation (the Aboriginal first contact episode in the pageant was quickly passed over, as one might expect), but swelling and growing around the actions of the Ngarindjerri in Tasmania was something less expected: they were popular. The *Tasmanian Mail* reported that while

> time did not permit of the whole of the pageant being fully unfolded ... What interested the spectators as much as anything was the brief corroboree of the blacks, and the onlookers became quite excited in their delight over the display of boomerang throwing by the grey-haired powerful black native 'Poochy,' but now rejoicing in the British cognomen of Dan Wilson. He proved himself an artist in the throwing of the sickle-shaped missile.[54]

And later we were to learn that the singing of one of the women was a 'revelation' to a congregation packed uncomfortably in a church. This somewhat sublime quality of revelation is for me at the heart of the discussion I want to have about history and historiography. In their enactment the events of history exceed the possibility of their representation; this is why the performative aspect of history, which includes those elements normally left out (voice and music in this instance), adds something to the representation of the factual.

The exchange value of Aboriginal performance in general and of the Ngarindjerri in particular, was no doubt known to the Master of the Pageant, Mr JH Lyons, also a South Australian. In Adelaide he had probably seen the Point McLeay choir, the Glee Club, which had been performing since 1894 and had earned as much as £200 in

1900.[55] According to Graham Jenkin, only the year before the Hobart Carnival the Aborigines Friends Association in South Australia

> attempted to exploit the earning and influencing capacities of the Ngarrindjeri singers by sending a group on tour with David Ngunaitponi[56] and Philip Rigney as speakers. The musical items were the main attraction for the audiences, but they were really only the bait: the messages put over by the two speakers constituted the hook. Nevertheless, according to the Advertiser, the audiences found the messages even more interesting than the singing. In a patronising report, the Advertiser correspondent stated:
>
> > But it was when the adult 'David' took the platform and spoke of the tradition of his people, of their knowledge of astronomy, their intimacy with the science of botany, their bushcraft and folklore, that the audience gave most attention. In a simple way, and without any attempt at effect, this civilised savage spoke of the similarity of the Greek mythology and the Aboriginal fiction. He told of the knowledge of the old people, their idea that the world turned, and that certain stars had their places and times of appearing ... He told of the lore of the natives, of their fables and traditions; touched lightly on their uncivilisation; and held an interested audience for a good ten minutes in a speech unmarked by anything in the way of a faux pas.
>
> The strategy of the evening's entertainment was clearly arranged. It was David Ngunaitponi's role to show that in pre-invasion times the Aborigines were a cultured people: and that, at the present time, they were capable of reaching the heights of European civilisation. His own beautiful diction and the quality of the singing reinforced this contention.[57]

This, then, indicates something of the complexity of the oratorical machinery used by Unaipon and his people; Unaipon's speech was followed up by Philip Rigney's more pragmatic one, pointing out that the settlers had obtained one of the finest countries on Earth for nothing and that all his people needed was assistance to purchase roofing for their huts. There are further elements Unaipon used on other occasions, one being the demonstration of his scientific inventions (also used as bait in the way Jenkin describes it); the other is the religious oratory that he could deploy as a lay preacher. He didn't take any machinery to Tasmania, but the following gives an indication of the professionalism of the South Australians' conduct of church meetings:

> Probably the largest congregation ever seen at the Congregational Church at Richmond assembled on Sunday evening, upon the occasion of a visit of a party of the aborigines who are present in Tasmania in connection with the carnival ... after holding a service at Cambridge in the afternoon, where they were entertained at tea by the Hon James Murdoch, they journeyed by Houston's brake to Richmond to hold evening service. The church was very uncomfortably packed, doubtless many attending from curiosity. The native party consisted of three females and nine males, one of the number Mr D Uniapon [sic], presiding at the organ. Three of the members delivered very earnest addresses and were listened to very attentively throughout, and between the addresses part songs (sacred) were most creditably rendered by the native choir. The anthem, 'He shall feed His flock,' was also well-rendered; while the solo by a lady member, 'Say, are you ready,' was a revelation to many of those present.[58]

Moving between the church and the stage the Unaipon troupe thus carried out its missionary work. We may never know to what extent they sincerely embraced the church or to what extent it was a vehicle for the advancement of the Aborigines' cause. In any case, it is my contention that our appreciation of this period of Aboriginal history has to take its actors' performances into account as they occurred in highly public contexts where orality, song and other impressive skills were much more significant than the written word. The written word is, by contrast, still very much, though not entirely, the defining medium for historical knowledge.

Cultural historian Paul Carter writes, therefore, in *The Road to Botany Bay*, in order to dismiss theatrical metaphors of historical exposition:

> Such history is a fabric woven of self-reinforcing illusions. But above all, one illusion sustains it. This is the illusion of theatre and, more exactly, the unquestioned convention of the all-seeing spectator.'[59]

Visibility is not the only aspect of theatre of course, and rewriting history in spatial metaphors will not efface the important part that performance, including voice, has and will continue to play in creating history *in situ* with a participatory audience. As one of the founders of the American pageantry movement, William Chauncy Langdon succinctly put it, 'The pageant is a drama in which the place is the hero and the development of the community is the plot.'[60]

The existence of film footage of the Hobart Historical Pageant is significant, for cinema is one of the media that were destined to replace the pageant as a major form for the popular representation of history. In the United States the pageant had all but disappeared by 1920 when Frank Morton Todd observed

> that the public's threshold of wonder had steadily increased since the advent of the motion picture, the airplane and the radio. 'There was a time,' explained Todd, 'when great crowds could be attracted and helped by stereopticons, but it was no longer ... The public imagination had been 'speeded up' and to outrun it things must be swift.[61]

One can only feel sympathy and admiration for Unaipon's forbearance when one considers the extent to which he had to constantly prove himself and, as a representative of his race, also prove its abilities. So even before arriving in Hobart he had established his own reputation as intelligent, an attribute that extended to his party. The *Examiner* reported on 17 February 1910 that the group had arrived and that 'they are a very intelligent party'. The illustrative narrative offered concerns a

> gentleman on board the boat [the S. S. *Manuka* who] somewhat condescendingly invited one of the party to a game of draughts. This was accepted, with the result that out of 13 games one was a draw, and the aboriginal lost only one game.

There is every chance that it was Unaipon who took up the challenge to play draughts and beat the whitefella at his own game. Again, even in this more real life situation, performance is of the essence, not just a simple performance or game for fun, since in this cross-cultural situation there are serious judgments hanging on the result, judgments of a moral and political order. This is why, at least in this situation, Unaipon's life hovers somewhere between the church and the stage; church as the establishment and maintenance of community and morality, stage as visibility and voice (imagine a crowd around the draughts table on the steamer) and the framing of an individual whose every gesture is doubled in meaning: 'I', becomes 'we', 'he' becomes 'they'. It is a theatre of grandiloquence in which every gesture verges on excess and the actor becomes a curiosity or celebrity. The demand for performance is something that dogs every indigenous person in such situations, making everyday life hard to find in public. Even crowds of small boys are 'followers [who] add dignity to a person' as we shall see in the next report.

The *Examiner*'s 'Special Correspondent', writing on 21 February, reveals once again the disparity between official chilliness and popular interest for the party:

> Only one contingent was not received, metaphorically speaking, with open arms, viz, the aborigines, but though their reception was not enthusiastic, they have certainly attracted considerable interest, and their frequent walks together down Elizabeth street and through Franklin Square invariably draw a train of inquisitive white attendants, chiefly, of course, of the small boy order. Thus if followers add dignity to a person, and make his lot enviable these blacks should have nothing to complain of.

Some of us are a continuation, down through history, of these 'inquisitive white attendants', pondering how to write this event up in a way that does justice to … what exactly? The truth, of course, that's a start. Facts, judiciously chosen, and ultimately a genre of writing. That leaves the poetics of the text, the *bio* of biography. Wouldn't our writing fail to be appreciated if it did not in some way bring its subject to life? This, then, would mean that the writing would be performative and that it would add something ineffable to its subject, partake of the revelatory. In theoretical terms I am talking about not simply representing the subject as object, but mimetically reproducing an excess. We will have to write magically.

There is nothing metaphysical about magical writing, we do it all the time. It is the reproduction of illusion using professional or craft techniques. Such illusion presents strange paradoxes. Conventional historical and fictional writing is illusory to the extent that it reproduces familiar effects, what we call an aesthetics of realism for instance, or the trope of the omniscient spectator, which Carter identified. But if the reader is not enchanted it might fail to be illusory at all. So the paradox is that conventions have both to reproduce old illusions and create new ones through evolving apparatuses of representation. It seems that this paradox occurs because mimetic contingency – 'the skin of the real',[62] the efflorescence of the sensate that envelopes and possesses the charmed body of the reader and holds his or her interest – remains part of these apparatuses of representation.

The Aboriginal philosophers urge us to follow, to know someone by following literally in the footsteps of the figure, because knowing the character equals a capacity to mimic the character's gait. Sign language has a way of silently characterising someone by some physical feature, such as a limp or pigeon toes. Aboriginal practices of bodily mimicry have often been described as a 'primitive', so we get such statements as this of Charles Darwin, 'The Australians … have long been notorious for being able to imitate and describe the gait of any man, so that he may be recognised.'[63] It has been the task of modernity to eliminate this notorious or dangerous mimeticism, so close to its object that it runs the risk of losing itself in it. So our scholarly enterprises have made it their business to maintain distance with representation, using alphabetical signs, which, once pictographic, have acquired over the centuries a mysterious arbitrariness. This is what I am juggling with in this discussion: 'history writing' stands for this distanced representation. At the same time the mimetic and the performative surge back into our sensate world with the invention of the cinema, as noted by the writer Walter Benjamin.

In looking at David Unaipon's mimetic capacities we have noted the requirement coming from the Europeans that he should perform, for the historic pageant for instance, Aboriginality. But we know that the mimeticism also went the other way: Unaipon's performance of whitefella styles and skills, exceeding them in his abilities; a way of dressing in three-piece suits, the white surplice [from L. *superpellicum*, an 'overskin'] and his voice, often noted as 'refined', dignified, sometimes with Scottish inflections, gentle but insistent, persuasive, as those who remember him recall.[64] I myself could perform a mimeticism of his mimeticism, an everyday version of his speech, as he went about his rounds of Adelaide suburbs and

South Australian country towns selling copies of *Native Legends.*[65] It might go like this: 'Good day my good woman! I suppose you didn't expect to see a black man knocking at your door this morning. My name is David Unaipon, you may have heard of me, I am a Christian man, and an Aboriginal man, and I have here a little book that may interest you.'

To mimic in this way myself would border on the offensive, especially if it is perceived that I am parodying this often-noted refined English that Unaipon spoke, as if such a man should not have access to the signifiers of higher class. The parody would only work in the context of stereotypes of the primitive versus the civilised, where the trope is always one of an impending fall from grace, a slide back to primitiveness. Unaipon and I both risk this: my mimeticism collapses scholarly distance, his falls into the disbelief of 'he can't keep up the pretence for ever'. But Unaipon's cultivation (of speech, of dress, of Christian values, of a renaissance range of knowledge) was always natural (he was brought up that way) and it was self-created and motivated by his individual capacities: he was 'growing' a new culture for himself and his people. To the extent that it is intended to prove the point that Aboriginal people can do it too, his cultivation becomes a culture brought into battle against the primitivising and historicising tendencies to keep the natives in their place.

Now, does it matter whether he could really do it or he was just cultivating it? Should his hybrid culture, which has become second nature, be returned to that real nature that colonial imperatives demand? Michael Taussig says,

> To exercise the mimetic faculty is to practice an everyday art of appearance, an art that delights and maddens as it cultivates the insoluble paradox of the distinction between essence and appearance.[66]

So in my own cultivation of this character in this writing I am not interested in stripping away mere appearances and getting down to the 'real' David Unaipon. I am interested in the power of appearances, something my writing will not seek to disavow, but actively encourage. 'What is essential to grasp here is the strangely naive and ultimately perplexing point that appearance is power and that this is a function of the fact that appearance itself can acquire density and substance.'[67] For a book is not just writing; it is also a complex artefact with designs and images and its own ritual life. *Legendary Tales of the Australian Aborigines* was finally launched, with a little emotional turbulence for some of us, by Lowitja O'Donohue as she handed over the book to the closest living descendant, Melva Kropinyeri, at the South Australian Art Gallery in July 2001. Thus we returned a life to a location, the gathering of people on this occasion giving more body and density to a mere book and a particular cultural context to the text.

We are so used to mimeticism being criticised as a naive form of realism, naturalism or essentialism that its particular power has been forgotten. As Taussig says, 'mimesis has become that dreaded, absurd, or merely tiresome Other, that necessary straw man against whose feeble pretensions poststructuralists prance and strut'.[68] Familiar appeals to the constructed nature of reality deny mimetic power in favour of a representationalism that is only ever theoretical.

The mimeticism that could conceivably envelop both the practice of our writing of David Unaipon and our understanding of his own strategies of cultivation will carry us forward in its movement. I hope to have shown that the mimetic could have this power, 'the power of the copy to influence what it is a copy of',[69] Unaipon's mimeticism warding off the dangers of colonialism, our mimeticism bringing the subject to life again. In paying attention to David Unaipon's performative inventiveness as mimeticism in excess, we follow this inventiveness, maintaining in movement that sense of excess that Taussig also talks about as a postcolonial dissolution of subject and object: 'Mimetic excess as a form of human capacity potentiated by post-coloniality provides a welcome opportunity to live subjunctively as neither subject nor object of history, but as both at one and the same time.'[70]

David Unaipon is represented in a sovereign fashion on the Australian currency. His portrait in this honourable pantheon has made him a figure of familiarity, but not necessarily knowledge. His head is a token of the value that the Australian government, leading up to 1995, wished to attribute to the indigenous peoples of the continent. For Marcia Langton this honour is dubious to the extent that it is a symbol of domination:

> Coins, stamps and the imagery created to give the impression of a distinctive Australian way of life all incorporated Aborigines along with the faunal oddities – the kangaroo, the koala, the platypus and so on – in an imperial signification of the domination of civilisation over nature.[71]

Nature is dominated with this 'captured' head and I am still pondering the parallel with the fetishistic symbolisation and exchange value of other heads, such as the warrior Yagan from near Perth; massive cargoes of 'the primitive' were exported from the Pacific to European museums and galleries in the colonising period. But with the $50 note indigenous sovereignty is given some kind of cultural or political autonomy; even if people don't know who Unaipon is, they see his head as a symbol. The head on the currency is the prime place for the assertion of sovereignty within an economy. As opposed to the face value, it asserts power and cultural value, a cultural value that becomes particularly evident when the head is that of a colonial subaltern. The power aspect is then inverted: on one side of the coin imperial sovereignty, on the other the indigenous or the wild: Queen Elizabeth II's head and the kangaroo somersault over each other as the pennies spin in the air for the traditional game of two-up. There is no historical continuity between queen and kangaroo; they are both ancient and modern: Taussig concludes:

> The history I have presented thus forms a triptych that somersaults backwards then forwards through time, awakening mythical pasts for modern projects. 'In order for the past to be touched by the present,' wrote Benjamin, 'there must be no continuity between them.'[72]

Recognising the capture of sovereignty on the note is one step towards building up (or reconstructing) cultures with other symbolic acts and by marking historical events to do with figures such as Unaipon or Yagan. It is the task of cultural workers, I think, to fill out the meanings of such symbols. Where the official symbols tend to the deadly earnest and ponderous, somehow the filling out might be able to aspire to the light and satirical,[73] the human, in other words, making David Unaipon count for more than just a token position on the 50, making his image count in other ways that resonate through society.

What interests me, as I wonder about economic versus cultural value, is to unpack the particular history of David Unaipon's activism. Recounting this history has led me to make theoretical reflections about the writing of history. David Unaipon made his own history by travelling to places and performing there in particular ways. We are familiar with the idea that people make history through their actions and that the historian reports in writing on the documents about these actions. And while there are those who would like to see history writing itself become more performative, what it should at least take into account as it writes across cultural differences are the different representational, performative and conceptual/philosophical strategies of Aboriginal versus Western culture. It is not enough, I would contend, to make the strange familiar, as if David Unaipon's life were destined to become only what it seems to be: a bust in an imperial gallery, a head stamped on the currency of the realm, endorsing, as it were, a banal token of the capitalist economy. It is not enough if one is prepared to concede that underlying this token value is an enigmatic bundle of forces and meanings called 'cultural value'. And that it is this bundle of forces that has the power to create and change Australia's history, as Henry Reynolds's work has so forcefully shown. Reynolds has demonstrated the changes that documentary truth can bring about; I am insisting that there is another avenue for historical renovation and change: attention to performance, the mimetic power of history enacted and re-enacted. Far from being a primitivist appropriation of Aboriginality, as some critics have suggested, it is designed to show the operation of 'primitive' mimeticism in everybody's versions of modernity.

7

MORNING COFFEE WITH CLARRIE

Clarrie Isaacs was standing by the Rottnest Island jetty on a fine Saturday morning in September 1997. We were both delegates to a landscape architecture conference and had been sharing one of the cottages. When I came walking by he asked me if I wanted to go for coffee. I said, 'Sure', and once we were seated on the terrace of the café he showed me, without saying a word, his copy of the *West Australian*.

Here was the latest episode in the saga of the recovery and loss of the heads of 19th century Aboriginal warrior Yagan. At the time the real head was in the process of being recovered and repatriated from a grave in the United Kingdom by Ken Colbung and others, the Perth statue of Yagan had been decapitated a couple of times by person or persons unknown:

> CLARRIE TAKES YAGAN HEAD PROBE
> BY SCRUFF OF THE NECK
>
> We can't help but feel for the poor plods tied up with the hunt for Yagan's other head. Clay Gwilliam, the affable copper of Argyle fame, was called in to look for the bonce the day it departed Yagan's statuesque body on Heirisson Island.
>
> First Nyoongar elder Ken Colbung pointed the bone (his words, not ours) at a 'scruffy-looking Aboriginal man' seen leaving the area in a car hours after the beheading. The lead took the coppers to well-known stirrer Clarrie Isaacs. Clarrie went down to the island on behalf of Aboriginal spokesman Robert Bropho, who wanted to know if the statue had indeed been desecrated.
>
> Clarrie then gave Ken a spray: 'Ken says that a scruffy

> Aboriginal was seen leaving the area in a car. Well that was me, and I'm no scruffier than he is.'
>
> Police divers then searched the Swan River, raising to the surface every rock that resembled a noggin. Quite an exercise.
>
> But then a breakthrough. A caller to a radio station said the head had been dumped in Strickland Bay, Rotto.
>
> 'We probably should go out there on the first day of the crayfish season and have a good look around,' Det-Sgt Gwilliam said.
>
> Sounds like a bit of skulduggery to us.[74]

Then Clarrie handed me the copy of the fax he had sent to the *West* that morning while I had been taking a swim in Strickland Bay. He had joined the spirit of the exchange by writing me into the script. At his insistence, apparently, 'culture professor' Stephen Muecke from Sydney had made a thorough search of the bay that morning without finding the head.

For the cultural consensus that is the *West Australian* and its readers, Aboriginal issues are currency, generators of discourse and opinion. But the important thing about editorials such as this is the normalising and consensual function of the 'we', the satirical trivialising of Aboriginal concerns (head becomes 'bonce', 'noggin') and people are made to ignobly debate relative 'scruffiness': these events (unlike 'Argyle fame', whatever that is) are excluded from knowledge and from the history-making process. It's not all that strange that Aboriginal leaders such as Isaacs and Colbung participate in this by providing good copy; their media savvy tells them it's important to stay in the news. So I guess my job as the culture professor is to reconnect these stories to those other planes of immanence we call knowledge. But the question is, how?

I shout the coffees and pay with a 50. 'Know this guy?' I ask Clarrie, pointing to the note. Clarrie knows a lot about David Unaipon. He treats the waiter to quite a narrative as he weaves his own involvement into the Unaipon story. So, *that's* how you get knowledge moving.

8

DEVASTATION

There is a significant ritual that marks that movement from the world of the living to the world of the dead, where the power of life is converted into a subterranean force as the new member of the line of ancestors becomes also a new storyline in a community mythology. Our intense feelings, even of sadness, are recruited to the sustaining and vitalising force of myth, which is what Flaubert might have meant when he said, 'Few will guess how sad one had to be in order to resuscitate Carthage.'[75]

In 147 BC the Romans sacked Carthage.

> For ten days or more the fires raged in the city. Reserving the gold and silver and sacred objects for the state, Scipio allowed his troops to plunder. Those who had surrendered were sold into slavery and all the arms captured were ceremonially dedicated to Mars and Minerva and burned. Finally, everything that was still standing was levelled; Scipio pronounced a curse over the remains, a plough was drawn over the site and salt sown in the furrow, to signify that it was to remain uninhabited and barren forever.[76]

In the theatre of the emotions intensities dip and surge. Someone can be beaten and humiliated, reduced almost to extinction, but in what remains of their vitality a curious power can emerge. Two men circle each other, snarling and hunched like animals, and fall into a fight. Isn't it the case that each is prepared to destroy his opponent as long as he is strong, but when one is at the end of his powers and lying on the ground the other can feel pity or compassion? But this sorrow (which might be sufficient to resuscitate Carthage) cannot be felt in advance or, as John Berger has said, one cannot claim compassion: 'I don't think that anybody can reasonably claim compassion. Because I think that when compassion occurs it's a kind of miracle. And it only comes by a kind of grace.'[77]

Our emotions and their associated virtues are thus fickle and dangerous. Individual anger can turn to compassion in a second, and feelings can ripple through a crowd like waves of firing synapses in the contours of the brain. Any attempt to collectivise a virtue such as compassion, by claiming a tolerant or compassionate society or legislating for humanitarian values in a government, can only be cold comfort or, at worst, hypocrisy. On the other hand, these feelings of pity, compassion or charity cannot be legislated out of existence either. They flow from positions of strength to positions of weakness in and around social bodies. And, of course, one influential religion tells us that the meek shall inherit the earth. The moral virtues are proposed as antidotes to their corresponding vices, cruelty and hatred, yet they cannot cohabit with these emotions.

How deep are the reservoirs of sadness? We cannot know. But these reservoirs can only be tapped with the kind of images our poets know how to produce: images of devastation, literal or figurative. Ruins and images of things lost or laid waste harness the power of the dead. The state can commission powerful images of imagined past glory so that it can inflect the present and spin even more dangerous feelings into the crowd: patriotism, for instance, with a them-and-us logic. But these images can also be gentle and interpersonal. Another image of the power of the dead will take us, at the end of this section, to the most banal and inevitable of events that call forth that power: a funeral, in this case, that of my colleague and friend Nyigina elder Paddy Roe.

We can experiment with different kinds of logic, both, in this case, atemporal, the first antinomical, the second reproductive. These are placed, montage-like, in this narrative of articulated fragments. So, to subject this image of Carthage to the calculations of antinomical thought:

> *Thesis:* If one community defeats another in battle, then it has won the right to absolute power and control in the territory it has acquired.
>
> *Antithesis:* A community defeated in battle retains certain rights in its conquered lands.

> *Proof of the thesis:* Two communities engaging in battle, whether both are willing or not, come into it with unequal strengths: technical, organisational, or even spiritual. Victory is marked by the surrender or retreat of the loser, and the territory gained is held by the victor, at least until the next battle. It would make no sense for the victors to give back the land they have shed blood for, as if the battle were just a game.
>
> *Proof of the antithesis:* There is never a total elimination of the defeated, there are always survivors who return and who retain powers and resources which the victors remain ignorant of, like traditions and cultures.[78] Power has multiple paths, it is neither singular nor absolute, as if the end of one war were the end of history. In any case, power is always working against a resistance; if there is no resistance, there is no power. History continues with the survivors, whose power begins to build up again until it is a power of action rather than resistance.
>
> *Discussion:* It is not a question of resolving the thesis and antithesis in a synthesis, as if this were a higher truth. The thesis and the antithesis represent generalised positions pertaining to war, but for the purposes of this discussion they can be used to highlight concrete differences as they have emerged in the much more recent past in the real encounters of Europeans and Indigenous Australians. A number of questions remain, brutally disrupting the smooth calculations of antinomical thought: Do both sides have the same understanding of 'war'; are they obeying the same rules of the game? Has war been declared? Has it been declared won or lost at any stage? Are the same things at stake for the two sides: territory? occupation? ownership? freedom (individual, national or communal)?

There was a modernist arrogance about the forward march of the armies of progress. They didn't feel the need to declare war against these 'savages' (or conversely negotiate a treaty). If there was no war, there is no peace to be established. As Bruno Latour says:

> The modernists were never really at war since they did not recognize the existence of possible conflicts, except in the realm of superficial representations ... Is it not astounding that the modernists managed to wage war all over the planet without ever coming into

> conflict, with anyone, without ever declaring war? Quite the contrary! All they did was to spread, by force of arms, profound peace, indisputable civilisation, uninterrupted progress. They had no adversaries or enemies in the proper sense – just bad pupils. Yes, their wars, their conquests, were educational! We should re-read Captain Cook or Jules Verne: there were fights everywhere and all the time, but always for the good of the people. 'That should teach them a lesson …'[79]

In any case, the almost total destruction of some communities, for instance in Tasmania, proceeded without the colonists attributing the status of 'war' to this series of events. 'Punitive expeditions' are so-named as if their objects are already-guilty prisoners; it is the equivalent of lynching. Similarly, 'guerrilla tactics' is a phrase used (no doubt post-Vietnam) to describe indigenous fighting methods. However, one thing is certain, there is a division in indigenous communities between those who think that reform and the progressive acquisition of land is an effective enough decolonising strategy, and those who think that 'sovereignty' should be challenged with a notion of an unfinished war, or a 'total' political challenge to the State by an indigenous Government.

It is for this reason that Mick Mansell, a descendant of the survivors of the Tasmanian Aborigines, had to take his battle outside the country in 1988, amid hysterical press-coverage,[80] to Tripoli in Libya, to talk to Colonel Gaddafi, whose ancestors had once been among the best fighters that Hannibal had taken across the Alps where they clashed with the Romans in the Po Valley. And it was the Libyans who fought side-by-side with the defenders of Carthage, the ruins of which lie near the present-day city of Tunis. No doubt both Gaddafi and Mansell were aware of their shared status as survivors and empire-resisters. The association with terrorism made Mansell infamous, but his much more practical aim was to use Libya as a lever to gain a voice in the UN where indigenous 'nations' are not represented.[81] What made the coupling of Mansell with Gaddafi work so well was the genocidal devastations, and its poetic emblem, the desert, that both carry in their backgrounds.

> The ruin … refers … to the loosened building blocks (both semantic and material) out of which a new order can be constructed.[82]

'Reserving the gold and silver and sacred objects for the state,' says the historian of Carthage, pointing out where the conquerors made their fatal mistake: they should not have coveted the sacred objects along with the money. You cannot appropriate other peoples' magical symbols and make them part of state power; sooner or later they will reassert their strangeness.

Australia's antiquity, as everyone now knows, has been reclaimed by the indigenous peoples because their contemporary cultures trace the least interrupted connections to the ancient past the world can offer. But no one has teased out the aesthetic consequences for the idea of indigenous antiquity in Australian modernity. This antiquity does not provide any 'loosened building blocks' – ruins, such as old castles – out of which a new order can be constructed to look like European modernism. Were Australian modernism, or postmodernism, to build on indigenous antiquity it would look completely different. Despite modernism's attempted denial of the past antiquity's presence is fundamental to it and it gives shape and form to the convulsions into modernism brought about by rapid change. In Australia's case there was an imported modernism without any base here, and an indigenous modernism whose forms have, as yet, scarcely been recognised.[83] We can see a glimpse of the key contradiction in indigenous modernism as CP Mountford – who assisted in the creation of Namatjira's modernism in painting – sees the Gosse Range at sunset. His hallucination, or double vision, establishes the ancient–modern vision I am trying to show:

> At sunset Titus turned the camel string, led it to the crest of the range, and pointed to the scene beneath. For a moment the beauty of the sight robbed me of words; for there, in all the glory of eventide, like a ruined medieval city, with battered outer walls, and broken turrets, was the steep-sided Gosse Range standing isolated and apart in the middle of a yellow spinifex-covered plain and glowing almost as an ember in the late rays of the setting sun.[84]

The 'ruin' is, in Susan Buck-Morss's phrase, the 'objective determinate' for a modernist poetics:

> throughout the *Passagen-Werk* material, the image of the 'ruin,' as an emblem not only of the transitoriness and fragility of capitalist culture, but also its destructiveness, is pronounced. And just as the baroque dramatists saw in the ruin not only the

> 'highly meaningful fragment,' but also the objective determinate for their own poetic construction, the elements of which were never unified into a seamless whole, so Benjamin employed the most modern method of montage in order to construct out of the decaying fragments of nineteenth century culture images that made visible the 'jagged line of demarcation between physical nature and meaning.'[85]

Desert and wilderness are the allegorical correlatives of Australian modernism, just as the ancient ruin is for European modernism. Each draws on the power of the dead and seeks redemptive aesthetic outcomes. Decolonisation – an interminable process it seems – cannot be about the removal of one kind of state power; it is about the creation of a new assemblage. A new Australian modernism connects along multiple lines with indigenous antiquity. This involves recognising the political devastation, the destruction of Carthage as it were, and mobilising the sadness. What is often called the indigenous sacred represents the cultural capital only slowly made visible to the Nation, haunting it with a strange power, the power of still living indigenous legends and heroes.

In the dust lies a broken orange cassette tape, BASF, its looping entrails lost down the way. Vibrations are magnetised into its ferrous or ferric molecules, only a micron of plastic coating away from their cousins, the red ochre dust whose very being lies in colour, not sound.

For some archaeologists coming through here, the cassette is not their kind of evidence. They are mapping and photographing old fences, 44 gallon drums, ruined bower sheds and old chains and tools. These are the relics of the pastoral industry in northern Australia and the old man they are working with will tell them stories that valorise this material, this junk, in terms of his life spent among the cattle.

A linguist from the Australian Institute of Aboriginal and Torres Strait Islander Studies (AIATSIS) had come through here only a few years previously and spoken to the same old man, eliciting word lists, sentences and stories for comparative and reconstructive analysis of his language. The cassette somehow slipped out of his bag and all its evidence is now decaying. The work of the linguist is at another archaeological stratum: the pastoral industry and other domains, such as contemporary linguistics and anthropology, are kept separate in the so-called rigours of disciplinary thought. But interdisciplinary method, particularly the experimental, facilitates the indigenous connection to various domains of knowledge because of its focus on the unsaid or the not-yet-seen. We can see then how methodologies need to be continually worked on as they sort the useful from the trivial or invisible. To each their own junk, or waste, which will return one day to fertilise knowledge.

I stop at the bakery in Chinatown to pick up sandwiches and cool drinks before heading out. Paddy Roe carefully places his drink on the dashboard to warm up. He says you get coldsick drinking things too cold; he rubs his chest, grimaces.

We have all sorts of problems with bad stuff these days, problems of accumulation and disposal. Some time ago I told Paddy off for throwing stuff out of the window of the car, so this time he sneaks the empty can out when he thinks I'm not looking (but he knows and I know; that can be our secret now). Why are whitefella sensibilities shocked when blackfellas throw stuff out of car windows? Maybe these blackfellas are just dispersing the rubbish, as they go, so that it can reintegrate, while it seems whitefellas want their rubbish to accumulate in a rubbish tip. They want to gather it all together to make a really big stink. Well, they don't want to, but the demand for economic growth means the growth of the population and its inevitable waste accumulation.

In the interval between finishing a drink and throwing the can out the car window there is a fundamental human decision to be made about purity, about what is connected with our body and what is not. Waste has that kind of magical liminal status of both being and not being in a relationship with our bodies. As Paddy throws the can into the arms of Nature, confident that it will be consumed, he might experience a healthy release. That bit of waste has no connection with me, he might say, but, by this same logic, other highly significant things are connected with me. He can assert belongingness to some things with a greater passion for knowing clearly those he must let go. He turns to point out a place; my reverie is broken: 'Lake Eda,' he says, 'that way.'

An eastbound caravan is approaching, first vehicle for hours. My finger rises briefly from the steering wheel in greeting. Others, I think, constrained to take their rubbish with them, may feel quite righteous, but are confused about what the significant connections are. In the assertion about the importance of waste, dealing with the shit end of capitalist processes, an ecofascist could forget the importance of life. This ecofascism (I am describing a tendency here, rather than any social movement) could see landscape defined by conflict and contradiction (sharp edges and the finality of decisions), such that other liminal figures, such as feral animals, also uncertainly belong – 'What's *this* doing here?' they might say, like that gesture of dangling something at arm's length with two fingers. Some might want to exterminate such animals or rogue plants, such as weeds, on the basis of a general principle of not belonging or of competition with good pure life forms. Others, including some Aboriginal people, see feral animals not so much as an impure or ambiguous category, but in their singularity, having a right to live like anything else and on this basis being connectible with us. A 'pussycat', for instance, could be 'good tucker', giving life.[86] At Minarinj, up the Lurridjarra trail, Paddy will point out a stand of three or four trees, acacias, I think, right on the sand dunes. What is extraordinary about these trees is that they don't belong here; they are montaged into the landscape: this gives them a kind of sacred power. A positive one, like you wouldn't go and cut them down because they are being ecologically anomalous or useless, rather, you would be charmed by this anomaly or singularity. And the next thing you know there is a story about them.

In Aboriginal country bodies are integrated with places via stories. It is not an anthropocentric world, so the bodies are also those of trees and stones. A stone is a body because it is simultaneously the egg of a rainbow serpent. Consider this cosmology as radically distinct from the Western philosophy in which, says Edward S Casey, 'By the seventeenth century place is largely discredited, hidden deeply in the folds of the all-comprehensive fabric of space.'[87] The early modernists were in thrall to the infinite and space was composed of geometric abstractions relatable only to the mind, not the body. In this period, Aristotle's thought that place 'has some power' was forgotten,[88] because the arguments that nature and place make to us were ignored in favour of masterful cognition.

But today there is a greater anxiety and loss of power among people who are literally and metaphorically 'out of place', so we are tempted to take a little more seriously what people say about the sacred power of places. Here there may be some inexplicable phenomena to deal with. There may be things that do not reduce to meanings, which are subject to alphabetisation in a Western logocentric effort. To say that there may be things that exceed explanation is not to make a little space for the other's beliefs in one's own system; it is to recognise that this system also has its metaphysical *topoi* (for example, a logocentric drive, the *Aufhebung* of transcendence, or rhizomatic distribution). An example: Aboriginal sacred sites are sometimes labelled (in order to conserve them, but sometimes with the opposite effect) 'Site of Significance'. Why not 'Site of Power'? What happens when one is moved by a site (it incites to action, it produces feelings of fear or elation, etc.) as opposed to being simply meaningful? The awe-struck tourist looking at the Gosse Range at sunset has perceptions and feelings trained by the European sublime. The indigenous perceptions of the same site are motivated by feelings no less cultural, historical, and motivated and yet not reducible to any function of context as such. Aboriginal Australia classifies places in country as 'sacred', 'good', 'dangerous', 'rubbish' and in singularity rather than in the generality that this classification suggests. A sacred place has an ancestral life pulsing within it and approach is restricted to certain initiated people. A 'good' place in Deborah Bird Rose's terms is 'one in which all the elements do their work. They all nourish each other because there is no site, no position, from which the interest of one can be disengaged from the interests of others *in the long term*'.[89] Rubbish country is where there is nothing of significance or power.

Marcia Langton's work has transformed the Aboriginal sense of power in the land into knowledge that European Australians can understand.[90] The savannah, the characteristic open spaces of much Australian landscape, and certain sorts of vegetation are the product of about 60 000 years of Aboriginal land management and firestick farming that have in effect 'imprinted a human signature on the land'. In many cases what Europeans want to classify as 'wilderness' or 'nature' may be simply neglected Aboriginal 'gardens'. While I use the term 'garden' to suggest cultivation, there is clearly no horticulture in the European sense. 'Cultured landscape' might be a better phrase than 'garden'. The neglect of these landscapes may have consequences as serious as the environmental degradation (deforestation, salination, erosion, reduction in biodiversity) brought about by up to 200 years of pastoral and mining exploitation. Protecting the country *as* wilderness may not be the solution, according to Langton:

> Pleistocene Australians come 60,000 years ago, approximately, and start to impose a fire regime based on mosaic season burning, controlling a fire-prone continent. Now we know that the sclerophyll forests and other vegetation forms are dependent on fire, and we know there are fire-sensitive plants and ecosystems which require refugia from fire, and Aboriginal burning creates these buffer zones around gorges which act as refugia for monsoonal vine forests in the northern landscapes.[91]

Far from being a wilderness, this is land management, which Aboriginal people would be prevented from continuing if they are locked out of national parks, and this is indeed an issue with some parks. In the end Langton argues for collaboration between Western and Aboriginal systems of knowledge that are 'parallel, co-existing, but different, ways of knowing'. Lesley Instone also argues compellingly that wilderness is a gendered, racialised and classed category that has to be structured in performance to exclude all but a small group of people 'able' to appreciate it. Its construction as pristine means that non-wilderness areas have to be devalued and can thus be surrendered to development:

> The discourse of wasteland that originally surrendered Australian lands to exploitation and irresponsible use is reversed, so that non-wilderness areas are discursively discarded, and, as waste, no one has to take responsibility for them.[92]

So land clearance proceeds apace, devastating the country,[93] but leaving pockets of so-called wilderness in the form of national parks, righteously protected for some people while others, notably the traditional owners, have their traditional activities restricted. These bits of country are so loaded with cultural values and shot through with contradictions that their status as nature – the very conservation category at the centre of discourses of conservation – is almost totally compromised. George Seddon notes:

> I have heard [of] a tattered few acres that has been logged, burned and cleared three times in a hundred years, and is now tertiary regrowth Eucalyptus woodland choked with blackberry and watsonia, described and ardently defended as 'natural bushland'.[94]

Thus the precision of science cuts through the romanticisation, which, like the introduced blackberry, chokes our perception. Let us consider all these ways of knowing against each other, because they all go back in history; the romantic perception emerges, in one respect, from the framing and stillness and of landscape painting as a way of knowing which makes landscape amenable to aestheticisation. At the same time other discourses (some more traditional versions of science, economics and progress) construct the landscape as an exploitable adversary. This is the '"dreamwork" of imperialism' spoken about by WJT Mitchell as

> unfolding its own movement in time and space from a central point of origin and folding back on itself to disclose both utopian fantasies of the perfected imperial prospect and fractured images of unresolved and unsuppressed resistance.[95]

Against the utopian logic of usefulness versus waste I would like to entertain the possibility of the return of waste. Indigenous people do not have a splitting or arborescent mode of classification for the use of things, but rather an overlapping one where something may be useful to humans or to birds, or both, in different ways. Deborah Bird Rose says that even if something is classified as 'rubbish', indigenous people might add that

> 'it's just for itself'. Being just for itself is an ontologically stranded sort of category, but not, in my experience, a despicable one ... so everything non-rubbish is enmeshed in relationships of mutual benefit ... rubbish country, I suspect, would be country that was not enmeshed in a system of mutual benefit.[96]

Even then it might be conceded that such country might be useful to some other group of people. It thus carries the preconditions for its return from waste. The network of mutual benefit, which the phrase 'multiple stakeholders' entertains in its open-endedness, is the more complex logic that I would propose for ecocriticism. So if value is suspended in such a network, it also has to be considered three dimensionally, since values are generated to be passed on rather than accumulated. One could hardly forget the reproductive dimension of living ecosystems, which have, as intellectual corollary, the capacity to generate history.

David Halperin says that our lives are necessarily wasted and that there is an ethics in deciding just how to do that.[97] I agree that the injunction to make a success out of life (not to waste it) is a foolish moral and transcendent command that tries to 'locate in the flickering presence of value something stable'. Halperin distances himself from this moral transcendence, which derives the inherent value in things from the singular and absolute value of a god. 'You make my life meaningful', one says to a god or to an adored loved one. Then, suddenly, that person is gone. A spouse is lost after so many years of togetherness that it seems as if the value had become permanent. A community loses a valuable leader whose absence creates an ethical (if not moral) void: the bereaved start to drift, asking themselves, 'What can we do now?' But it is the ritual, not the moral position, that will provide an anchor. Ritual makes no judgment on life; it integrates people – and ghosts.

There was labour at the beginning and the end. We took turns shovelling the red earth onto his coffin as the women, and some men, cried. The Catholics repeated the Hail Marys endlessly, and Franz said, 'I guess we'll have to let you go, old man', like Paddy himself used to say, sitting under his old tamarind tree, sending us off so he could have a break from all that work dealing with whitefellas.

They all came to his funeral, those he hadn't outlived. Daughters, grannies, great-grandchildren, countless numbers it seemed. These lives are the product of a life. Their birth, their lives, are the easy part; their ethical inheritance is more difficult to think through. Paddy Roe's children inherit the country north of Broome and he tells the story of how this came about. His wife picked up the *rai*, spirit children belonging to that country, who were supposed to go to Djaber-Djaber women, but these women were past child-bearing age. For this reason they gave the country into the custodianship of Paddy Roe and his descendants, who were in a way also their own through those *rai*.

When Paddy, in about 1933, said he couldn't understand why they were handing the country over to him, they were all astounded: 'What! Can't you *see*?' they said, and all got up, about 20 or 30 old people, and approached him:

> 'See we gonta die with no babies, we can't have any more babies – no babies, that's why we tell you this country gonta be yours, you've got three daughters,' they told me –
>
> 'Ooh I see,' I said –

(soft voice) 'Ooh,' I didn't take much notice, 'cos the girls are still small, my daughters all small yet –

'You gonta have plenty babies,' they tell me, old womans tell me –

'You gonta have plenty baby, we got no baby to take country, take this country, you gonta look after him, with your family –

when the childrens born' –

'Oh,' I said, 'Oh that's the way.'[98]

David Halperin wrote about a house in Sydney he remembered, this reverie not unlike that of the Bachelard of the *Poetics of Space*, in which the house is so poetically layered into a European myth structure.[99] Such places, which one loves, just get sold or abandoned to crumble over time, but their spatial structure remains in mind, reproducible in the next house. Places remain, however, unless the contours of the land are bulldozed, something that Paul Carter has discussed in *The Lie of the Land*.[100] It is in an abandoned house that Halperin declares a love for a boy that remains incomplete. This is how his ethics grow and flower, because they are carried by a beautiful writing, the parentheses of which remain unclosed.

Aboriginal desert country, however, is not as easily commodified as a building, nor are its ancient ruins visible, except when one hallucinates in the manner of CP Mountford. The semantic building blocks are there, however, the meanings and associated ethical forces asking us to consider what we do. Paddy Roe, to whose life these words are always humbly dedicated, left us bereft, somewhat devastated, in his departure. And yet, for those of us who have wondered, sometimes, as we do, grumpily, why we waste our time having children, he has provided an answer: 'They have to look after the country, I s'pose.'

Albert Namatjira, *Haasts Bluff*, c. 1956, National Gallery of Australia

SECTION 2

COUNTRY

1

HOW DO YOU GET TO ALICE SPRINGS?

You take a plane, or you drive there or you even go by train. But I learnt from Aboriginal television that, in the old days, people had to come in single file through Honeymoon Gap, following exactly the footsteps of the person in front:

> Harold also talks about how travellers who come to Alice had to enter through Honeymoon Gap and only when escorted by our elders ... Each person travelling through here had to follow the footprints exactly, each footprint on top of another ...[101]

There is a lesson here for people interested in landscape or wanting to find out about places, as one does, for one reason or another. If you are a tourist you might be interested in the indigenous peoples' views on the view or if your purpose is professional you may have to get the expert opinion of the custodians of sites. In both cases you observe the protocols. In the observation of following the rules, that is, the footsteps in the above case, you can get new insights into the land and its significance. As you approach places you might wonder what really being there might be and you recall a related slogan: the preparation of the ceremony is the ceremony. You might then think in terms of processes, ways of living rather than results to be gained.

And if in your search for Aboriginal versions of landscape you find nothing but tracks being covered by drifting sands, this may be a consequence of the imposition of the European institutions of Time and Distance, as the 'killing times' of historical invasion and displacement caused ideas of Death and Disappearance to soak into the landscape and name the anguish of whites or blacks: Cape Tribulation, Blackgins Leap. Seeing things from some kind of standpoint, perspective or distance was also invented, a long time ago as the notion of landscape as a feature to be viewed, rather than land as lived in. If one is looking at the land like this, as 'out there' and separate from the abstracted position the viewer has had created for him or her by the famous renaissance perspectivity, then it makes it so much more difficult to imagine participation and connectedness for those of us who live here.

The European institutions, for their part, have to leave friendly tracks if they want Aborigines to follow them, but all they know is the law of cumulative time and time itself leaves no permanent trace. But who follows whom? It seems that there is a realisation among scientists that, in matters of Land, Aboriginal people are leading the way.[102] The European institutions are starting to learn how to follow.

A few years ago I started following the traces of the first Aboriginal writer, David Unaipon, and was wonder-struck by this statement: 'A friend will always leave a footprint – this is the teaching of the Aborigines.'[103] The logic is that the absence of a clear sign is a danger and that it is wise to avoid the unfamiliar. Unaipon's story goes on, and I feel compelled once again to follow: 'So he thought to himself, like all wise men do, that he would always be on the alert; and during the day he was not seen.'[104] So in arriving at an Aboriginal place the unseen is important. You often call out to the dead. This is a way of talking that maintains a reciprocity across the dividing line of death and unites those in attendance: 'I want your goanna, sugarbag, bush yam. I got all the *karu* [children] here hungry,'[105] calls Hector Wartpiyarri. Then, when he goes hunting, the country will benevolently respond.

2

'... A BURLY SALT WATER WOMAN OF ABOUT MY OWN AGE'

Visitors to indigenous Australian communities, typically, anthropologists, have time and again learnt things through defamiliarisation, a concept and practice favoured by the poets who burst open words as if they were seed pods and all our certainties suddenly lie scattered on the ground. Anthropologist Marie Reay, for instance, went to Borroloola years ago; her queer descriptions revelled in the sexuality and laughter of the women. She was there to find out about the mythic story of the sexually voracious Mungamunga women. To elicit the stories Reay had to 'satisfy [the] addiction' to analgesics of her informant, 'Clytie': 'This girl, whom I shall call Clytie, gave beautifully full accounts of the Mungamunga on eleven Aspros each morning. (More than that, I found, made her as silly as a rabbit and her stories unintelligible.)' Clytie, she goes on,

> was a particularly expressive performer in the women's ceremonies, preening her breasts as she danced and portraying in the rhythmic trembling, the shaking, the twisting and always graceful jerking of her lower body all the sex manuals have to say about the orgasm ... [106]

Clytie had an 'arpeggio of giggles' as carefree as 'a magpie's song', while another woman, Big Taylor, 'had a habit of shaking with gargantuan laughter'. Reay's writing expresses her distance from, if she is not indeed sublimating, her longing to participate in this life, made vivid through her metaphors. It is in this way that her descriptions of this everyday laughter and sexuality become defamiliarising. But there is no way she could accept the offer of Beulah, 'a burly Salt Water woman of about my own age':[107]

> Beulah called to see me on her way home to the single women's camp and I could not always be away somewhere else. On these occasions she would place her chair so that she faced me directly and was as close as I would tolerate and gaze fixedly at various parts of me ... Embarrassingly, Beulah described with relish certain acts she would like to perform on various parts of my anatomy.

These are some of the strange things that can happen when one visits any community, not just Aboriginal ones. What is curious is that Reay writes about it the way she does. She is not always highlighting sexuality, but it is the raw energetic material coursing through the relationships of the kinship system into which Reay is describing her integration. She takes up her roles not only in relation to these women, but also in relation to the Mungamunga myth, which the people's lives 'reproduce'. Even what she can do with her fieldwork becomes modulated by this system, as the ethnographer is constrained by kinship rules for cooperative or avoidance behaviour. But Reay keeps her distance with the strategically placed negatives you can see in these brief quotations. Some connections must remain closed because of the nature of 'our' sexuality – that sex must be referred back, implicitly, into the intensely private realms of one's real or imagined home, the couple, the bedroom, who knows?

Another similar story involves a real person I met in Perth, Gloria Brennan. When I arrived in Perth in 1974 for my first job teaching linguistics in the Anthropology Department at the University of Western Australia, I was advised to consult with 'Prof' before heading north to do fieldwork. A venerable and benevolent figure puffing his pipe in his study, he ordered tea and then issued me with two prohibitions to equip me in the field. 'Don't have anything to do with Aboriginal women,' he said, 'or Aboriginal politics.' The two great modernist repressions, ones we associate with the originating discourses of Freud and Marx, here poignantly focused on the indigenous, the site of the nation's founding repression.

I was embarrassed, for only the other night I had been in Gloria's bath. When I had moved into the Everett Street flats, my hot water was out of action, so Gloria, immediate neighbour across the hall, recent acquaintance and Aboriginal student at the uni, had invited me to use her tub. She was amused, popping her head around the door as I enjoyed the bubble bath, offering a towel, and then, a bit later, 'Would you like a martini?'

Like Marie Reay, I was being integrated. Gloria possibly didn't see herself as an atomistic individual meeting another such free agent. Her work doing politics in and for her community had the effect of maintaining ties that actively affected her life down to the smallest actions. I was a young single man enthusiastically embracing my new life in a new city and, for years afterwards, the effects of Gloria resonated through my life, to the point of even writing a book based on a story she used to tell.[108] But at the time the effects were immediate and social, and this brings me to the point of my story. I couldn't understand why I was so much in demand as a date in those early days of my arrival. Was there a shortage of men? But no, it was Gloria's work. She had been praising me to her girlfriends, white and black, talking me up. This was unfamiliar. I was used to exclusive relationships; romantic interest focused within the closed circle of the couple, relationships based on some possessiveness and even jealousy. Now I was looking at a situation in which a man seemed to belong to a whole group of women. How was this possible? If you look at it in the light of a philosophical concept, he can. This is the concept of connectedness, or relatedness, which can be contrasted all too easily with the concept of individualism associated with the rise of modern Western philosophies. This concept of connectedness is, of course, the basis of all kinship systems and indigenous Australian kinship systems have a concept of 'skin' or section, which places a group of men of one category in the relationship of husband to a group of women in another category. Getting married, in this case, is not just pairing off, it is, in a way, sharing each other. The point of my story about Gloria is therefore not just about one system of relationships (my culture) meeting another (her culture); it lies in the way in which her conceptual system became action in everyday life. I was behaving a bit differently though I didn't know it at the time and, while there were even different feelings spinning off; jealousy and possessiveness certainly didn't seem to be among them.

Coexistence is the word for different cultures living together in the same place and within the cultural bounds of the nation and this coexistence extends from the micro level of interpersonal relations to the image of the nation. Once *my* place expands into *our* place circles of responsibility lead to contested ownership, land rights and a variable sense of belonging to a national identity. There has been an indigenous cultural reawakening over the past 30 years and it has moved through numerous receptions.[109] For whitefellas it has meant taking more and more seriously the achievements of Aboriginal people, taking their narratives on their own specific cultural terms, that is, in all their difference and singularity. This ethics of reception means not reducing difference to the self-same by finding a classification from among the available genres, including the national narratives that have repetitively looked to the indigenous for completion of a national lack, to recolonise histories and cultures even as they are being brought into visibility.

For instance, the staging of the Sydney Olympics in 2000 saw an outpouring of pride in Australia's indigenous heritage less than a decade after indigenous title to land past was legally acknowledged. In the televised opening ceremony indigenous Australia was celebrated in dance, music and other iconic displays. But as the narrative unfolded, it emerged that there was a kind of transfer of significance and power between the two main characters: an Aboriginal elder and a very young white girl. It was impossible, it seemed, for the White Nation[110] not to stop itself transferring its symbolic investment into a figure of innocence, subsuming all Others, past and future. The indigenous was thus made ancient – the old man – while the future was made white with a cute and innocent image of a white girl. After all, she cannot be responsible for what happened in the past, can she?

I could put it another way: when it comes to national identity there is more than enough history and culture to play with; both are constantly transforming and being transformed. They are the product of a surplus of social energy. We have more energy than we need just to survive. Desire always exceeds the space it seems to occupy; there is always a spilling over. It is this surplus that makes cultural formations into a constellation of forces. Australia is not, as has often been said with the period of whitefella dominance in mind, a young country. It may be literally a young nation, but whatever is unique about its culture is linked to the ancient. For this reason there is no longer any need to speak of a cultural cringe, as if Australia needs to strive to catch up with the rest of the world. Most significantly, there was a radical rewriting of history – now hotly contested in the latest chapter of the Australian culture wars – that occurred as a consequence of the acknowledgment of native title, particularly concerning the birth of a nation. This moment of genesis is symbolised, as always, by sacrifice and death.

Death is at the heart of the formation of the nation, in as much as Nation is an entity that emerges from statehood. States can be set up as political entities, but they only become nations through the magical or spiritual agency of death. Mythologists and anthropologists usually explain it like this: a people recognises itself as a people, that is, as a culture, through the symbolic treatment of its dead. So that social order can be maintained, cultures don't just bury their dead and forget them; they have to attribute some power to the dead. A surplus of social significance or power is transferred to the dead so that their fixed and symbolic narrative can control us. The myths of the ancestors or the dead tell us where we come from, who we are and how we should behave towards each other. This is why we have monuments to the dead; this is why the sacrifice at Gallipoli is a crucial nation-forming narrative for Australians.

The Mabo decision in the High Court of Australia in 1992 gave us the opportunity to say that the country we thought was fully occupied, fully 'covered' by a history that has its point of origin in London (and regular and symbolic 'return' there), is not finished at all in that sense. The narrative would have to take a different turn. This turn happened when Mabo was made possible through historians such as Henry Reynolds showing lawyers that the *terra nullius* doctrine, itself only a few years in the public eye, was wrong.[111] We can now pay our dues to the dead in a different way, our cultural surpluses are now to be expended in an Aboriginal memorial for which the emblems are cultural genocide, the implications of child removal policy and the martyrdom of black deaths in custody. So the affirmation of new forms of Australian cultural life would mean that the national dead will become increasingly the Aboriginal dead. This would be a profound change – and one that is vigorously resisted by conservative writers – because it literally means the enhancement of Aboriginal cultural forces through each ritual that symbolically transfers power to their dead.

There is nothing morbid about this; it is just one theory about the way cultures work, which is with a certain amount of magic or spirituality. How else can one explain funeral rites, Anzac days and historical monuments? Mabo is an example that has invented a new politics, a politics contingent on the specificity of place. According to philosophers such as Algerien-French Jacques Derrida, a politics contingent on the specificity of place is useful because only the singularity of the example, adequately prepared, will enable us to examine the 'possibility of beginning not with a politics of which we would then give examples, but with examples out of which we might invent a politics'.[112] Derrida continues:

> One will never elaborate a politics of place and of taking place without a topographical and topological determination, but this determination itself comes out of the foundation of an indeterminability, of a possible substitution – of an iterability. Certainly, we must determine. But to saturate sovereignly in advance the determination of place, to program a *topolitique*, does this not sign the end of the political?[113]

Meditating Derrida's statement in the context of land rights as utopian reinventions of place, one is faced with the uncertainty, the interminable struggle. For, to achieve sovereignty, to reterritorialise country already transformed and alienated by its state and economic framing in the capital (Canberra), is not necessarily to wish for politics to end. It is perhaps to wish for the most powerful concepts to control politics. This is why we might need to elaborate something more philosophical about place, which has little to do with the political symbolisation of 'Left' and 'Right'. As Noel Pearson says:

> Indigenous political activity and philosophy are largely spinning in an orbit that does not have much relevance to, or impact upon, the dominant sphere in which many of the critical developments are taking place. We need a new political ideology for indigenous political strategy.[114]

3

TOWARDS THE CENTRE

We are still walking single file, like these words on the page, towards the Centre, towards Alice Springs, and wondering if we will get any closer to an indigenous philosophy of place, wondering if it is all worth it. We have had a quick look at the whole place (the nation) as an historically contested and fraught entity whose whitefella identity shimmers over it like a thin layer of something ephemeral yet rapid in its symbolisation and clever destruction of indigenous cultures. Under it, we are tempted to say, deeply pulses a chthonic heartbeat whose ancient forces break through into flashes of innovation with a different kind of logic. We have seen Noel Pearson make such forces into a continuity – he has never forsaken tradition – for his vision of a modern indigenous Australia. Swain has helped us with an approach to dreaming places as well as with an understanding of the innovation of modern Aboriginal cults as these too reinforce place, but also prise meanings loose from places and release them into the flow of historical whitefella time.

This was, no doubt, a means of survival. But instead of saying blackfellas 'learnt to adapt' (like Darwinian creatures) to whitefella concepts of time, why not say they captured them for their own purposes? And some white scholars have been captured by the power of this intellectual project as, fascinated, they follow, mumbling to themselves: 'It is only in the past few years that Western scholars have realised there might be a profound price to pay were the Aboriginal way of existence to be lost.'[115] What can the power of an indigenous philosophical project be, one may ask, if it is about the orientation and distribution of particular bodies in particular places, never 'rising' to the conceptual level and thus made general? It is easy, as one habitually performs the critique of power, to equate that power with universalisation.

The 'universal' is only a danger when it claims to have succeeded. The usual situation is that it is being negotiated with particular arguments, so we say, for Australia in particular, let the indigenous philosophers become part of the negotiation as they observe their own time-honoured and well-placed protocols and practices. It is a philosophical approach that the whitefella learns: obligations for exchange both within communities and in the so-called fieldwork situation which has been the terrain in which most Aboriginal knowledge has been elicited. Being a philosopher in an Aboriginal community, we find, will be a quite different thing from being a social scientist there. The philosopher is not on the lookout for information to take home, he or she is alert for concepts which by their nature are generalisable.

So we are there. I am remembering another scene, one from a trip to see Paddy Roe in Broome. It was our first meeting and I wanted him to work with me, a first year PhD student recording oral narratives. It was at the old Anna Street Reserve and he was dismantling some old sheds to take the materials out to Coconut Wells to build a new place there. When I asked if he could tell me a few stories he responded by saying, 'Things must go both ways.' When I ask what he meant he laughed and asked if I could start by loading that corrugated iron on the truck.

4

'OK IF WE CAMP HERE AGAIN?'

Coral Oomera Edwards, in a discussion of her 'Aboriginal Solutions' project, told a story outlining a particular Aboriginal philosophy she calls *Guyanggu* ('way of being').[116] I paraphrase:

> I have developed a program for Catholic education, for little children. It is based on the principle that we have a connection with places, with any kind of place. Our habitual and sustained presence, passing though, camping in the lee of a hill, always going to the same place for fishing. All this presence, modulated by absence, establishes a sense of connection. Eventually we might address these presences, in a place, with whom we have become familiar, as we approach:
>
> 'Hello, only us mob coming up, OK if we camp here again?'
>
> Relations can thus be established with any sort of place. Even classrooms. Children might be encouraged to perform a little ceremony, to change each time they enter a place, to modify their behaviour at the threshold. They might be induced to address the room:
>
> 'Hello, my name is Tommy, is it OK if I spend a year with you here?'
>
> This is long before the didactic element is introduced, long before the child is introduced to the word 'respect'.
>
> Imagine all sorts of children brought up in this way. Imagine if they have the same attitude when, as teenagers, they get into cars.

In this example of the approach to place, the children keep in mind that the place has a prior existence and history of its own long before they show up. Their arrival and its impact are considered as additions to the place; in establishing a relationship they acknowledge the prior existence of a context they now seek to become part of and perhaps this performed ethic opens into sensations such as 'seeing' the place for the first time, which is another way of seeing it differently.[117]

According to Deborah Bird Rose, Aboriginal cosmologies (understanding of the world) incorporate a non-human-being-centred view of the world, which also tends to be an ecological one.[118] 'Man' is just one living being among plants, animals, even the inanimate environment – all are kin.[119]

For instance, Rose recounts how, in the field, she was given advice about how to get rid of her daughter's head lice. What the girl should do is place them on a classificatory son-in-law. The lice, having fed on his blood, would know because of kinship obligations to then avoid the mother-in-law. Rose found this advice 'profoundly expressive of a whole way of being and knowing, implying the consciousness which different entities have of themselves and of systems.'[120] This world is thus composed of singular and discrete phenomena, animate beings and inanimate things, whose encounters create surprising relationships full of potentiality.

5

LANDSCAPE AND COUNTRY

While political issues to do with country are vividly alive in Australian national awareness (Aboriginal land claims and ecological issues are being hotly debated), their cultural representation remains less focused. Let us say that the cultural representation of country is discussed as landscape. In Australia, then, it is the 'wide brown land' gathered and brought into the orbit of perception via the recontextualising device of a 'frame': framed as a landscape painting or photograph, conceived of as a suitable site (with marked boundaries) for building (as in landscape architecture) or captured as a moving image in the cinema. The cultural representation of country has, no doubt, an aesthetic dimension, but the beauty thus presented also has a political dimension. Aesthetics can be politics carried out by other means, for what one learns to value in landscape, indeed, what is included in the frame, enables the promotion of what is considered valuable and worthy as an object of aspiration. So, in considering the politics of Landscape, we may need to look at the origin of the framing device that allowed Land to be recontextualised as landscape. WJT Mitchell thinks that 'Landscape is a medium of exchange between the human and the natural, the self and the Other. As such, it is like money: 'good for nothing in itself, but expressive of a limitless reserve of value.'[121]

One of the classic critical takes on European postrenaissance landscape painting can be found in John Berger's *Ways of Seeing*.[122] Here he takes the case of Gainsborough's *Mr and Mrs Andrews*, in which the aristocratic European landowners are located in the foreground, while the estate extends into the background which has a perspectival vanishing point on the horizon. Berger didn't believe his conservative teachers, including art critic Kenneth Clark, who said that 'Landscape painting marks the stages in our conception of nature. Its rise and development since the middle ages is part of a cycle in which the human spirit attempted once more to create a harmony with its environment.'[123] The lost harmony was, of course, brought about by the rise of Enlightenment rationality and instrumental reason and, eventually, the alienation of the industrial landscape and the death of any illusions of the pastoral ideal.

Berger's account, acutely aware of the politics of distance, ran like this: the painter's job is to amplify the landowners' sense of their property and their solid occupancy within that property. Hence, the economic exploitation of the peasantry, which makes this ownership possible, is not depicted ('the sentence for poaching at that time was deportation').[124] This, very broadly speaking, is the tradition of landscape painting-cum-land-ownership (with its value embedded in its imperial vision, as WJT Mitchell would say), which was imported into Australia, but which began rapidly to change under local conditions. By the turn of the century Australian landscapes were searching for a new idiom eventually, degenerating, by mid century, into some very ugly Russell Drysdale's (the angst-ridden central Australian paintings) or moving towards a minimalist abstraction with Fred Williams. While early landscape painters, such as Streeton and Roberts, struggled to depict accurately the specific tonal palette of the environment peculiar to the light in Australia, they also continued to struggle with the perceived inhospitality of the environment and securing a means by which to represent their identity in relation to this 'new' Land amid the disorientation of displacement and distance. The emergence of indigenous painting initially from Papunya in the 1980s, has almost eclipsed the whitefella tradition of landscape painting and its attempts to 'come to terms' with the new country, for here all of a sudden was a seemingly authentic expression of places, and 'expression' is certainly a better term than 'representation' or 'depiction'.

One contemporary white Australian painter, William Robinson, has continued strongly as a landscapist precisely because he too is expressivist and challenges the distance between viewer and image, re-engaging with an understanding of land as personal and lived in, rather than as viewed from a distance:

> I want to move away from observing the picture as some sort of representation. I want to sweep the observer down the gullies and up into the sky. The observer is drawn into the landscape – not physically, but as a sort of connection with memory.

> The painting reminds us of experiences we might have had when walking in the bush ... I am only presenting personal experiences to be shared, but I would like to give some clues that may help the observer to experience the picture. These works are the outcome of my own experience and they are totally to do with feeling and walking over the landscape. Such pictures cannot be understood if they are not felt physically.[125]

His primary instrumental strategy is to use multiple viewpoints (clearly, the 'vanishing point' of renaissance art has been long left behind) that engage the viewer in a feeling of being surrounded. Robert Dixon, in a paper concerning versions of the Australian pastoral, relates Robinson's explanation of how he came to solve the technical problem of multiple perspective:

> One evening after rain he stood outdoors looking down into a pool of water. In it he saw the reflection of the sky and the moon. He was at once looking down and looking up. This showed him that a composition could be arranged not just from one viewpoint, but from many viewpoints.[126]

In his paintings, Robinson began to experiment by moving the horizon line to the bottom of the picture. He painted trees sideways, on a dramatic angle, and then upside-down to capture the vertiginous experience of looking upwards at the sky through a canopy of trees. He arranged compositions in which the trees formed a circle around the edges of the picture, the sky with the moon or floating clouds in the centre. As Victoria Hammond puts it, in these new works, 'Robinson pulls you through the Renaissance "window on the world" and draws you into this curved world'.[127] Robinson himself continues:

> Because the paintings are the result of experience, they are not 'instants' of time any more than they are instants of place ... the observer and painter are included in the picture as a traveler, in the same way we would walk around a landscape. The development of a multiview point requires much explanation, but all I seem to return to are the fuges of Bach. They begin with a subject, this is repeated in other subjects and answered in various voices. They are interconnected with sequences and layer on layer of key modulation. They can be inverted, augmented, diminished and partial or fragmented. Similarly, my paintings have a subject with movement throughout and use visual inversions, augmentations or their equivalent based on physical feelings for the landscape.[128]

Dixon suggests that the content of Robinson's late paintings are increasingly empty of human habitation and that Robinson has displayed 'an increasing obsession with the idea of wilderness' since the 1980s.[129] But with Robinson's description of his own work in mind and the means by which he attempts to overcome the objectifying distance of the gaze, it is curious that Dixon suggests Robinson's intention is to represent wilderness, particularly when it leads to the idea that

> Robinson ... has increasingly taken a deep ecological view of wilderness. His paintings of the 1990s embody a vision of rainforest landscape as it might symbolically have existed in 1788, prior to European settlement yet also strangely devoid of Aboriginal presence ... In the wake of the High Court's landmark Mabo and Wik judgements, this is indeed to see the national landscape once more – almost wilfully – as a *terra nullius.*[130]

The attribution of the term 'wilderness' to the subject of Robinson's paintings allows Dixon scope for interpretation, and yet he forgets it is the term wilderness itself that excludes people, European or Aboriginal. Whether his intentions are as divisive as Dixon suggests, 'symbolic existence of landscape' prior to European settlement is a description indicative of the Romantic resacralising response to the rationalism of enlightenment, investing nature with primordial origins. This reading of Robinson's work sees nothing as divisive as Dixon suggests, and yet perhaps we may never know. In any case, what is certain is that European settlement is responsible for the importation of representations of the Land in this county and, specifically, of the concept of distance that informs the categories of wilderness and landscape, terms that 'occupy' our relationship with the Land.

The critical terminology that circulates around indigenous art has other things at stake. It has shown a propensity to locate contemporary Aboriginal art as the endpoint of tradition, deploys the cliché of spiritual connection and tries to have modernity as well, not by virtue of the art's own contemporaneity and inventiveness, but through unestablished connections with 'abstract' art conventions of the West. Bernice Murphy (one of the two judges of the Telstra Indigenous Art Awards in 2001 for which Dorothy Napangardi won first prize) does it all as she describes *Salt on Mina Mina* (2001):

> This painting proved outstanding as a work exhibiting both the depth of its cultural background (emerging from a continuing observance of spiritual connections to the artist's own Land) and a powerful demonstration of capacities to express those connections in new ways – of extending tradition itself through experimentation, and reaching out into the broad domain of visual language in abstract painting, a rich seam of continuing cultural production in the wider world of art.[131]

The contemporary painting of country works in such a way as to present the Aboriginal relationship with land to a wider audience and its reception according to the protocols of a commodified art market are just one of the realities of the hit-and-miss nature of interpretation. Napangardi's work is no less 'authentic' because of its innovation and transformation of traditional modes of production. Just as the permanence of painting the Yuendumu Doors and the Papunya murals were transformations of painting usually reserved only for ritual, they were a response to the conditions of settlement. The maintenance of relatedness to country and the network of kin relationships and custodial responsibilities that sustain the continuity essential to survival were under serious threat so the elders found a cultural expression that transformed one kind of ritual into another. This works to maintain cultural continuity in innovative ways despite (and in conjunction with) the imposition of the coloniser's technology, philosophy and economy.

We began with a discussion concerning the specificity of place and Coral Edwards's way for children to establish relatedness with the contexts they meet. In response to the distance manifested by the enlightenment encounter with space, we saw how the loss of attunement to the specificity of place tends towards a loss of contextually, ethically derived behavioural responses. This was furthered by the instrumental means of framing Land as pictures of landscape in making possible the recontextualisation of the environment at a distance from ourselves and, by implication, under our control. William Robinson challenges this distance in a way that usefully contrasts to the indigenous place-paintings that maintain relatedness by remaining anchored to the specificity of place. These indigenous place-paintings had their origins in ritual and thus there was no distance inserted into the process of their creation; they were created as re-enactments. Whether they continue to defy the label of representation depends on the relationship of the viewer to the place painted. Uninitiated viewers most likely understand the paintings as representations of places, since they do not share relationship with the place painted. Yet for initiates, who share substance and relationship with the particular place, the painting embodies place presented in the relation; that painting, they might say, *is* my country or, indeed, that painting *is* me. The same cannot be said of European landscape paintings, for they represent places via a quite different conceptual instrumentation.

Aboriginal paintings of country have defied description by the term 'landscape', despite being paintings the subject matter of which is country. The strength of Aboriginal relatedness to country stands over and against the imposition of distance assumed by the European tradition of painting the land. Napangardi's paintings are transformations of traditional methods, of ingenuity and adaptation towards new expressions of indigeneity, which draw the continuity of her past with her. Robinson's paintings are also transformations of tradition, challenging the distancing of the viewer and attempting to re-engage a viewer as a participant.

Land is not landscape, but the concept of representation allows us the illusion. It does this through the habits of perception and memory, as the technologies of convention work up the viewers' feelings of, for instance, belongingness. Thus can the romanticism learnt from painterly convention subtly mediate the terms of our relationship with our actual surroundings, while other more shocking conventions can defamiliarise such a relationship. In principle, indigenous paintings should be largely incommensurable or incomprehensible to outsiders, but the apparatuses of primitivism or abstraction are there to allow some connection, a connection that has more to do with the contingencies of visual knowledge than relative levels of embodiment between land and its painterly expression. Commodity production and novelty have the effect of leaving the task of connection to the country, or to the past, up to the apparatus of representation. And into the space it allows flows a complex of modern affects like cynicism, irony and insincerity. The continuity becomes feeble and temporal as this modernity tries to shut off the tap to the reservoirs of the ancient. As we have seen the ancient is always there, but what kind of ancient is it? What conceptual apparatus or process can harness its energy without falling into the trap of romanticism?

Ross Gibson, who has developed a long-standing project of working on landscape and cinema, asserts the primacy of landscape in Australian film. '[T]he country has come to represent something much more than an environmental setting for local narratives. In so many ways, the majority of Australian features have been about landscape.'[132] Discussing his 1993 film *Wild*, Gibson explicitly makes use of the concept of suture to discuss the stitching in of the viewing subject into landscape. Film operates, he says

> to conjoin citizen and country, subject and object, in a way that breaks down a functional separation between the two entities.
>
> Film is well-suited to this kind of task, particularly in the way it folds a spectator into the scene through the all-encompassing environment of sound and through editing sequences which lay out a space over and around a viewer, who is being 'shifted' constantly in vantage point to a profusion of possible sites-of-being and sites-of-seeing.[133]

Gibson concludes that 'the place of the film enters the spectator's mind and soul.'[134]

While there is a temptation to assert the current naturalising power of cinema over painting or, indeed, architecture, the definition and analysis of landscape as cultural representation of country can more usefully avoid the primacy of any particular medium and extend the conceptual tools to include intervals, moving frames, multiplicities and folds. It is precisely this conceptual technology that avoids the traps of romanticism (which, to operate well, need both a transcendent concept, such as a god or a muse, and a subject over-inflated with interiority).

If the landscape function (the 'suturing' of the subject into representations of the country) has survived, it is possibly through its extension into the moving image. Its value, as property, as dwelling or as destiny constantly transforms. As WJT Mitchell says, quoting Marx, its value is that of a ' "social hieroglyph", an emblem of the social relations it conceals',[135] and one would only have to think of a John Ford western such as *The Searchers* alongside the epigraph from Jimmie Durham at the beginning of this book to illustrate that point.

A landscape (painting, garden, architectural construction, scene in a movie) is a forceful piece of communication because it naturalises the already natural. Landscape sites are often conceived as points of consent between Nature and Culture, where homeliness billows forth in a dream of harmony, or where, as in a Japanese garden, yügen flashes like Cézanne's 'sensations'.[136] If, in the 1960s, movement was installed in landscape via cars and movies, then this was the dreamwork of driving empire to distraction and individuals to a certain amount of self-destruction as postwar Australia spasmed and metamorphosed into a modern shape.

What I am driving at here is that things and people are mutually transformative: the place changes according to who comes to occupy it and what they do there; the people change as a consequence of the place, which is itself defined not just by its form, but also through the potentialities introduced in the intervals in its territory. This has consequences for seeing landscapes and, eventually, building them. Joseph Mallard writes, 'As transient lives pass through it, we represent it and it represents us.'[137]

Lest one think that this effort is one of idealising landscape again, using indigenous and contemporary ideas to confer a new value or naturalise the cultural, let me assert that this perception of landscape is really only something to think with, the continuation of the poststructuralist project, which, whatever one might say about it, still always had a kind of intellectual courage. Michel Foucault, for instance, used the concepts of radical singularity and heterotopia to speak of a non-Cartesian logic of space:

> [I]n such a state, things are 'laid', 'placed', 'arranged' in sites so very different from one another that it is impossible to find a place of residence for them, to define a *common locus* beneath them all ... *Heterotopias* are disturbing, probably because they secretly undermine language, because they make it impossible to name this and that ... because they destroy 'syntax' in advance, and not only the syntax with which we construct sentences but also that less apparent syntax which causes words and things (next to and also opposite to one another) to 'hold together'.[138]

In terms of intellectual history, this passage represents the break from structuralism and the linguistic paradigm and a reversal of its terms. For us now, thinking in terms of landscape, it offers a new mode of construction, an aesthetic practice that allows for (continual) response to an image, site or building, as if the project was never finished and the site always already occupied. Ancient Aboriginal ownership of the land – and more recent Aboriginal history – gives us this latter sense of a flickering palimpsest of change. Landscape architecture's response to what architectural theorist Alberto Perez Gomez calls a 'non-discursive embodiment of knowledge born from a concern for the Other'[139] might then be cross-cultural and mutually transformative in a heterotopic sense, and not based on perceptions of conflict or contradiction within the same spatial or temporal plane.

Concern for the Other necessarily means openness to different kinds of 'logic'. Another example: if listeners perceive what they think are contradictions in Aboriginal discourses, hearing a voice composing an argument in which the premises shift and change so that the logic doesn't seem to hold, then these shifts can still be read as the work of rhetoric. These could be responses to a logic based on environmental variability, on shifting relations (say, of kinship: what one says or does with one's mother-in-law is different from words or actions with others within the same system; if one has to address a diverse audience, one tries to say something for each constituency – this is what the whitefellas might read as contradiction). The philosopher John Rajchman develops this idea of non-contradiction in architecture with the help of Deleuze's 'fold', a questioning and form-generating construction:

> when a question comes into a space ... the space discovers its free complexity; and conversely, when a space freely complicates itself it always opens itself to question. This perplexing sort of complication is thus not a matter of resolving a contradiction, as with Venturi, but rather with what Deleuze calls 'vicediction' or the weaving together of a multiplicity.[140]

Consider, by contrast, the idealism of sustaining a discourse that assumes a homogeneous audience responding evenly. With the former, 'contingent variables' are in play, enabling the value of statements to change as one moves through a discourse (as if through a landscape), speakers perceiving change and responding to it as they go, implicitly addressing different sections of the audience. Contradiction, it seems to me, can only emerge as a logical possibility if there is an 'outside' position held constant, sitting in judgment on the two propositions deemed to be in contradiction. The judge thus sits immobile in a virtual ideal space. The judge's word is an overarching logos blocking perception of difference on one level, sustaining uniformity on another.

6

BACK TO ROTTNEST

It is September 1997 and I am sitting in the Quokka Arms on Rottnest Island, Western Australia (the long trip across the Nullarbor Plain over; several days, several hitchhikers and flat tyres behind me), having a quiet drink before dinner and getting ready for my talk at the W Edge Landscape Architecture Conference. There is an advertisement on the pub television for the Jeep Cherokee. The camera is tracking past a series of expensive front gates. We come to one which, instead of having a gate, is built up with boulders. Simply because the 4WD can drive over them, it does, with ease. Surreal inanity. As a particular sort of machine the 4WD creates new sites of possibility, just as the playing field reveals the possibility of athletics. In all these recent ads for 4WD vehicles it seems the Australian landscape has been turned into a simulated obstacle course reminiscent of a video game.

In his book *Earth Moves*, philosopher Bernard Cache writes: 'Architecture would be the art of introducing intervals in a territory in order to construct frames of probability.'[141] He argues that architects, working from a site, do not 'bring out' or reinforce an already existent identity of the place. Nor do they totally construct that identity; rather, they work with its singularity (defined mathematically as points on a curve) to change the probabilities of what can occur in that place. Genius loci, then, becomes the perpetual transformation of identities in a site (which could simply be something like a primary school becoming a market at weekends). Architecture, as 'the interlocking of frames',[142] involves basic figures such as the *wall*, which separates, the *window*, which selects, and the *roof*, which singularises and provides the definitional effect of, for instance, 'the domestic.'

Cache applies this mathematical analysis to the Swiss city Lausanne as a site composed of vectors and forces, inclines and intervals. The spire of the cathedral on the hill is the actualisation of a vertical vector in defiance of an opposite force: gravity. The genius loci of the mountain or the hill is not the same as its identity, for every attempt to use a built environment to bring out, realise or express this genius (defined as the identity of a place) is already an interpretation. In the case of the cathedral it is the vertical principle of up and down, transcendence and the fall (under the influence of gravity); it is the principle of hope ('the nearer my God to thee'). In Aboriginal Australia gravity (or verticality) is not an issue – it is lightness, movement, impermanence. In Aboriginal dance there is dispersal and circulation rather than lift; feet drumming the earth.

Just as architecture can frame the environment, so too does cinema. The cinematic screen is a wall/window, separating and selecting, but it also moves, panning into its out-of-frame potentialities. This is not movement that comes one way from the screen to our perception of it. This version of cinematic movement, coming from Deleuze via Bergson, is about the types of encounter between one kind of movement and another, because the viewing subject is also in movement.[143] Cache develops this: 'Our brain is not the seat of a neuronal cinema that reproduces the world; rather our perceptions are inscribed on the surface of things, as images amongst images.'[144]

And in stressing the interval ('no value has been attributed to the interval that separates the cause from the realization of its effect'[145]) we can create a new 'logic' for the relations between things which is not based, for example, on linear cause and effect or on dialectical conflict. We might rather stress circularity and movement, folds and returns:

> as with the 'movement images' and 'time images' Deleuze analyses, we see things as functions of actions in and reactions to a milieu. But since such reactions are not automatic or deterministic and include 'zones of indetermination' from which unexpected movement might come, images involve what transpires in the intervals or disparities between things. They are connected through a logic where the whole is not given but always open to variation, as new things are added or new relations made, creating new continuities out of such intervals or disparities. In the unstable dynamic world in which they figure, images are therefore no longer defined by fixed relations between inside and outside.[146]

7

A CHARACTER CALLED '62 PONTIAC PARISIENNE'

In 1977 Phil Noyce directed *Backroads*, a low-budget short feature funded by the Australian Film Commission. It was the first feature for this Australian director who went on to Hollywood and now has work such as *Newsfront*, *Dead Calm*, *Patriot Games*, *Clear and Present Danger* and *Rabbit-Proof Fence* in his directorial CV. Film writers Susan Dermody and Liz Jacka considered *Backroads* one of 'the most interesting films of the period',[147] '... an existentialist road movie, directionless, on outback roads, leading nowhere'.[148] While atopia is in itself an interesting figure, the structure of the movie is more determinate than that. The following analysis will sketch some of the lines of influence which made the movie what it is, and then go on to relate it to concepts of Australian landscape.

Backroads emerges out of Noyce's background in the documentary genre. He had shot a number of short films, one of which was on 'poofter-bashing' kids from Sydney's western suburbs. In an interview made for the Australian Film, Television and Radio School (AFTRS) in 1978, after Noyce had made *Newsfront*, he gestured towards an aesthetic of *vérité* focused on casting and performance.[149] He distinguished his work in this area ('more realistic performance') from 'the ABC style' ('a studied sort of thing [with its] stiff ... and theatrical rendering of character').[150] Casting is crucial in achieving this because he is relying on the actual life experience of the actors so that their 'performance comes out of a sort of inner emotion ... the people look as though they've done all that before ... they mean what they are saying rather than a screen they've set up around their body to make them appear like that'.

So it was highly significant that Gary Foley was chosen to play the part of Gary in *Backroads*. Foley had reached a plateau in his political activist career. In 1971 he had hoaxed *The Australian* into believing there was a highly militant Black Panther chapter in Australia,[151] but, even though no Black Panther chapter existed in Australia, the members of this group were nevertheless part of a new generation of Aboriginal activists fighting for political ground, land rights and the promotion of Aboriginal knowledge and history. This group, which put Aboriginal affairs firmly on the agenda of the Labor government of Gough Whitlam, was associated with the 1972 Tent Embassy set up outside Parliament House in Canberra. Foley was also one of those who also worked on cultural fronts, taking part in street theatre, movies and the music scene and, eventually, appearing as a guest singer with The Clash on their Australian tour in 1982.

Backroads, Foley explains, 'was only ever screened once commercially in [Australia], at the Longford Cinema in Melbourne'. But it was

> a great success at the 1978 Berlin film festival, where it attracted high praise from German directors Werner Herzog and Wim Wenders. As a result, the film was a big success at the Cannes film festival later that year, and consequently was invited to screen at the British Film Institute in London. Backroads ultimately screened for six months at the Scala Cinema in London.[152]

Noyce explains the different levels at which this 'volatile and articulate' Aboriginal activist contributed to the production. Drawing on a short story by John Emery about an Aboriginal man called Noel,[153] Noyce is interested in exploring the notion of unmotivated crime (here, existentialist philosophy – the ghost of Camus – enters the picture) as much as Aboriginality. So Noyce's directions are that Foley should position himself as the rural Aboriginal male, but base the feeling for his performance in everything that had happened in his own life as an Aboriginal person.

Furthermore, Foley was involved in an ongoing critique of the film. *Backroads*, says Noyce 'went through a genesis right through until it hit the screen', and was even recut afterwards. Foley was allowed to modify the script as Noyce invited him into the screenwriting process. All the team was aware that the film was to be workshopped as it was being made and Noyce was prepared to admit 'that he [Foley] knows more about Aboriginals than I *ever* will'.

Noyce encouraged Foley to 'take that basic concept [of himself as a young rural Aboriginal man] and develop it himself in conjunction with the other characters in the picture'. We will see in the transcript below how he does this with Bill Hunter (Jack), who is also appropriately cast since he 'has bummed around the country with Aboriginals ... has had quite a close but conflicting relationship with Australian Blacks'.

Noyce's documentary aesthetic – 'filming what happens ... recording' – is reinforced with the performances of cast members drawing on their own life experiences, adlibbing the script and, finally, brought together in the editing, which is where Noyce seems to feel his authorial intervention is made: 'You editorialise later in the editing or manipulation by juxtaposition, you're making your statements later'.

Michael Carlton, in the interview, was keen to label Noyce the 'democratic film director' in recognition of this more communal effort in the production; for Dermody and Jacka there is a 'less didactic' style as such films 'tend to be those that play with the genre'.[154] And while the overall effect is 'a relaxed way by thinking through genre' the film also 'accurately articulates its time and place'.[155] In retrospect, it most definitely belongs to 1970s Australia, with emergent Aboriginal politics and cultural activism colliding with hippyism and so-called sexual liberation. At a technical level the film has the low production qualities of the nascent Australian film industry.

In the film, Gary and Jack meet more or less by accident when they steal a car (a 1962 Pontiac Parisienne) and head off on the backroads through outback New South Wales towards Sydney. The story opens with the following text:

THE STORY SO FAR

> Gary and Uncle Joe breezed into Colli yesterday looking for work around the wheat sheds. When Gary's old Morris packed up Joe pissed off to the Royal to spend his social cheque.
>
> The cops lumbered Gary for the night on a vagrancy charge, so Joe hitched a ride back to the reserve with some buds.

MEANWHILE ...

> Jack was passing through town on his way to meet up with some mates in Newcastle. He spent too long in the back room of the Exchange last night and his truckie mate cleared off without him.

They never reach Sydney,[156] but pick up Uncle Joe, Gary's countryman (Zac Martin), a French hitchhiker, Jean-Claude (Terry Camilleri), and a disgruntled petrol station attendant, Anna (Julie McGregor) on the way.

At a central point in the trip there is a sequence of events and images on which I want to pause, not to release a condensed or hidden meaning, but to examine the apparent meaninglessness of the sequence and to show how the intervals release 'new' probabilities. In speaking of the cinema of French director Jean-Luc Godard, Rajchman talks of 'a montage of "irrational continuities", where the "and" of cinematic construction falls free from the movements of the "is" of given identities or predications.'[157]

Gary is in the house at the Dodge City Reserve, Brewarrina, cuddling his son, saying goodbye. Jack is yelling at him and swearing; he's uncomfortable on the reserve; he wants to get back on the road. And at the same time we cut to Essie Coffey singing a famous Aboriginal country and western song:

> I spend the days in jail as they paid my bail
> and they opened up the big iron door
> I shook my head as I sadly said
> 'I never get drunk no more'.
> I made a vow I give it up for now
> and let the blood roll down my veins
> then a friend of mine he had a flagon of wine
> so I turned it on again.
> People in town they just runnin' us down
> and they gave us a big bad name
> so we drink and we fight but it's quite alright
> because the others is all the same.[158]

Then, the travelling companions are in the car again, the 'empty' landscape flashes past in side view or is framed as the disappearing horizon ahead. Gary and Jack have an argument over Australian race relations, while in the back seat Uncle Joe is drinking from a flagon and Jean-Claude and Anna are smoking a joint and getting friendly.

GARY [j]ust sorta, let us live the way we want to, that's what it's all about that's the way I think.

JACK You couldn't make it in fuckin' white society you fuckin' part Abo little cunt.

GARY What about assimilation and all it means, man … far as I can figure out we'll all get wiped out in the end, all us fellas, the Kooris, that's no good.

JACK Well it'd be better than what you're doin' now look at those poor bastards on the reserve man they got no chance. Look at you, you bum around the fuckin' country. I don't work but at least I always got a bloody quid in my pocket. I pinch, borrow or steal it. Chris' what are you doin'?

GARY That's what you gubbos can't understand eh? Ol' koori is different to you fellas, ol' koori is different, different ways.

JACK Well, what do you want?

GARY You s'posed to go to work six days a week, get yourself a house …

JACK Oh fuck, I don't work either.

GARY Yeah I mean, look at all those, maybe you're a bit more Koori (hits him on the thigh) than you like to think, mate … Look at those gubbos out there man, they slave their guts out all their lives and what have they got to show for it? You know? What you going to do with all that money, you know you can't take it with you …

ANNA *Oh I don't know I wonder …*
[in back seat, stoned]

GARY The old koori's got his way of life, everything that we've got.

ANNA *… it's the kid I worry about …*

GARY There's no such thing as what's mine in the Koori way of life, it's what's ours.

JACK Pack a fuckin' commos.

ANNA *Mum's looking after him*

GARY Maybe, but still, [laughs]

JEAN-CLAUDE *But still you look for yourself, huh?*

ANNA *I don't reckon I'll ever know myself.*

GARY Nah mate, we're different.

JACK You're livin' in a white society, man.

GARY Are we? Huh! Are we livin' in the white society man? Are we really in the white society. Why we on the reserve, if we in the white society?

JACK Well the fact that you're on the fuckin' reserve is pretty significant, isn't it?

GARY We're separate from the white society already, aren't we?

JACK Yeah, on white man's terms, gubbo's.

GARY Look at the dagoes mate, they've been brung out 'ere ...

JACK Oh come on, don't give me that shit. When a dago comes out here within two fuckin' years they got their own house paid for, the fuckin' two fridges and the two cars ...

GARY They still got their own language they still got their own customs.

JACK Yeah they're assimilated, they're assimilated, man!

GARY They're not assimilated.

JACK They fuckin' are! I've been down to fuckin' Carlton in Melbourne, I was down there.

GARY Well you wind up in the big smoke like that in Melbourne, but not me. What I seen, what I seen is, Eyeties and all these people man, what I like about those fellas anyhow they've kept their language, they've kept their customs, and they look after their own just like ol' Kooris, mate.

JACK Yeah.

GARY I mean what's a gubbo? ...

JACK Yeah they might kept their fuckin' language but they've taken all the bloody Australian money too mate, whatta you bastards doin'? Fuck all! Sitting on your arse drinkin' fuckin' flagons all day.

ANNA *Sometimes I think it would have been better to stay where I was ... I had everything I ever possessed ... I didn't know it ...*

JACK I'm not havin' a go at yer, mate, I just wanta understand it that's all.

GARY You're learnin', that's the main thing.

A semitrailer looms behind them, blowing its horn as the music changes from seventies cool rock to comic triumphant battle charge. A hitchhiker in the truck is waving and excited, taking photos of Jean-Claude and Anna having sex in the back seat of the Parisienne. The vehicles rush ahead side by side; the sequence concludes with a shot of a dead kangaroo by the side of the road.

I had already decided that this scene was pivotal to the film and this was confirmed in the Carlton interview in which Noyce describes the two characters' reaction to the script:

> [T]hey'd say: 'Your dialogue's rubbish, we're gonna change it' ... the two of them reach some understanding of each other – the white of the black, the black of the white – and they'd say 'Yeah, well look, we've been talking about this' [they'd been living together for three weeks] ... 'an' we reckon we know how to do it an' we reckon that we've had enough discussions out here just to play this scene right through'. And it's a great, it's a scene where the camera was strapped to the side of the car and there's a two shot looking over Bill towards Gary and they're arguing with each other about the black situation and Bill is coming out with stereotyped white responses to dirty blacks and their attitudes and Gary's trying to answer him. And that scene was filmed almost like a documentary, the camera has 400 feet, 11 minutes, of film in it, Bill Hunter's driving the car, I'm sitting in the back, the sound recordist's in the boot [Carlton: And away you went] and away we went. But you're still the director because afterwards you decide what material to use ... you're still sculpting all that material later on, dropping it into some statement. But you are making use of the energy, the enthusiasm, the passion of your actors.

These characters thus engage with problems of race by living through them as they are suspended in the goodwill of community and mateship and in an artistic project conceived and transformed as it is being made, carried by a popular genre. This is a 'working' solution, a *poesis*, to an ethical problem (what do you do about racism?), the solution emerging because the problem is conceived not so much in terms of identity, but in the intervals between shots, codes, voices, the viewing subject and the Australian landscape. Relating this ethic to landscape as a metonym for national identity, an important contextualising effect for the meaning of the film, means going beyond perceiving it in the old imperial sense as something to be possessed and built on and towards understanding it as the cultural transformation of country. Moving images, including those framed by car windows, give us the possibility of seeing landscape as variable rather than fixed, as in landscape paintings. In the intervals between sites stories can emerge.

This film sequence, like Foucault's heterotopic sites, is composed of heterogeneous elements. The appreciation and analysis of this heterogeneity means that, where race-based conflict and contradiction habitually intensify (over sites, landscapes), ways of thinking other than possession and identity may have to be found. The ethical solution I have described is not achieved didactically, but its 'relaxed' effect is achieved more in a ritual condensation of various codes – music, the road genre, sexuality, racism. This is a poetic effect with an ethical direction.

Rather than interrogate this sequence until it releases its meanings, I wanted to attend to its intervals and movements, the potentiality it creates for a posthumanist ethics in landscape.[159] In this case I want to relate this ethic to ideas for understandings of the Australian landscape that go beyond perceiving it in the old imperial sense as something to be owned and built on, and towards understanding it as a set of spatial intervals where transformations can occur. This sequence is composed of heterogeneous elements. In Foucault's terms it is a heterotopic site. This cinematic landscape can help us answer the question: What do you do about racism? It seems that race-based conflict and contradiction intensifies over sites (landscapes), so other ways of thinking may have to be found. One example of such a conflict was given at the W Edge Conference.

Ryan Healy, a landscape architecture student talking at the conference, described a violent reaction to his work. His project was one of analysing the Aboriginal burial ground on Rottnest Island, where he spent some weeks reconstructing what the site might have been like. But his ethical concern could not be contained within the moral safety net of his university discipline on a small place like Rottnest, which to this day has repressed its shameful history as a gulag for Aboriginal people. There are not even any sanitised cultural tourism versions of signage or museum displays that would inform us about this history; the placid dream of holiday-makers remains undisturbed.

Ryan used to have a beer and play pool of an evening with other local workers at the Quokka Arms, but he found to his dismay that, when he told someone about what he was doing, this erstwhile drinking mate now wanted to beat him up.

The problem is this: in a context of racist feelings, what landscape strategy will work to ethically reconstruct community in spaces for living without being seen to do good? This is raised by architect Mark Jackson who asks: 'How do we conceive of the efficacy of architectural practices outside the delivery of a social good by an intentional agent?' It means that the place has to do the thinking and feeling for us (or it has always done the thinking, if we listen to Coral Oomera Edwards) and that the place, in conjunction with the other beings and things that occupy it, gives rise to a new form of life because it has potential for growth and continual change.

And Coral Oomera Edwards has provided Jackson with one kind of answer: an ethical disposition is induced into subjects via a place, without didacticism or intentions to 'do good'. This could be an unexpected version of the posthumanism some have been looking for in contemporary philosophical thought.

8

A SPACE FOR ETHICS

It may be a bit far-fetched to say that the *Backroads* cinematic sequence is resonant with a certain kind of poetry, but I would say its aesthetic is the landscape function of offering a non-didactic space, suturing the subject into it. Jack's racist ravings (which are remarkably consonant with contemporary racist discourses; the unreconstructed 'innocent' dialogue of the 1970s meets reconstructed or staged racisms 20 years later) are dominated by the men's emerging feelings of mateship, while the comic sex in the back seat makes the whole sequence into a 'community formation' exercise. Essie Coffey's song teaches us that the ethical is not in steadfastness ('I made a vow I'd give it up for now'), but in the truth of the image ('and let the blood flow down my veins'), which is one of how jail relates to grog and how we relate to them ('the others are just the same'). But 'we' are the ones who get jailed.

Bachelard finds his phenomenology of space in poetic emergence, images without causality or history:

> to say that the poetic image is independent of causality is to make a rather serious statement ... the poet does not confer the past of his image upon me, and yet his image immediately takes root in me. The communicability of an unusual image is a fact of great ontological significance.[160]

He elaborates on this communicability:

> The image offered us by reading the poem now becomes really our own. It takes root in us. It has been given us by another, but we begin to have the impression that we could have created it, that we should have created it. It becomes a new being in our language, expressing us by making us what it expresses; in other words, it is at once a becoming of expression, and a becoming of our being. Here expression creates being.[161]

The consciousness of a society, what has become our memory (and it is not that far removed from the present), is carried by popular forms as these codes and forces are combined, articulated with a logic, not of causality, but with a more poetic logic of interval, movement, multiplicity of layers folding over each other in a heterotopic and variable space.

So it will not be a critique of racism produced as a statement that will work, a reduction to the law of the word, to the predictable syntax of a grammar of compulsion. The viewer must be 'enchanted'; as Bennett says, '… the ethical value of enchantment resides in its ability to persuade without compelling, to structure experience without insisting that this structure is the one that must be duplicated again and again.'[162] The effective critique (for want of a better phrase) is the one produced as something desirable: a form of life that is not just the film, text or building as expression, but the possibility of the viewer already formed or coming to being through other such articulations. Having been in one place (say, Dodge City Reserve in Brewarrina), one emerges via an interval in another (a car moving on a road). This is not just a vector of freedom (and certainly not a symbol or metaphor of it). Rather, it releases an ethical lifeforce through utterances ('JACK: I'm not havin' ago at yer, mate, I just wanta understand it that's all') or acts (sex in the back seat). The assertion of this life is offset by the dead kangaroo as a figure of Australianness, destroyed by the same ongoing mad rush that is Australian modernism and prefiguring the death of Gary hunted down by gleeful police at the end.

So WJT Mitchell's dialectical or binary conception of landscape as 'a medium of exchange between the human and the natural' is not what is envisaged here. This is a cosmology that places humans too centrally and instrumentally and it fixes the natural as a resource in a way similar to James Corner:

> nature's infinite complexity will in itself continue to challenge landscape situation and metaphors, demanding hermeneutical reflection through the (re)building of critical landscapes that do not stand still but continue to be revisited and transformed through time.[163]

The philosophy of variability envisaged here is an informal philosophy of the singular (with open-ended variability or iterability) rather than a deductive philosophy of the general (with particular variants).

Landscapes, therefore, are not constructing or drawing out the inherent identities of sites as if they were always approaching an ideal type. The landscape that is of interest here is one which, in a cycle of movement, releases potentials – forces and meanings that have real effects not established by 'principles'.

Rajchman reports Deleuze's opinion that, as an art form, cinema is closer to architecture than to theatre.[164] This enables us to see the potential of an unsettled postcolonial architecture, with its movement similarly rhythmed to road travel: we sit still in a car or the cinema as images and sounds flash and change; cars and films are continually linked with our occupancy of houses. Accordingly, Rajchman is interested in using Deleuze to create 'a new sense of "construction" neither purist nor transgressive nor utopian',[165] and, I would add, one that does not seek the redemption of Man in Nature, nor in indigenous spirituality, nor in anything other than the experimental and intelligent use of media that find chance points of articulation.

So we have seen a film, vehicled by movement, thus folded into the space of landscape, on the wings of a song, as new aspects of landscape continually emerge.

Gordon Bennett, *Black Swan of Trespass*, from the *Home Decor* [Preston + de Stijl=Citizen] series, 1996, Sutton Gallery.

SECTION 3

TECHNOLOGY

1

'HE THINKS, HE DESIRES'

In the very beginning everything was resting in perpetual darkness: night oppressed all the earth like an impenetrable thicket. The *gurra* [bandicoot] ancestor – his name was Karora – was lying asleep, in everlasting night, at the very bottom of the Soak of Ilbalintja; as yet there was no water in it, but all was dry ground. Over him the soil was red with flowers and overgrown with many grasses; and a great *tnatantja* [pole] was swaying above him. This *tnatantja* had sprung from the midst of the bed of purple flowers which grew over the soak of Ilbalintja. At its root rested the head of Karora himself: from thence it mounted up towards the sky as though it would strike the very vault of the heavens. It was a living creature, covered with a smooth skin like the skin of a man.

And Karora's head lay at the root of the great *tnatantja*; he had rested thus ever from the beginning.

And Karora was thinking, and wishes and desires flashed through his mind. Bandicoots began to come out from his navel and from his arm-pits. They burst through the sod above, and sprang into life.

And now dawn was beginning to break. From all quarters men saw a new light appearing: the sun itself began to rise at Ilbalintja, and flooded everything with its light. Then the *gurra* ancestor was minded to rise, now that the sun was mounting higher. He burst through the crust that had covered him: and the gaping hole that he left behind became the Ilbalintja Soak, filled with the sweet dark juice of honeysuckle buds. The *gurra* ancestor rose, feeling hungry, since magical powers had gone out from his body.

As yet he feels dazed; slowly his eyelids begin to flutter, then he opens them a little. He gropes about in his dazed state; he feels a moving mass of bandicoots all around him. He

> is now standing more firmly on his feet. He thinks, he desires. In his great hunger he seizes two young bandicoots; he cooks them some little distance away, close to the spot where the sun is standing, in the white-hot soil heated by the sun: the sun's fingers alone provide him with fire and hot ashes.
>
> His hunger satisfied, his thoughts turn towards a helpmeet. But now evening is approaching over the earth; the sun hides his face with a veil of hair-string, covers his body with hair-string pendants, vanishes from the sight of men. And Karora falls asleep, stretching his arms out on both sides.
>
> While he is asleep, something emerges from underneath his arm-pit in the shape of a bull-roarer. It takes on human form, and grows in one night to a full-grown young man: this is his first-born son. That night Karora wakes up because he feels that his arm is being oppressed with the weight of something heavy; he sees his first-born son lying at his side, his head resting on his father's shoulder.
>
> Dawn breaks. Karora rises; he sounds the loud vibrating call known as *raiangkintja*. The son is thereby stirred into life. He rises; he dances the ceremonial dance around his father who is sitting adorned with full ceremonial designs worked in blood and feather-down. The son totters and stumbles; he is still only half-awake. The father puts his body and chest into a violent quiver; then the son places his hands upon him. The first ceremony has come to an end.[166]

I was going to let this passage sit without commentary, but this connection is too good: What *is* the most significant body of Australian literature? The one that stretches from the first European literature set in Australia to the current European literature set in Australia? Or ... what? Langton has spoken of 'the grand tradition of ethnography in Australia that has produced, arguably, the most important literature in our history'.[167] I think she is thinking of passages such as the above, carefully translated from Arrernte by Strehlow, who was perfectly bilingual. But there are other significant gems of Australian literature that seem to empathise with an indigenous philosophy.

I am thinking of author Donald Stuart's wonderful novel *Yaralie* (1962), in which the individual identity of the main character is not as significant as her position as 'growing girl' in the Garadjeri group of northwest Australia (in Anna Plains country): '... *She had no special name, this girl – none that anyone remem-*

bered. She was just Girl. Young Girl. Not child, but growing girl. She was Yaralie ...'

The novel starts with a sentence that snakes and winds through the country, imitating in its form, it seems, the form of the country itself. It sings like the rippling cadenzas of Garadjeri song:

> She sat at the open side of the boughshed, the side that looked down to the well on the flat and to the old road coming out from the hills that squatted darkly secret on three sides of the flat. Behind the camp the hills marched northward in disorder, and eastward and southward where she looked they climbed and fell and staggered in broken bulks of red and brown and tawny gold.[168]

On this first page of the novel Yaralie remembers finding her first slug of gold in country where her white father and Garadjeri mother are drifting prospectors, working the lines of the country, equipped only with a hunter-gatherer alertness for the traces of a living to be gained. She is helped by ants who lead her to this wealth:

> There had been a line of black ants moving slowly from a nest at the base of a dead bloodwood, a slight skeleton of a tree that had never really lived, and she had followed it, watching its slow movement that was made up of a multitude of frantic jerky individual movements.[169]

She had followed

> the pattern of the line, its continuity and flow, swallowing each ant, leaving only a long slow line of ants, that went on and on, by quartz pebbles and flakes of schist, across sticks of dead wood and round a giant spinifex.

What Stuart has captured here is an abstraction of continuity and flow, so that the girl always loses sight of the individual ant, but becomes mesmerised by the pattern, so that in this antlike, snakelike country with its twisting creeks and gullies, her eye becomes able to see:

> As she had turned to go back, she had seen the slug, with her eye, but not with her mind, and had squatted to look closer. It had been almost covered, but the finger-tip piece that was above ground was the unmistakable dull heavy gold colour.

So engaged is she in her childish reverie – and Stuart in the writing – that the transformations continue and her heart becomes a bird: 'she had leaned forward, the flutter of her heart like the wings of a small bird in the wiry cage of her ribs, her mouth half open, her tongue and throat dry' and her newfound wealth, the 'enormous slug' is something she can talk to in a language that flickers between English and Garadjeri. Stuart has no interest in purity or continuity of language; he gives the situation its true sounds and language its regular code-switching, its 'foolishness' and incantatory rhythm.

> Squatting, heels wide apart, bare feet splayed on the hot ground, She had reached her hand out and touched it, and pulled at it, and it had come out, heavy, shapeless, the red earth sticking to it, an enormous slug, heavy, and she had turned it over carefully, wary of scorpion or centipede, sitting, then talking softly, foolishly, childishly, to the gold, of the gold of her mother and her father, of herself, and to herself, in her father's English and the language of her mother.
>
> 'I can find you, I have found gold, yenali, midji-midji mana, oh yes, and a big gold, see, big and solid; my mother and my father, oh, they will be pleased, and ngahdjoo ngalba, very good I am, that's what they'll say to me, and it was the pingah, the little black ant hurrying that led me to you. I'll take you to my bibi now, and she will be happy.'[170]

And, indeed, when she gets back to camp her mother's smile and the country have the same golden shine, which unites body and place (as, of course, Aboriginal philosophy does), and mother and daughter persist there in that place while time disappears: the hours do not 'pass', the day 'wears away' like the dissipation of energy from a labouring body.

> It had been heavy, that slug of gold, as she took it to her mother, holding it in her dress pulled up by its front to make a pocket, and when she had stopped in front of her mother and sat down, to roll the slug out at her feet, all the midday air, the shade, the sunshine the high clear pale sky, the silent world of flat and well and camp and waiting secret hills had suddenly become golden and hazed with the smile in her mother's eyes, and yes, her mother had said it, softly, 'Yenali, nyoondoo midji-midji mana. Ngalba.' Softly, with warmth, 'Just walking about, you found gold. Good.' And her mother had hefted it in her

> fine slim strong hand, and had put her head on one side, and clicked her tongue, and they had both drunk from the black billycan of cold tea till it was all gone, and had walked up the slope in the heat of noon to the camp, and had sat waiting for the day to wear away.[171]

So from those early days when whites and blacks, separately or together, made their lives nomadic in search of sudden wealth or, more likely, bare subsistence on the prospecting trails, we can shoot forwards (sideways, perhaps; the fossickers are still there) to the situation where the big businesses of extraction of mineral wealth still depend on indigenous cooperation.

2

INDIGENOUS CAPITALISM

Noel Pearson's Cape York Partnerships is a modern initiative that aims to empower indigenous communities within the economic domain. It is driven by moral force and seeks to link politics directly to the economic without too much 'empty' symbolic trickery in between.[172] It sprang from the belief that uncoordinated, centralised governments and their promotion of an epidemic of passive welfare dependency, have failed Aboriginal communities in Cape York, and that what was needed were solutions tailored to the particular situation in each region. Pearson says it is as simple as dusting down a big table in each community and sitting everyone around it who's involved in decision making.[173] Its called joined-up government, all fifteen different departments involved in the situation of youth in the community, each with their budgets, across the table from community people who are dealing with the daily situation – it is a kind of Third Way political thinking. To Pearson the concept of responsibility has always been as important as that of rights, as outlined in his book *Our Right to Take Responsibility.*

The call for people to take responsibility has certain connotations in white society, but when Pearson talks about it, it is in the context of traditional Aboriginal culture.[174] Pearson's controversial Family Income Management plan is one element of a three-pronged approach adopted in the Cape. This plan has been criticised as New Right politics, consonant with the views of the current federal government under John Howard. But Pearson is adamant that the problems that people who are marginalised face, such as his community, are less ideological than practical. Practical reconciliation is the platform of the current government's indigenous policy.[175]

For Pearson, alcohol prohibition and an economic development initiative, Indigenous Enterprise Partnerships, are the other two programs. Pearson believes the way forward is specific to place and particular situations and it begins with people taking responsibility for their futures and freeing themselves of that 'soul destroying passive welfare', which had been a general strategy of governance and one that failed to provide an active economy.[176] Crucially, he argues against the use of symbols:

> When you've got foetal alcohol syndrome and petrol sniffing, you're wiping out generations of kids. We could say those are casualties until we get the big symbols into place and we've got everything right at the Canberra end of things. I just cannot accept that we should let more generations of young people suffer and lose their lives and destroy their potential through the drug and grog abuse problems that exist. A lot of progressive thinking is preoccupied with the symbolic and it has little relevance to and offers little assistance to people who are trying to grapple with these terrible social and economic problems. It is absolutely critical we get a change of thinking about what is the priority because I don't think that positive social progress is going to follow symbolic reconciliation. It's just not going to happen. The symbolism should follow the practical social progress so we don't end up with something that's hollow.[177]

Pearson's injection of entrepreneurial thinking into Cape York via Indigenous Enterprise Partnerships has involved Boston Consulting, the Body Shop, the Myer Foundation and Westpac. The role of these private industry groups is to deliver expertise and to help support existing efforts, working with local people as they try to develop economic development programs.

> You don't send a bureaucrat in, you send a social entrepreneur. [They] don't have some kind of preconceived program, they are people who can see that there are not just problems here on the ground, there's opportunities, there's talents ... we actually go in and compile an assets [rather than needs] list.[178]

While cynics may suspect the involvement of private enterprise is merely a way for the government to pass social welfare responsibilities into private hands as an aspect of the charity economy, the approach Pearson has taken in seeking capital involvement is intended to be a contemporary manifestation of enduring Aboriginal principles; that a way of being will be specific to the resources and needs of a place and that one's conduct will be informed by responsibility specific to that place. However, while Westpac has no necessary links with rural communities, a small indigenous start-up business, say, in tourism, finds itself in competition with local whitefella businesses that are loath to go into partnership with blackfellas because they say the market isn't big enough. Richard Ah Mat of the Cape York Land Council argues that there is a 'moral case for indigenous capitalism', and the picture of an indigenous kind of capitalism starts to emerge in his description of 'strong families', the decline of a 'communist' or community model, the specifics of cultural difference and multiculturalism or biculturalism.[179]

The moral pressure seems to be largely on blackfellas not to see themselves at odds with the inevitability of the market economy. Morality, however, is a very dubious concept, playing little part in the organisation of either government or capitalist enterprises; it is unavoidably associated with judgment of the good and the bad and with the will of individuals to pull themselves out of the kind of dysfunction Ah Mat describes repeatedly. This dysfunction is not only endemic it is structurally associated with the kind of economy Cape York wants to embrace in principle: capitalism. Only morally disinterested governance, however, can regulate capital when it seeks to squeeze more out of workers; only education and training based on knowledge – including indigenous knowledges – can create new opportunities. It is impossible to avoid the symbolic; indeed, the label 'indigenous capitalism' is itself a symbol of a new way forward.

In 1997 at the Defence Force Academy I had a chat with historian Jackie Huggins, asking her if I should continue to struggle with the topic of Aboriginal philosophy, maybe working towards a book, and she said yes, kind of, tentatively. I eventually came to see that it would be too hard for a white boy to do anything really strong; I could only approach the topic with a kind of humility because while there *is* something 'out there' that is the accumulated wisdom of countless generations of Aboriginal peoples' living in their places; a mere book can scarcely contribute much to that. In any case, Jackie had a strong position on knowledge relations:

> Foremostly I detest the imposition that anyone who is non-Aboriginal can define my Aboriginality for me and my race.

> Neither do I accept any definition of Aboriginality by non-Aborigines as it insults my intelligence, spirit and soul, and negates my heritage. The reincarnate anthropologists have made a stunning career out of a continuous 'Daisy Bates' serial. There are no books written by non-Aboriginals that can tell me what it is to be Black as it is a fiction and an ethnocentric presumption to do so. I would never presume to know what it is to be white (except when I dine at the Hilton).[180]

Given the highly specific community procedures for producing Aboriginal knowledges, a book is hardly the right sort of medium to perform that sort of cultural reproduction. A book is a whitefella artefact destined to be used in the processes of dissemination, exchange and commentary, which characterise my academic culture. Aboriginal knowledges have specific contexts of disclosure, situated within larger processes of responsibility. The fixity of knowledge recorded in texts stands apart from the dynamic and continuous flux of process. Fragments recorded on paper get stuck in time and left behind after they are read. Once recorded, knowledges are open to be traded, manipulated and reinterpreted; the agency governing disclosure, crucial for Aboriginal knowledges, is appropriated if there is no longer a guardian present each time a book is read supervising the reading. Books are disseminated haphazardly; each time one appears it finds a new context – it is placed here and there – in a classroom, a library, a sitting room.

While we make no apology for this, it is crucial that one considers how each little development in the academic curriculum could also be seen to change incrementally the institutional structure of that environment. In other words, teaching author Sally Morgan in an English Department, for instance, shouldn't just involve getting students to rehearse the same sorts of responses they perform in relation to other literatures. In those contexts literary scholars agonise about speaking positions and placement: Who speaks for whom and should this text be read next to Shakespeare or should there be a special section for indigenous literature so that it doesn't get contaminated by other literatures? In this present context, *My Place* is beginning to look more and more like a perfect title for a book about the personal discovery of Aboriginal Being, which in fact it is. The real trick is to get the literature to increase, which means making it immanent to its *milieu*. Or, in the words of novelist Kim Scott: 'We gotta be moving, remembering, singing our place, little bit new, little bit special, all the time.'[181]

3

TRAVELLING THE SUBTERRANEAN RIVER OF BLOOD

> When this mixed host reached the border of the Ilbalintja territory[,] which is owned by Bangata-Panangka men, they decided to continue their further journey under the ground, lest they should trespass upon the ancient soil belonging to men of strange classes.
>
> They arose from Ititjankerama and continued their journey. They marched onward; they entered into the mulga thicket. Ntjipurara, the leader of the combined hosts, sat down with his legs crossed under him. The iliara seated themselves around him in circles. They all opened their veins. Thereupon a wondrous river of blood swallowed them all; it engulfed them deep in the ground; the blood rose to the top. Underneath the surface of the ground they continued their journey in the direction of Untjuiatjatua.
>
> The host emerged from the ground when Unmatjera territory was reached, and continued to march on the surface.[182]

As much as the linguist TGH Strehlow disliked hybrid languages, the above is *his* literary crafting of an ancient myth or performance that was originally in Arrernte: a hybrid of Arrernte content and English form, if you like, but missing are the bodily movements, the music and the ritual acts. All these elements necessarily come together in ritual; there is no indigenous content waiting to pour into any available form, such as the genres of English, which would remain untransformed by that process.

Contrast it to the 'Last Post' ritual, another ceremony describing the spilling of blood for one's country. For me, the relationship is heuristic rather than genuinely culturally comparative. Travelling this trope of blood allows for metonymic associations: giving of lifeforces for the communal good, creating this community in corporeal transformations focusing on death. In such rituals mimetic effects touch the participants; the contagious magic uniting them seems not to be explicable in the distancing vocabulary of sign, structure or function, which is why I would argue that one needs to rethink the apparatuses for understanding. Call them academic disciplines.

A piece of music is played on a brass instrument by a lone man at dawn. It is a trace of rhythmic energy, an almost perfect sine-wave emerging from a body and entering every sympathetic, permeable body in the listening host, which, in its life-movement, alternates inside and outside, self and Other, sound and the whisper of breath. The sound swells, other forces come together and intensify into something that might be called an event, perhaps a ritual. Its performance is designed to ensure cultural growth, or at least instil a structure of feeling. And as the final tone of the 'Last Post' fades on the breeze, there is hardly a dry eye at the Shrine of Remembrance.[183]

This 1920s war memorial is described by Dening as

> harsh and heavy, like some pillbox standing in Flanders fields, it is all contradiction in architectural design, a ziggurat on top of a columned temple ... through the ziggurat is carved a shaft. At the eleventh hour on the eleventh day of the eleventh month every year, the light of the sun beams through this shaft directly on the Unknown Soldier's tomb.[184]

Dening adds, wistfully, as he describes yet another kind of magic: 'Or it used to, before daylight saving. It is all done with mirrors now.' I am starting to think that, if the older magic was more à la Stonehenge, cultural events were always done with mirrors, the necessary seductive illusion being part of their force.

The crowd gathered there recreates the nation every time with this multiplicitous event: myth of origin, ceremony, music, bodies full of affect. The force of the myth lies not just in its meaning construction, it rather derives from the power of death as a vital force, this derivation as complex as the seeming necessity for music on this occasion and even for smells. There is the scent of the sprigs of rosemary worn in buttonholes by participants. It is also the transformation of the bodies of those present at this ritual. Michael Taussig talks of the 'magical harnessing of the dead for stately purpose', the state's:

> attraction and repulsion, tied to the nation, to more than a whiff of a certain sexuality reminiscent of the Law of the Father and, lest we forget, to the specter of death, human death in that soul-stirring insufficiency of Being.[185]

There is a vitalism, encapsulated by Ngarinyin elder David Mowaljarlai's 'Everything stand up alive', which can be read into foundation myths and rituals as the condensation of positive forces in the transformation of bodies in space. Death is a positive force to the extent that it makes gifts to the living; in return the living must make sacrifice, which, of course, literally means 'make sacred'. There is no greater sacrifice, we are told, than the gift of one's life for the nation: the unknown soldier stands for the universal and arbitrary grandeur of this gift. The state, relentlessly secular in its definition, remains nonetheless the highest form of the sacred-in-death ('the horror of the mute-absurd of the violence upon which all states are founded'[186]). Blood has been spilt. The political stakes for the sacredness of the state are high. The political question, however, in a multiracial and multicultural nation, is whose dead will count on the rolls of honour? In Australia the quasimagical force of Aboriginal cultures far outweighs the political calculations of numbers (now 2 per cent of the population) and representation, something Prime Minister John Howard seems determined to counter. Where is all this damn cultural force coming from? And so, the prime ministerial emotion concerning the stolen children will be one of anger not sorrow.[187]

4

LIFE, ABUNDANT LIFE

The field of traditional anthropology that has come closest to a description of Aboriginal philosophy is that of the study of religion. In that field the work of WEH Stanner touches on the problem of the relationship between philosophy and religion. Earlier, in a famous speech in 1969, Stanner established with the powerful evocation of the 'Great Australian Silence'[188] the force of historical forgetting, the repressed potential of which may be later released in that spasm of community feeling that is the sacred.[189] But the problematic of the sacred is not here his concern. Here he actually develops a description of a pan-Aboriginal philosophy, with statements such as 'The known evidence suggests that Aboriginal religion was probably one of the least material-minded, and most life-minded, of any of which we have knowledge.'[190]

Stanner does not qualify 'material' here, but he is probably referring to the minimal physical necessities for transitory lifestyles and a non-accumulative economy of exchanges in which objects have cultural rather than inherent and arbitrary value. By 'life-minded' he means an

> Intense, one could almost say obsessive, preoccupation with the signs, symbols, means, portents and evidences of vitality. The whole religious corpus vibrated with an expressed aspiration for life, abundant life. Vitality, fertility and growth; the conservation, production, protection and rescue of life … Vitalistic things obtruded throughout the myths and rites – water, blood, fat, hair, excrements; the sex organs, semen, sexuality in all its phases, the quickening of the womb; child spirits, mystical impregnation and reincarnation; the development of the body from birth to death; the transitions of the human spirit from

> before organic assumption until after physical dissolution; apparently animated phenomena such as green leaves, rain and the seasons, lightning, whirlwinds, shooting stars and the heavenly bodies; or things of unexplained origin, unusual appearance and giant size.[191]

This text has a sympathetic libidinal economy – Stanner is getting excited with his tropes of listings, metaphors and climaxes. Aboriginal philosophy is making connections happen in the mimetic and intersubjective sense of making things come to life, move, like his text quickening with poiesis. But elsewhere in his text his operative vocabulary centres upon 'signs', 'symbols', 'symbol function' and 'symbolism', a thoroughgoing representationalism that I will argue takes him down the wrong track, that is, significantly *away from* the religion he is describing. At the time he was writing it was intellectually mandatory, it seems, to say something stands for something else, or that a sign or symbol is a vehicle. He defines 'symbol' as 'the patterns, structures and designs that connect arrangements or systems of vehicles and their elements' (p. 167). A whole range of things are patterned in this way: iconic markings, such as 'zig-zags' and 'lines', semiotic things, such as 'silences' and 'facial expressions' and ritualistic things, such as 'drawing of human blood', 'laying on of hands', etc. He gives an example of how a whole range of things can come together:

> In certain initiatory rites a blood-smeared bullroarer is thrust between the loins of young men. Blood, bullroarer and loins are all symbolic of something else, but the significations may vary with context. In this case, evidently it is the pattern of structure or arrangement of the whole act that is 'the symbol'. But what is symbolized by it is not revealed directly or necessarily in the immediacy of the act itself.[192]

Stanner is searching for words, for an explanation, 'evidently it is the pattern of structure or arrangement', and now puts 'the symbol' in inverted commas, perhaps because its meaning is getting out of hand. 'Thrusting' no doubt signifies something else too, for this mode of analysis. Now, certain directions in poststructuralist thinking have given us grounds for doing a pretty solid critique of this sort of representationalism. One does not have to postulate another side to be revealed, away from the immediacy of the act. 'The presence of the sign is not an identity but an envelopment of difference, of a multiplicity of actions, materials and levels,' says philosopher Brian Massumi in the 'Meaning is Force' chapter in his *A User's Guide to Capitalism and Schizophrenia*.[193] 'Blood', 'loins' and 'bullroarer' are not metaphorical displacements either, they are planes of consistency intersecting in this particular ritual. They contribute to a build-up of intensity that makes this ritual work as it is in itself, to have the powerful effect of initiating someone.[194] Their significance is not elsewhere, as if thrusting really has to do with sex. Rather, thrusting is all over the place. Everything is thrusting, more or less; it just quickens in certain times and places. And it is movement going on here, not meaning; rapidity, not *logos*.

Stanner will later claim that one of the reasons there is no Aboriginal philosophy is that there is no tradition of intellectual detachment. True, there isn't an Aboriginal philosopher standing to one side observing this ceremony, stroking his beard and saying, 'Hmm, yes, definite sexual symbolism going on here.' That's the anthropologist's job. And we would have to reverse the gaze and ask Stanner just how intellectually detached he was about his *own* sacred rituals (seminars, advancements of science). Just how seriously was he taking himself? Philosopher Ludwig Wittgenstein would no doubt have intellectual detachment pegged as just one language game, perhaps the everyday version of negative theology. And we have to bear in mind that seriousness is not sustained in Aboriginal ceremony; there are significant periods of hilarity, lewd behaviour, clowning around, alternating with the most serious, life-transforming ritual. What's all that good fun supposed to mean, since anthropologists traditionally bracket it out? Later, Stanner's language performs his confusion:

> One studies symbolisms for the sake of the symbols, and the symbols for the sake of the symbolized. The things to which the symbols point are metaphysical objects, in patterns, structures and designs that, in religious study, are the true objects of inquiry.[195]

So the real reason for all this symbolism is so the 'true object' can become metaphysical! And his object of study has shifted. The contemplation of these (almost visual) patterns and designs will no doubt produce religious study, but not, I think, understandings of 'Aboriginal religion'. He goes on: 'In Aboriginal religions they form a highly involuted complex which anthropology is only beginning to break down.'[196]

If it is highly involuted, why not at least try to understand it as such, with an analysis for which the breakdown is less obviously non-Aboriginal? Stanner goes on:

> Whether such objects are 'real' is a question for philosophy, not for anthropology. It is sufficient that the Aborigines use symbols to conceptualize and express them, or features or aspects of them, in perceivable or inferrable ways. The symbols, by pointing to, stand for; by standing for they represent; by representing, they objectify; by objectifying they betoken ultimate or metaphysical things, which they thus mediate to living men by means of images. The vehicles conveying the images attract to themselves the sentiments, thoughts and acts properly due to what they ultimately designate. The vehicles are not themselves 'the religion', though they have sometimes been confounded with it because of a failure to distinguish the symbols from what is symbolized. They are but the husk around a kernel; means of symbolizing something else; tools or instruments ... [197]

He is floundering around with a circular representationalist model in which things have to be objectified and made metaphysical, converted to images and fed back into the ritual complex from which they originally emerged. The process he is describing is not an Aboriginal process of understanding, but the process of his own science's rationalisations of Aboriginal religion. The Aboriginal people he is talking about did not, of course, have the specific vocabulary he is using, a vocabulary designed to separate meanings from acts. In any case, Stanner himself denies any Aboriginal person could have conceived of the functions of representation because there was no 'tradition of intellectual detachment', no 'class of interpreters'.[198] No hermeneutic tradition, so the ritual, like the initiation, has to be taken on its own terms: it means what it does via immediate relations between objects, things, feelings, words, music.

The work of anthropologist José Gil can help us here. Gil advocates taking seriously tribal peoples' own words that they use to describe things and formulates a new approach in terms of forces:

> to stop giving prime attention to the *meaning* of signs, to their representational contents, in order to focus instead on their *practical effects*. To give up trying to decode the significance hidden behind symbols, but to ask what forces they draw on or shore up, and through which mechanisms they are likely to trigger certain effects.[199]

Taussig also offers a political critique of anthropology's reduction to the symbolic, the function being to create understandable and exploitable 'traditions' out of the force and magic of the primitive:

> How often we have been told that ritual's function brings spirit and matter into a divine unity as with the romantic understanding of the symbol (the understanding implicit in anthropological discourse). How often we have been told that rites, especially healing rites, recruit the passions in order to consolidate the cake of custom, sustaining the normality of the norm, the internalization of the convention (and so on).[200]

Gil again:

> In other words, and we must stress this notion, it is not a question of studying forces (magical, religious, prestigious or whatever) according to their representational contents, but to grasp them in the way they function in their own right, that is, in the way they may differ from the signs and symbols that are attached to them.[201]

Now, Stanner has given us the words of an Aboriginal informant or, rather, a kind of scenario that is instructive in a number of ways:

> Scholars familiar with Aborigines have usually had one impressive experience in common: to be taken by Aboriginal friends to places in the wilds and these shown something – tree, rocky outcrop, cranny, pool – with formality, pride and love. Conversations follow rather like this: 'There is my Dreaming [place]. My father showed me this place when I was a little boy. His father showed him.' Perhaps a child stands near by, all eyes and ears. Here is a tradition being made continuous, as in the past, by overlapping life-spans. What had his father said? 'He said: "Your Dreaming is there; you want to look after this place; you don't want to let it go [forget, be careless about it]; it is from the first [totemical] man." ' The historical link is thus made: from the now old to the still young; from the living to the anciently dead; from the very first true man to next true man; from the oldest time to the here and now. (Down with a crash come the needless postulates of racial and collective unconscious.) What did the father do there? 'He used to come here every year with the old men, the wise men; they used to do something here [hit, rub, break off pieces, brush with green leaves, sing]; that way they made the [totem] come on, come back, jump up, spread out.' *How* did that happen? *What* is it that is in the place? 'We do not know. *Something*

> is there. Like my spirit [soul, shadow, invisible counterpart]; like my Dreaming [naming the totem entity].' Will he think more? What else did his father say? That there was something in the Dreaming-place? The dark eyes turn and look intent, puzzled, searching. 'My father did not say. He said this: "My boy, look! Your Dreaming is there; it is a big thing; you never let it go [pass it by]; all Dreamings [totem entities] come from there; your spirit is there." ' Does the white man now understand? The blackfellow, earnest, friendly, makes a last effort. 'Old man, you listen! Something is there; we do not know what; *something*.' There is a struggle to find words, and perhaps a lapse into English. 'Like engine, like power, plenty of power, it does hard work; it *pushes*.'[202]

Let us take the informant at his own word. More important than the explanation (the *logos*) is the quasiritual (the approach to the place, the things one must do there, the way of life). In any case there is a 'struggle to find words'. And, most importantly, there is a force in this place ('it *pushes*'), not a meaning.

The anthropologist Ian Keen reads the same passage without the notion of power or force and comes down on the side of ambiguity. First, he sees the possibility for religion: 'A theist might argue that there is a spiritual reality towards which Aboriginal belief, as expressed in this passage, is groping. Stanner himself seems to have been of this mind …'[203]. While Stanner suggests that there might be determinate Aboriginal beliefs that are not easily understood by people using 'abstract, discursive symbol-structures', Keen argues that the beliefs are '*constituted* in the use of imprecise terms', that 'religious mystery was created through ambiguity'.[204] This may be so, but nor does it have to be a special case for Aboriginal material. It is the condition of language itself to be imprecise and it is the further condition of culturally elaborate materials (poetry, ceremony and the like) to have multiple layers of meaning. Keen may be telling us nothing specific about the Yolngu and nothing new about language. The other aspect his reading ignores is the layering of translation. If there is 'groping' in the Stanner passage, it is filtered and translated. His 'informant' is translating, perhaps from an indigenous language or concepts, then Stanner translates via the mode of recording used (memory? notes?) and then into English, into the specific discourse of social science. How does one eliminate the effects of all these indeterminacies to get to understand something about the indigenous expression?

Stanner's argument about why there is an Aboriginal religion, but not a philosophy, is based on the need for stated 'axioms' to be non-ritual and non-mythic, that is, to be 'scientific':

> There were no Aboriginal philosophers and one can thus speak of 'philosophy' only metaphorically. But there is ground for saying that they lived – and therefore thought – by axioms, which were 'objective' in that they related to a supposed nature of man and condition of human life. Myths presented the axioms in intuitive-contemplative aspect. Rites presented them in passionist-activist aspect. No Aboriginal put the axioms into words but the existence and efficacy of anything – including intuitional awareness and insights – do not depend on someone's formal affirmation of them in words. Myths would not be stories, and rites would not have an invariant structure, if axioms could not exist by other than formalized means. I shall try not to do more than state what I believe to have been the principle of Aboriginal philosophy in the metaphorical sense. I propose to call it a principle of assent to the disclosed terms of life.[205]

As he says elsewhere, 'Religious belief expressed a philosophy of assent to life's terms.'[206] It seems that the dominance of a certain kind of philosophy led early scholars of Aboriginal societies to opt for the category of 'religion' for these peoples. Even Stanner is not sure; since Aboriginal peoples had no gods as such there could be no theology. The problem is how to recognise the 'potencies'[207] Aboriginal people understand, since Western categories flip between the theistic and the scientific.[208] To his credit Stanner ends up saying that the 'Aboriginal religions must be described and analysed as significant in their own right, as expressions of human experience of life; as essays of passion, imagination and striving',[209] which is a broad, almost philosophical, definition, certainly one that is in tune with my interest in a philosophy as a way of life. As I have argued above, the intersubjective element will mean that the approach to the problem is as significant as its attempted solution.

Legitimate occupancy of the country, currently much contested in Australia, is about what peoples' bodies can conceivably do there. For this, Gil has created the term 'exfoliation', which describes the ways in which the body opens into the spaces it can occupy or articulate with; I can use it to 'read' (that is, displace, move from there/then to here/now) the story about the subterranean river of blood. The body, Gil says, is a volume in a perpetual state of disintegration and reconstitution through exfoliations.

> The anatomical diversity of the body and its various articulations show us that the space of the body is in itself diversified. There is no sole space, but multiple spaces; no sole relation, but a multiplicity of relations ... The body 'lives' in space, but not like a sphere with a closed continuous surface. On the contrary, its movements, limbs and organs determine that it has singular relations with things in space, relations which are individually integrated for the decoder. These relations imply *exfoliations* of the space of the body which can be treated separately. Relations to a tree, a prey, a star, an enemy, a loved object, desired nourishment, set into train certain privileged organs inducing precise places of the body. Exfoliation is the essential way the body 'turns onto' things, onto objective space, onto living things. Here there is a type of communication which is always present, but only makes itself really visible in pathological or magical experiences. Nevertheless the ordinary experience of relations to things also implies this mode of communication. Being in space means to establish diverse relationships with the things that surround our bodies. Each set of relations is determined by the action of the body which accompanies an investment of desire in a particular being or particular object. Between the body (and the organs in use) and the thing, is established a connection which immediately affects the form and space of the body; between the one and the other a privileged spatial relation emerges which defines the space which unites them as 'near' or 'far,' resistant, thick, wavy, vertiginous, smooth, prickly. The use of these metaphors in order to characterise the space of communication simply shows that the body is a foundation for metaphorization; because a 'petrified space,' for example, speaks of nothing but the quality between the body and the objective space – something of the order of 'petrification' comes from things and affects the body. And something of the order of the body (its capacity to qualify space, to transform it through affective investment) comes to affect things.[210]

There are many examples of this in Aboriginal Australia. In some mythical account of metamorphosis, round stones are the petrified eggs of a snake who is an ancestor figure. The body has become animal and then stone or, rather, a transformative relationship between stone, human body and animal is set up that is flickering in perception.

A perpetual transformative effect is the consequence of some blockage in narrative or ritual, such as that of Lot's wife who was turned into a pillar of salt because she broke the law.

So many Aboriginal stories seem to culminate in metamorphoses, beings turning into trees, stars or tracks. But these are not everyday stories; they are magical stories that are part and parcel of the strong beliefs and rituals that intensify the (bodily) energies of the participants in the ceremony. A ritual performance is an event in which codes (music, dance, myth, organisation of space), which are normally, in everyday life, quite separate, are brought together and condensed so that actual transformations can be brought about on the bodies of the participants or a single participant: an initiate to be made into a man and imbued with knowledge, a sick person to be cured. These bodies turn into the body of the ancestor-snake or the pain in the body is transformed into, for instance, a shard of quartz. Ritual exfoliations, therefore, are extraordinary compared to standard exfoliations of the body, which involve the ability to walk down a path, sit in a chair, drive a car – the body exfoliates into these spaces; leaves or laminates of surfaces as extensions of organs are involved, not the unitary body driven by a total self-image or central motor.

The subterranean river of blood story is about the bodies of the participants collectively joining the flows of their lifeforces, their blood, to create a fluidity that dissolves all borders (between their individual bodies and the sacred ground, the ground made sacred). The exfoliation is almost absolute, but it retains these features: vitality, movement, transformation (the bodies return to normal when they re-emerge). The movement is into country (at a place that gives life, like a soak) and out of it again, like ceremonies that are culture-made to 'move', 'stand up alive', and go down into the ground, 'quiet again' at the end. The force of the metaphor is also a powerful oneiric image of being moved, effortlessly, in a warm, fluid space, absolutely red when the light is shining through.

As Gil says for indigenous peoples:

> The Earth is not limited by a border which has precise contours tailored to the needs of the military, administration, customs, taxation or politics. The Earth is the magical territory perceived in the extension of the community body in relation to the ancestors.[211]

In the subterranean river of blood story, blood is spilt in order to avert possible danger and conflict with other people; in yet other stories the sight of spurting blood from a leg wound is a sign that a debt has been adequately settled.[212] Elsewhere, donations of this precious fluid fall into the domain of charity, for the moment, still for the collective good, not yet privatised, the aura of the sacred still isolating this substance from normal commodification.

Many indigenous accounts of the death of individuals are not so much about bodily death as about a return of energy to the place of emanation with which it reidenitifies. In this life-affirming philosophy death has a significant place: as in any philosophy people arrange things so that their beliefs about life and death become the effective means of their power.

In this section I have tried to show that the secular state finds in its foundation myths and rituals the same magico–religious forces observable in the rituals, and the cultural poiesis, of non-state societies. Accounting for the force of the cultural means accounting for the persistence of ritual in state-run societies, not to mention the persistence of the rituals of Others in these multicultural societies.

> The history of the State in the West has been a long process of disengagement of political power from its religious roots, while at the same time seeking out a new sacred foundation for its authority. This would be an interminable task. Where is the transcendence of the secular State to be sited, if it is away from religious or divine sources? It seems that no modern State has satisfactorily resolved this question. But history is revealing; in the absence of being able to give itself a religious foundation, the State will transfer aspects of its sovereignty and authority towards the 'nation'; and the latter will be founded on the power of the dead.[213]

The resurgence of the power of Aboriginal cultural formations in the context of Australia as nation in recent years is not just as a consequence of calculations about politics and justice, but also because of the resurgence of the power of Aboriginal rituals and of Aboriginality in rituals. This would be most significant in revisions of history and nationhood that seek to pay homage to the Aboriginal dead. Making the unknown soldier in a shrine of remembrance someone – anyone – from the Aboriginal wars would be the radical gesture that would honour all dead and those particular dead. It would change the site of our foundation myths to this country (rather than its current location in overseas wars) and create the possibility of seeing in Australia's Aboriginal wars the real horror and violence, yet also gain a new legitimation in the sacrifice of the Australian dead in these places and the gift brought by those dead each time we remember and honour them. This gift can be interpreted in a few ways: as glory for the metaphysically minded, as the reconciliation of the nation for the politicos and for me: some comfort in the idea that minor philosophies not only survive, but they are also the seeds of future thought.

5

BOXER DECONSTRUCTIONIST

Aboriginal power haunts Australian politics like a spectre. Like the Phantom, the ghost who walks, there are activists out there who are the children and grandchildren of people who refused to lie down and die. Perhaps in the way that Marxism has been the spectre of world politics, Aboriginal power has asserted itself through the patient exercise of sovereignty, intellectual invention and appeals for justice. And, despite all the struggles, the regular announcements of victory, assimilation, reform or ten point plans, Aboriginal power persists. Marxism, too, for that matter, continues to haunt the languages we use to analyse politics and history.[214] How does one understand the persistence, even the growth, of Aboriginal power, the power it uses to unravel those often-held certainties of whitefella politics and history?

In answering this I shall have to avoid that language which seems to aim towards certainty and closure (history and politics) and warily stray into philosophy again, a mode of activity that rarely engages with Aboriginal knowledges (or is, indeed, rarely seen as a kind of Aboriginal knowledge. You have religion, but not philosophy. Why is this?[215]).

My discussion will centre around a famous Kalkatungu man who lived with the Duracks in the east Kimberley when they started their pastoral empire. 'And on the more benign stations,' says Tony Swain, 'there was room for the creative philosophic thought of people like Boxer.'[216]

What kind of philosopher was Boxer? Mary Durack also mentions philosophy, in a book talking a lot about Boxer, *All-about*, 1935, in which the dedication, the most significant encapsulation of the book, ends by saying: 'Yours is the gift of laughter and human kindliness and true philosophy. Were you ever savages?'[217]

'Were you ever savages?' is the question picked up by historian Tim Rowse for his significant article, his historical and political analysis of the turn of the century frontier in the east Kimberley, '"Were you ever savages?" Aboriginal Insiders and Pastoralists' Patronage'. Why this interrogation about savages, from Durack in 1935 and then Rowse 50 years later, when the thrust of the question is that you can no longer be considered 'savages'? We know this from Durack's change of tense: 'Yours *is* the gift of laughter …' becomes '*Were* you ever …? [emphasis added]' But 50 years later Rowse still asks the same question; I will ask why again later.

Now I want to ask about that gift, that precondition, for not being savages: 'Yours is the gift of laughter and human kindliness and true philosophy.' Unlike Rowse I want to begin with what Durack asserts in that present of 1935; *true* philosophy (and *laughter* – not many jokes in historical and political analysis; these are no laughing matter) and *kindliness*, which is, of course, about kinship – knowledge and kinship, kith and kin, go together in the philosophies I am speaking about. Laughter, human kindliness and true philosophy are, of course, the opposite of savagery, as Durack implies, questioning the assumptions of her readers (just as Latour was to do in 1993, telling his European readers, *We Have Never Been Modern*[218]), so my interrogation of the analysis of certainty might just have to pop the question: Might your analysis not be getting a little bit savage, or at least a bit blunt, to the extent that it does not incorporate laughter, human kindliness and true philosophy?

So I am going to tell the story of the philosophy of Boxer (Warramungu was his bush name), an 'insider black', a 'magic', a *maban*, and how his work made Aboriginal power persist. I am going to reread the available texts, which give us just about all we know about Boxer. I am going to make these texts work a little bit harder – this is deconstructive method – finding the words in them that have given up and, it seems, can go no further on the road to truth. Exhausted words that fall back on our old assumptions. Critics of deconstruction say that it is apolitical, that it is all negativity and has nothing positive to offer, that it denies the existence of reality. Polemicist Keith Windschuttle, for instance, says: 'Because we are locked within a system of language, Derrida argues, we have no grounds for knowing anything that exists outside this system. "What one calls real life," according to Derrida, is itself a text. Hence it follows that all we have access to are texts. "There is nothing outside the text", he has claimed in a famous aphorism.'[219]

Derrida would never make such arguments and the quotations are not referenced. For a book that is supposed to take questions of history and truth seriously, it is very short-sighted and self-serving. It aims only to create a skirmish in a little academic field. However, I want to take some of the accusations on, to correct them and reveal more of the method I am using. The thrust of 'there is nothing outside of the text' – *il n'y a pas d'hors texte*, better translated as 'there is no outside position on a text' – is not to deny the existence of objects in the world, but to argue that a philosophical project, like deconstruction, does not consist in bringing a theory to a situation, or text, as if the theory would enlighten it, but rather to scrutinise what is being said in order to 'articulate the problematic foundations of our currently conceived political programs.'

In other words there is no 'outside' in the sense of a stable, overarching or commonsense position from which all things can be examined for their truth values. If deconstruction works from the inside, then its aim is to question the most basic assumptions and concepts underpinning a project. To neglect them is to surrender to political stasis. Elisabeth Wilson states the problem for feminism.

> Feminism's complicity with patriarchy, for example, is the structure of violence that is the "origin" of feminist politics in general. An examination of this "origin" is neither a disinterested pursuit nor a leeching [parasitic] one; on the contrary it is the hard political work of feminism itself. Without such (self-)scrutiny, that is without an examination of how this violent origin enables feminism in general, feminism may be tempted to declare itself a sanitized and sanitizing political practice.[220]

Now, this can be argued for Aboriginal political situations and the notion of inside and outside is most relevant to the frontier as reality and as metaphor. There is indeed a founding violence in the colonial or frontier situation. Many have experienced that this violence can be perpetuated by the words used in the analysis of it and that another kind of critical or symbolic violence has to be performed on those words to open up a space for new political conception and action. This is deconstruction. It works from the inside, it does not bring ready-made concepts from somewhere else and apply them. And if we agree that there is no Aboriginal politics that is not complicit with the colonial violence that created the need for them in the first place, then there will be no pure Aboriginal position outside to provide a critique of what is going on inside Aboriginal politics. Those doing these politics are working within and continually on the symbolic violence of colonial history, in which that history can never be purely a whitefella imposition nor a pure blackfella revolution from the other side. So, for this story, Boxer is the enigmatic figure of frontier ambivalence whose work should be able to cast some light on how we think about Aboriginal politics and power.

The power of words and the inside/outside problem articulate Rowse's text. He knows that the arrival of the Europeans on the Kimberley frontier was a massive disruption of the old way of life: 'a world in such ferment'[221] and, 'the unprecedented nature of the phenomena confronting Aborigines'[222] are phrases he uses. And before too long he divides the frontier between 'insider' station people and 'outsider' wild blackfellas – which is pretty convincing – yet he uses too quickly, for my liking, the word 'order' to describe station life: '... the universe of Kimberley Aborigines came to be divided between the pastoral *order* and its dangerous exterior',[223] and, 'to be lost, as in Jack Bohemia's police tracker stories, is "to be in a state of moral *disorder*" '.[224] The crucial question is, whose life was more ordered? Whose law is wilder, the cattle spearers' or the blackfella-shooters' (and there is evidence that the Duracks, as well as their insider blacks such as Boxer, were among the shooters, though they were almost surely not the worst of them).[225] Old Bulla (from Kununurra) puts the same question, talking about magic: 'Who's the powerful? Who's the strongest? The white man or the blackfeller, see, out of those two?'[226]

Now, having posed those questions, I am not going to be in a position to answer them, here, and it is not my place to do so. I have simply woken up a sleepy word, 'order', which was happy to go along with the assumption that the whitefella world was taking over on this frontier, that this would be the new world order, so to speak, what Rowse calls the *Pax Durackia*, and what others have called the 'golden age' in Northern frontier history:[227]

> Here is a lasting ideology of paternal responsibility – timeless compared to the shifting government philosophies of protection, assimilation, land rights and self-management ... It is this ideology, as much as Durack's books themselves, which enjoys

> classical status in Euro–Australian culture. An ideology as secure as this must have reason to be so. Jack Sullivan's memoirs have shown us one reason: he and his fellow stockmen were able to expound their good fortune as subjects of the Durack's peace.[228]

After many thousands of years of Aboriginal reign in the Kimberley we have a picture of a 'lasting' new peace, a 'timeless' and classical ideology installed at Argyle under the benevolent patronage of the Duracks. But what happened? Charlie Court had grander plans for the Kimberley: in 1971 the lands around Argyle were submerged by the waters of the Ord, a veritable biblical flood. On the scale of Kimberley history this new order hadn't lasted too long.

Yet it lives. The Duracks transformed this pastoral order into books, Mary wrote a fine pastoral classic, *All-About*, which included Elizabeth's drawings, and Elizabeth went on to create a fictional indigenous *persona* for herself, Eddie Burrup, based in part on Boxer.[229] Boxer, for his part, transformed all that local material into a new cult, his *djanba*, the ceremonial boards of which are disintegrating along with the remains of the station (the homestead itself was relocated) under all that water.

Whose magic is the more powerful? I can only keep asking that question, but I am an outsider critic, one of a group Rowse perceptively included in his discussion. Who were the enemies of the Duracks' order?

> From the Durack point of view there were two sets of outsiders to de dealt with: the urban critics of pastoralists' apparent enslavement of local Aborigines; and those local Aborigines who distanced themselves from the homestead's regime of rationed work and remained a danger to people and to cattle. For the Duracks and their contemporaries 'the insiders, both black and white' enjoyed an accord that neither the critics with pens nor those with spears could share.[230]

The critic with the pen is wild in the sense of being out of line. What would those city folk know? For instance, there is a profound accord, a loving trust, that makes Mary Durack able to write in the following way about the housekeeper who comes up from the camp to wake up the people in the homestead each morning:

> Nubbadah's coming marks the beginning of the day for the white community. She pads noiselessly, from one to the other,

> and upon the sounder sleepers lays a firm black hand. 'Cub-a-dee!' she says, thrusts a cup and saucer into half-dazed hands and disappears.[231]

Do a bit more work on the text. There are two sorts of hands; 'firm black' ones and 'half-dazed' [white] ones. Each day her coming 'marks the beginning'. Who is running this show? And already on the previous page we have met Boxer for the first time, as a young boy, insisting that a boab tree be planted in the garden against the wishes of the gardener who found them

> hideous ungainly things; but Boxer the ten-year-old rascal, had brought it in to be planted in the garden and called after himself. Boxer thought very highly of boab-trees (particularly boab nuts), and what Boxer said, even in those days, went. 'Boxer' the boab tree is nearing its forty-fifth year.[232]

Where did this powerful boy come from, who could boss around the white gardener? Mary Durack tells us that he was

> from the Mt Isa area ... the eight year-old Boxer had come across from Queensland with his mother and a man called Wesley Lyttleton, then on their way to the Halls Creek goldfields. Pumpkin, so the story goes, took a fancy to the boy and acquired him in exchange for a good packhorse and a tin of jam.[233]

This boy grew up to be so trusted by the Duracks that he virtually ran the cattle camp, as did Jack Sullivan who followed in his footsteps and left his oral history with Bruce Shaw. As a Queenslander, grown up by another Queenslander (Pumpkin), Boxer had some conflict with the locals, but at the same time learnt the local languages and mediated strongly between inside and outside: 'Boxer was a man who flowed around like the wind,' said Bulla.[234] He was always turning up just as he was needed; whitefella and blackfella testimonies agree on this.

Most importantly, for my argument, he was a cultural innovator. Was he happy with the order the Duracks had installed or, rather, the order that his peoples' cooperative effort had installed with the Duracks, which was only to last a little more than his lifetime? There was obviously such a huge disparity between these two ways of life that he could not help but be highly stimulated by it, to do something with it. Not totally unlike Mary Durack writing *All-About* to make sense of it all from her point of view. But while Mary Durack's text was sent off to the *Bulletin* to be published far away from its source ('You will never read this, for to learning you have no pretensions ...' she says in her dedication to her 'all-about' mob, adding, as if in anticipation of intellectual property issues, 'You cannot sue us for libel'), what Boxer did was performative. He created a new cult, *djanba,* which would have been quite opaque to the Duracks (they too, had no pretensions to learning).[235] This *djanba* that Boxer created really took off:

> Old Daylight ran that Djunba from down near the jetty road at Wyndham. He just flew around like that, all over, like this Mulalai who started from that way too. Djunba flew in the sky, Mulali went on the ground. Djunba started from Wyndham and came this way past to Argyle right back this way to Darwin. The corroboree belonged in Queensland to those Kaukadunga, in mixed English ... They were really clever men and flew over just like the wind.[236]

Rowse quotes the full text from Lommel, who observed the cult in the 1930s:

> In the myth of *Tjanba*, some of the characteristics of this ghost are borrowed from modern culture: his house is of corrugated iron and behind it grow poisonous weeds. *Tjanba* is able to impart the hitherto unknown diseases of leprosy and syphilis by means of little sticks which have lain in those weeds overnight. Men who possess [name deleted, but incised boards thought to have circulated from the desert Aborigines] are able to infect other people. *Tjanba* hunts with a rifle and ornaments his slabs with iron tools. To distribute his slabs to men (some of his slabs are stolen, others he himself sends out) he uses aeroplanes, motor cars and steamers. When showing the slabs to fellow ghosts, he asks them for tea, sugar and bread. Following the myth, the modern cult demands exuberant feasts with tea, sugar, bread and as much beef as possible but no meat from any indigenous animal. The cult places have to be in the vicinity of farms and stations. The cult language is Pidgin-English. The cult is directed by a 'boss', the slabs are stored away by a 'clerk', the feasts are announced by a 'mailman', and order and discipline during them is maintained by some specially appointed 'pickybas' (from police-boys).[237]

Swain has written about this cult and others like it in interesting ways. Swain's habit when citing these Aboriginal innovations is to talk of the 'cosmic marriage' of two laws: '... having of necessity allowed White Law to impose itself on them, they have sought their salvation partially by employing its representations, but pre-eminently by conjoining it with the law of the lands and their spirits.'[238]

To which one has to ask: Is 'salvation' what cultural innovators, even philosophers, seek? Are these two laws conjoined, married? All of these metaphors suggest closure, the pious end of the story. But *djanba*, like Boxer, knows how to flow around and put himself inside every ceremony: As Swain says:

> Jack Sullivan [says] ... Djanba 'was a wild human' ... The multifaceted Djanba has a chameleon-like capacity to conceal himself within ceremonies; 'he puts himself in every corroboree; just fits himself in'. His ability to appropriate perhaps reached its height when, at the request of the Catholic priest who asked that traditional songs accompany mass, Djanba entered holy communion: 'he goes through the white fellers now that Djanba'.[239]

Swain makes a strong case for power coming from the east, not only the colonisation by the Durack mob, but also a tradition of new cults emerging from Arnhemland. Coming on that wave Boxer seemed to have brought, from his own country around Mt Isa, a way of thinking that coupled fierce loyalty to the whites with a culture which, according to Swain, was 'more subtle and dangerous' than the millennial cult of *Mulunga* (see p. 19), born about the same time as Boxer, in the late 1880s, and spreading right down through the centre to South Australia. Six hundred warriors were supposed to have died at Battle Mountain. Boxer would have been about three at the time, though we don't know if he was anywhere near there.

Now, unlike *Mulungu*, the argument goes, *djanba*, Boxer's cult, does not promise as its outcome a return to homelands free of whites. It does three rather new things. First, it articulates Aboriginal power with white objects such as cars and aeroplanes, giving it speed of transmission. Second, it morphs culturally, performing insider work – 'he puts himself in every corroboree; just fits himself in'. its third innovation is that it opens up time by proposing a future, personal immortality, in the form of stories about Boxer's resurrection after death, the introduction of the subsection system (by Boxer) and Moon stories that involve recycling of individual bodies than places and, possibly, also the promise of equal coexistence with whites. Swain is assertive ('Time is central to the innovations of Boxer …'[240]), but not entirely convincing on these questions; like so many of us he lacks evidence.

How does a deconstructive attitude attend to the fact of the persistence of Aboriginal power in the face of the opposing power of white philosophies? Take another innovative object, as described by anthropologist Bob Tonkinson in Swain:

> Crayon drawings made by Aborigines of *badundjari* [dream-spirits] sometimes resemble aircraft, and vehicles said to be used by *badundjari* to transport others are depicted as aeroplanes, complete with wings, tail, windows and headlights, but with sacred boards, not propellers or jets, supplying the power source.

Swain concludes:

> In other words, these spirit aircraft were propelled to their lands by icons manifesting the potentiality of place. Beyond dreams filled with invading places are visions of place-planes offering a ride home.[241]

This innovation, which articulates Aboriginal power with white objects of power, speed and travel, has a poetic resonance in the very shape of the propeller boards and the sound they make. But we all know those blokes must be quite wrong to think that *that* is what gives these machines power; it is, of course, the engines, the petrol … unless we make one little shift, which is to humanise the object, not fetishise its technology. The plane articulates with the bodies that use it; the seats and controls are made for bodies to occupy. It cannot function without them. The object has emerged out of human invention, out of bird-dreams. How far is it from them in the ways we enjoy it? The power is ultimately human. Whether the humanism is relevant, understanding the plane from this perspective makes the Aboriginal version no longer primitive. It sees it from what we might call indigenous connectivist (relation-based or pattern) thinking, rather than thinking in terms of discrete objects and beings. In any case, all objects are assemblages; they are not 'pure' constructions, even in respect to time:

> What things are contemporary? Consider a late-model car. It is a disparate aggregate of scientific and technical solutions dating from different periods. One can date it component by component: this part was invented at the turn of the century, another, ten years ago, and Carnot's cycle is almost two

> hundred years old. Not to mention that the wheel dates back to neolithic times. The ensemble is only contemporary by assemblage, by its design, its finish, sometimes only by the slickness of the advertising surrounding it.[242]

We can ask once again – with an old Aboriginal man, Bulla, comparing whitefella and blackfella magic, 'Who's the powerful? Who's the strongest? The white man or the blackfeller, see, out of those two?'[243] – not to decide that contest, but to use this image-thought to pragmatically rethink (in a singular context) a fundamental value (power). Power was never an *a priori* value; it is made and remade as a philosophical concept that can also be used. How can we explain the paradoxical power of political weakness, the persistence of indigenous magic? In Deleuzian terms it makes connections that modernist technological fetishists have forgotten: these connections spark across potential differences, mobilised as they emerge. Indigenous political thought, one might add, seems to be characterised by the patience of the gatherer-hunter, waiting for the right conditions, unlike the individualist and forced will-to-power of the European politician.

Rowse supports his history of the stability of insider station life, opposed to the 'landscape of terror'[244] on the outside, with narratives in the 'police tracker genre', as documented by linguist Bill McGregor. In these narratives, understandably because told by a police tracker, there is no safe return for outlaws; people would generally die out there. 'The safe return of the lost is a non-event in Bohemia's narratives because, in the moral order that gave rise to police tracker narrative, people had no business being out of place.'[245]

But there is another genre that contradicts this one, one that suggests to me that people such as Boxer, who had no terror of the outside,[246] might just as soon have been inside on the outside, so to speak, flowing around, getting in with the locals. So when Boxer is put in goal he can escape at will with his magic:

> They put the poor bugger in the jail house in Wyndham, locked him in. He'd done nothing. They just put him in the jail, that's all, and he came out and went away. After a while they saw Boxer walking round in the pub out there. 'Oh blimey', the policeman said, 'There Boxer outside walkin around.' 'Oh well', old M.P. Durack said to him, 'You can getim and putim in jail if you wantim.' They went up. The policeman caught him and took him back and locked him up in the jail house. As soon

> as they walked away, two or three hours after, they saw Boxer again walking about outside. 'Ah well, give him another go.' The third time they tried again and saw Boxer sitting down in the store in a chair, the old bastard. They didn't know what to do. The policeman couldn't do anything.[247]

This escape narrative has exactly the same structure as Paddy Roe's 'Mirdinan', even down to the three part structure.[248] Mirdinan goes further afield, down to Fremantle, to escape dramatically from the noose as he is hanged, transforming into an eaglehawk and flying back to his country. Boxer's magic *persona* shares some of these features of freedom of movement – self-transformation (changing into an emu, also in Paddy Roe's stories), letting his guts spill out and putting them back and creating songs and stories – all in explicit assertion of blackfella power.[249] This, I would argue, is inside work on the representations of both black and white culture. It is less the mediation of the clever man, creating a syncretic culture by going backwards and forwards, and it is certainly not the culture of a radical outside, as in the Mulunga cult (or Pigeon's guerrilla warfare in the central Kimberley), which would bring whitefella rule to an end and take things back to the old ways.

Boxer's infiltration and conceptual change of both laws is open-ended. As Swain says, it incorporates time, perhaps for the first time, in a significant way in Kimberley cultures. We don't know what happened to Boxer in the end. Unlike Paddy Roe's Mirdinan, who was defeated by a whitefella power and alcohol and dumped in the deep water off Broome (another source of ceremonial power, according to Swain), Boxer, in a way, still lives. One source says he was 'in our cemetery down at Argyle'.[250] Jack Sullivan says he was buried in Darwin, but then, years later, seen in a pub in Hughenden, north Queensland, by a white station manager who returned to Darwin to find his grave split open.[251] 'I don't think magic people die,' concludes Bulla.[252]

So this 'history experiment' starts to conclude. We have seen deconstructive method work with the changing stories of Aboriginal power, leading up to the radical challenge to historiography posed by Boxer. Yet, as always, we are left with further questions: What is the most appropriate method for understanding that frontier history? As Rowse says, 'The most difficult part of frontier history for Europeans is the history of Aboriginal understanding: How did they make sense of the invaders ...?'[253]

My feeling is that we have to go further than the opposition of inside and outside, that the method will also involve simultaneous enquiry of how the invaders understood the Aborigines. I also think that it is not just a question of getting the words right, for, if the Boxer story has taught us anything, it is about the importance of performance. The stations and the country of the east Kimberley were the theatre of his life as 'a magic'. I haven't been able to reproduce any of that drama in my poor performance today (maybe I should make an excuse, like old Bulla: 'I could dance it but my knee's buggered'[254]). But that is the question: What forces does history writing mobilise that reach truths other than – or as well as – the factual? What will be their poetry, their magic?

And in deconstructing the insider/outsider opposition, let me recall that spectre of communism with which I began. Tim Rowse quite rightly warns against city outsiders who are too quick to condemn exploitation on the stations, armed as they are with a Marxist theory insensitive to the more 'human' relations of affection on the Durack stations, for example, that enabled survival and cultural innovation for the station Aborigines, pretty much on their own terms, running the stations almost as much as they were run by them. Now, what is curious is that Swain's book concludes with another haunting of that marxist philosophy, but one that works its way up from the Pilbara, becomes known as Don McLeod law, infiltrates ceremonies such as *Djuluru* and perhaps culminates at Wave Hill with the revival of the land rights campaigns. This is the law of the fair go, of the historical, future oriented promise of equality and moral rights. Was it Boxer, perhaps the first Aboriginal modernist, who paved the way along this frontier for the passage of these ideas?

How can it be that communism, now pretty dead as a social system and capitalism triumphant on the world stage, came inappropriately from the city as European theory and secret English and from the bush as insider knowledge, to produce, in conjunction with local cultures that I have been unable to expand upon, a radical transformative cult that still lives in the name of Boxer? Boxer's story has the power that is often attributed to European theories, stories with the power to change our understandings of things. Boxer is dead, we are pretty sure (maybe we should check that grave again),[255] but as that Algerian-French philosopher says, 'The dead can often be more powerful than the living.'[256]

6

INDIGENOUS MODERNITIES

In 1873 Rimbaud urged his European compatriots to be 'absolutely modern'; if they understood what he meant, they no doubt already were. Being modern, it has been claimed for individuals, is 'one of those all-or-nothing conditions: either you are or you are not'.[257] But when it comes to social groups or communities 'modern life' can only appear under propitious social, economic and philosophical conditions. These include the rise of rational and scientific thought, secularisation (yet redemption in promised worlds), the mastery of Man over Nature and materialism. In this body of thought and activity time is crucial in assuring man's social destiny. Those who are already modern are busy creating the artefacts of modern life, the whole trade fair of industrialisation, while any aspirants to the modern condition find themselves with the wrong artefacts and in the wrong place at the wrong time.

In Australia indigenous communities have been targeted for development in a way analogous to Third World countries. This has roughly been the case from the adoption of social and economic policy towards these communities and, as they 'evolved', from anachronistic 'savages' to welfare dependents to partially autonomous communities, but never quite, it seems, contemporary modern subjects. This section aims to turn this developmental and historicist thinking around.

Europe, traditionally thought to be the place of origin of modernity, has forms of (aesthetic) modernism and (material) modernity that are varied and stratified. Modern ideologies may have aspired to social and economic uniformity, but this never happened. In any society considered modern there is the minimal and the overabundant. The street dweller on the banks of the Seine in Paris claims to be a modern subject, as does the multimillionaire in Neuilly-sur-Seine. So not only does modernist uniformity not exist in these most likely places, but whole regions and social strata in northern hemisphere countries are also 'underdeveloped' like the Third World. Some communities of migrants and guest workers in the heartlands of Europe *are* Third World and they have upset the white dreams of uniform modernity and national identity. And dreams they are: there was always a proletarian underclass before there were migrants to blame. This class – or these migrants – have not slipped back into poverty; their material, cultural and even spiritual poverty was always cyclical and endemic.[258] There are more and more people today who would not understand what Rimbaud meant.

So even at the heart of the modern project there is a quarrel over the empirical conditions for modernity that is not due to the failure of economies or governmental will to make everyone comfortable and up to date. The quarrel arises from the fact that modernism and modernity are conceptually split across what is a shifting colonial divide, not only between the West and other countries of the world considered to be in development, but even within Western countries. This conceptual split leads us to claim that an absolute modernity cannot be a simple attribute or achievement. It is full of contradictions and each of its manifestations carries its own ancient forms, for instance, the mimetic. Rather than leaving behind the primitive, modern inventions such as the cinema re-enchant the machinery of mimesis; there is, says Taussig, a 'surfacing of "the primitive" within modernity as a direct result of modernity.'[259]

The narrative of modern disenchantment, which Jane Bennett has so skilfully described, brings alienation (a sense of embeddedness of human life in a cosmological order) and a loss of the 'primitive' magic of events in favour of a calculated telos. This disenchantment causes the moderns to be nostalgic for those 'fugitive experiences of magic [that] persist within the calculable world … mysticism, eroticism and other curiosities of the "cultural" field.'[260] Her 'alter-story' advocating a re-enchantment of modernity finds a 'pagan' enthusiasm for a 'materialism wherein matter has a liveliness, resilience, unpredictability, or recalcitrance that is in itself a source of wonder for us'.[261] No longer, therefore, do 'we' have to pester indigenous peoples as curiosities and bearers of 'magic' and at-oneness with the world that we have lost, for the contemporary world is replete with that same magic: Walter Benjamin found it in cinema, Jane Bennett finds it in nanotechnology and an optimism of the spirit. Indigenous peoples, for their part, can escape the anachronism of playing the primitive (or endorsing the sad story of how the industrial world has betrayed them as well) by asserting their own forms of modernity.

The modern is most often constructed – as much postcolonial thought has taught us – by contrast with the primitive, such that the modern/primitive is a paired concept. Hegemonic modernism is bolstered by apparatuses of representation (literature, cinema, art), which function to provide glimpses of the primitivism of the Other, for instance, in the unconscious – that holiday home of the eternal savage, which is itself a modern invention – only to constantly reinforce civilisational logics as the moral narrative is spun out, according to which the modern is both good and inevitable. And we are familiar with how the story of a nation can emblematise a whole people, often the indigenous, as its internal primitives.

Gil's definition of a primitive society is one in which only one system of power is in operation, where, in response to interrogation, people will assert that the law is singular, ancestral or immutable.[262] To this we must add that while there is no such purely primitive society either, it is possible for a 'primitive' political mode, for instance a totalitarian one, to dominate in some societies, while its contestation (underground resistance, for instance) is necessarily modern because it differentiates power.

Let us assert, then, that primitivity is something that has never been effectively left behind. But understanding primitivity in modernity is less about an historical dialectic than it is about the recognition of multiple primitivisms and modernisms in all sorts of cultural practices and in any culture. A primitivism is a reduction to the self-same, to the always was, to the non-historical and circular. Concepts too can be primitive; these are the key concepts so packed with common-sense assumptions that they are ripe for deconstruction. If a social science bases its discourse on words such as 'function', 'language' or 'power', these become the necessary givens on which other concepts can be elaborated or a method can proceed. These, then, are also the words one might interrogate if one is no longer satisfied with a given conceptual framework.

What is the essential difference between the ancient and the modern? Philosopher Charles Taylor identifies two useful models for thinking about this.[263] One says that the difference is cultural, that the difference between, say, medieval and contemporary Europe has come about through a radical reorientation of the structure of values and concepts such that the difference is analogous to the difference between medieval India and medieval China. The other model says that there is a social evolution that is rational and culture-neutral: the older culture, aided by social changes such as industrialisation and urbanisation, gradually sheds its superstitions as it acquires reason. Here, the acquisition of reason is seen as 'the exercise of a general capacity, which was only waiting for its proper conditions to unfold'.[264] This acultural model lends itself to the idea of the spread of modernity as an inevitable historical transition and the expression of human destiny.

The culturalist theory, on the other hand, allows for a theory of alternative modernities, which would see difference in terms of ruptures and breaks.[265] Different modernities would result in different societies as they come from divergent starting points in their particular traditions, adapting, borrowing or having imposed on them aspects of the modern. These other modernities don't just happen; they can also be the product of forces such as the expression of political desire, for instance, for independence from colonial annexation. In such a process, in which identity is both maintained and protected from being flooded by some other culture, it is necessary to keep up the link to native antiquities and civilisational roots as the sources of moral worth and the spiritual foundations of such societies.

In Europe, the 'ruin' has a special emblematic status as the magical source of ancestral power. Europe is seen as building its modernity on these ancient ruins, something of a Walter Benjaminian idea: 'the loosened building blocks … out of which a new order can be constructed'.[266] But this constructionist metaphor is far too historical in its orientation for our purposes. It implies progress and linear chronology and ignores the fetishistic uncovering and display of ancient ruins that came with modernism, so that the ancient was very much made to live in a spectacular fashion within the modern, like the colosseum in the modern city of Rome. The pilgrimages towards history, known as tourism, began as the everyday manifestation of this power and the millions of individual pilgrimages close the circuit by which the ancient and the modern were constantly fed into each other from the Enlightenment onwards. What we would add, therefore, to Taylor's culturalist version of modernity is the specific engine that powers it: the link that flashes between the coexisting ancient and modern.

When the European modern gets transported to a place such as Australia it becomes dislocated from its sacred sites, disorienting the settlers. In the first instance they cannot recognise the new places as home and go back to the old country whenever they can in their imaginations or on actual trips. In a second movement they begin to construct significant sites, monuments and associated myths to pay homage to. Aboriginal peoples, for their part, because of the late date of colonisation, were not even expected to play the civilisational catch-up game; for the first 200 years their primacy and antiquity were scarcely recognised as having any value for contemporary life.

The forms of indigenous antiquity are less material than the constructed European monuments in Australia; and precisely because they seem less immaterial they seem more philosophical. They are enshrined in a massive oral literature and an extensive set of relationships with country. Were Australian modernism – or postmodernism – to build on indigenous antiquity it would look completely different to the ruins of European culture. The standard option for modernist discourses, the conversion of history into novelty-commodities, has happened to indigenous cultures in Australia, but this obviously takes the form of kitsch objects such as tea-towels or tourist boomerangs. Aboriginal history is a more serious but also relatively new phenomenon and is a great source for new material for understanding a broader and more multiply stranded Australian history. But our concern here is not historical; it is with the indigenous past and its operation as a co-past (with Europe) in contemporary Australian culture. The presence of this antiquity is fundamental to the alternative being posed to a European antiquity. I would suggest it was always growing, organically, as it were, out of the country and that the indigenous ancient gives shape and form to the convulsions into indigenous modernism brought about by the rapid change introduced by invasion and colonisation. The forms of this indigenous modernism have scarcely been recognised yet.

It might be useful to clarify my terms, since I am dealing with a conceptual domain where meanings of words such as 'indigenous' and 'modern' are used in a variety of ways. 'Indigenous' most often describes people who identify as such and are accepted by their community as such.[267] They are linked by a network of kinship and other associations to each other and to specific parts of their homelands. But 'indigenous' is more than a political identifier for a person; it is also a basis for a conceptual package of other concepts, such as nativism, autochthony and ancestral or ancient connections with country. Here, it seems to sit very uneasily with the modern.

Let us deal, then, with the modern, which can be split into modernism and modernity. Scholars, such as literary critics, working in the field of aesthetics have a fairly good idea of what they mean by modernism. It is a movement of the early 20th century, ushered in especially by the First World War. In writing it would be associated with the formal innovations of writers such as Gertrude Stein and James Joyce: streams of consciousness, strong metaphors, language and form overpowering content and narration. Cognate movements in the visual arts, such as cubism and abstract expressionism, music and architecture, have similar strategies; all are conscious of posing as the new in favour of tradition. This, then, is the cultural-aesthetic discourse of modernism.

Now, there is also the 'philosophic discourse of modernity'.[268] According to Christopher Norris this Enlightenment modern philosophy starts with Descartes and is consolidated in Kant. It is about shoring up certain values against scepticism. It is 'enlightened, critical, progressive [and] aimed towards extending the public sphere as far and as wide as possible'.[269] Critical theorist Jürgen Habermas calls this the 'unfinished project of modernity' and defends enlightenment and rationalist values against the incursions of poststructuralist philosophers of various sorts who may be interested in the kinds of cultural differences and incommensurabilities that might debate and challenge the fundamental values of European philosophic modernity. Chakrabarty's *Provincializing Europe* is a recent example of this sort of incursion. And, being a historian, Habermas's challenge is not just via the device of citing cultural difference, but also through an historical and intellectual analysis that throws up native concepts that challenge and refigure mainstream historical thought such that it can never be solely identified with Europe any more.

The conditions of emergence of European modern philosophy also included enabling factors such as the distribution of global wealth. This kind of analysis is found among the postcolonial economic historians such as André Gunder Frank.[270] Modern European cultural infrastructures were funded by imperial trade and, at a more human level, the emergence of European modern philosophical thought is an expression of the cultural confidence of the wealthy:

> civilization, especially in France, marks the triumph of modernity, in which the modern world was for the first time confident enough to set itself up as equal to or better than antiquity, at the same time European explorations of other worlds had demonstrated the potential relativity of European culture and values ... [271]

So this is the familiar argument that European modernity didn't develop without close (culturally) comparative and (economically) exploitative links with the colonies. But we mustn't forget the significant link with the ancient, which was made by Enlightenment thinking itself, creating for its modern purposes the radical discontinuity with the ancient past.

Cultural theorist Marshall Berman defines modernism as 'the aesthetic means by which an urban and literate class subject to the invasive forces of modernization seeks to create ... a sense of being at home in the modern city'.[272] This seems to leave out a lot of people on the urban and rural frontier, including the indigenous. But the definition is adaptable. Let us say that, when these forces of modernisation and colonisation arrived on the Australian frontier, there was a range of indigenous responses: compliance and collaboration, resistance and inventive adaptation, all of which I am prepared to call parts of a modern way of being because first, they differentiate power and second, develop new forms of language and culture that involve lots of translation work. No one, this is saying, was ever a pure primitive, for this would mean steadfastly refusing to admit that the power of the Other had any existence ('only our way is true'); it would also mean refusing to accept any changes. But any culture, including the ones that see themselves as the most advanced, will display moments of primitivity.

'Indigenous modern' sounds like an oxymoron because the indigenous has always been the emblematic primitive against which the European Other defined its modernity. The reflective distance introduced by the cartesian *cogito* allowed this aspect of European thought to step out of its relatedness to place, its 'provincialism' (as

Chakrabarty would say), and aspire to the universal. Yet emerging in recent years, and mostly out of postcolonial thought, is the challenging idea that there is more than one modernity, even more than one enlightenment. If this is the case for India, Ireland, China and so on, why is it not also the case for indigenous peoples? I want to tackle this question from a number of directions.

1 By extending the usual definition of modernity. The indigenous modern could be defined as the inventive adaptations – aesthetic, social or technological – to the rapid changes brought by colonisation.
2 By dissociating modernity from the belief in technological progress, *pace* Heidegger. Are there not less technological ways of being modern?
3 By arguing against the recently-revived 'modern' project of cultural assimilationism in Australia.
4 By asserting that the modern and the primitive coexist in multiple forms, abandoning the historicist argument that the former is the process of the elimination of traces of the latter.
5 By installing the idea of everpresent antiquities and primitivities in modernity. Only thus, by giving up the exhausting and inexhaustible work of purifying the world of the irrational, ritual and magic, can cultural analysis stop relativistic comparison and see new growth in minor connections.

7

THE RELIGION OF TECHNOLOGY

Another significant point from Taylor is that Western modernity is 'sustained by its own original spiritual vision'[273] and that the drive towards instrumental reason and secularity has not displaced a belief in what is 'good' about this project of modernity. These positive aspects of modernity can be identified, rather than treating its values as simply the good things remaining after one has stripped away the negative ones such as old superstitions and legends. One of these positives is an endorsement of the technological that emerged not simply for its own sake, but out of a particular configuration operating in early Christianity. In the monastery, *techne*, the 'useful arts', stopped being kept at arm's length and came to be associated with an acceptable conduct of the religious life. Historian David Noble, in *The Religion of Technology*, claims that 'The dynamic project of Western technology, the defining mark of modernity ... is actually medieval in origin and spirit.'[274] His example is that of the Benedictine monks from about the time of Charlemagne, who found in the useful arts a key part of their religious life. His comments underscore the magnitude of the cultural changes involved:

> This unprecedented enterprise reflected a profound cultural shift, a departure from both classical and orthodox Christian belief, whereby humble activities heretofore disdained because of their association with manual labour, servitude, women, or worldliness came to be dignified and deemed worthy of elite attention and devotion. And this shift in the social status of the arts, if not the artisans, was rooted in an ideological innovation which invested the useful arts with a significance beyond mere utility. Technology had come to be identified with transcendence, implicated as never before in the Christian idea of

> redemption [and] salvation ... Christianity alone blurred the distinction and bridged the divide between the human the divine. Only here did salvation come to signify the restoration of mankind to its original God-likeness. (pp. 9–10)

Noble bases his thesis on the fact that Enlightenment secularism and scientific reason have not displaced religious authority and that, indeed, even today there is a continued salvationist belief in technological progress that in no way contradicts, or is contradicted by, renewed religious fundamentalism. To put the case somewhat more crudely, some of most fundamental (and primitive?) Western beliefs are associated with faith in progress and technological innovation.[275] In Australia, for instance, there is a whole complex culture of reverence towards the motor vehicle that is in no way shared by indigenous Australians. This can often be observed in the bush where fellas are puzzled – and sometimes enraged – by Aborigines who seemingly have so little respect for cars.[276] The focus of Aboriginal spiritual fidelity, it must simply be said, lies completely elsewhere. Aboriginal inventiveness, these peoples' own ways of being modern, did not include the invention of 'the chariot', an unfortunate example thought up recently by a conservative federal minister.

8

'I DON'T THINK THEY INVENTED THE WHEEL': NEW RIGHT ASSIMILATIONISM

In 2000 Philip Ruddock, the then Federal Minister for Immigration and Multicultural and Indigenous Affairs, was quoted by the *Washington Post* as saying: 'We're dealing with people who were essentially hunter-gatherers. They didn't have chariots. I don't think they invented the wheel.' That was July.[277] When in October he produced similar statements for *Le Monde*, the Australian press picked up the story and the ensuing scandal brought widespread calls for Ruddock's resignation.[278] Prime Minister John Howard declined the opportunity and defended his minister and close friend by saying Ruddock's heart was in the right place and that any criticism was 'a trivial and demeaning example of political correctness'. He went on: 'The public is tired of endless debating about how you describe the past and what they want is some action into the future.' By virtue of holding the Indigenous Affairs portfolio, Ruddock was supposed to support the process of reconciliation and it was argued that his insults had set this process back considerably. This observation would miss the point entirely if that was Ruddock's – and the government's – actual aim.[279]

While some observers were amazed that a government minister could produce such a naïve view of technological progress as an index of civilisation, other politicians, including the then leader of the Opposition, were not able to come up with any incisive critique. Beazley countered with 'they [the Aborigines] were the first to discover the opportunity of movement by sea', and the premier of

Western Australia, Richard Court, with 'they've taught us how to survive in incredibly desolate type conditions'. These comments suggest a model of thinking that places civilisations in competition with each other on a timeline of largely technological progress, Man as master of Nature. On this model the politicians were all in the same boat. Archaeologist Bruno David and his colleagues analyse this problem as one to do with racial and civilisational rankings established in the nineteenth century and say that Ruddock's attack shifts from the question of land rights towards something much more embodied, the racial type.

> If it is publically accepted that the 'real' problem is not one of historical injustice but rather of the inherent nature of the Aborigines as 'racially' inferior, then acts of injustice against Aboriginal people need not be judged by the standards of civil society; in this horrible logic, they cease to be amenable to moral or juridical consideration ... it is not land that Philip Ruddock evokes ... but an understanding of Aboriginal disadvantage revolving around a notion of Aboriginality defined as a series of other pre-existing absences: agriculture, chariots, the wheel and a hierarchical, evolutionary or developmental order. Such absences are treated by him as a measure of the (in)ability of Aboriginal people to position themselves socially above a 'very low base' [Ruddock's words] from which they came before the advent of European civilisation, the very society to which Ruddock traces his own roots.[280]

Bad old ideas can thus be revived if they are politically useful and, as the wind of government policy was changing and blowing backwards, they were. Assimilation was on the agenda again, having been considered for years a phenomenon of the 1950s. Barry Haase, Federal Liberal Member for Kalgoorlie, supported Ruddock and argued in a way that would have been impossible ten years earlier: 'I don't believe there is any real attempt by the majority of indigenous people in Australia to become part of Western society, there is no desire to be Westernised, so to speak.'[281] The assimilationist argument continues to be put as the only 'practical' way to solve problems of social disadvantage. Those political Wets who have upheld cultural equality and difference have now become the usual 'urban elites' who are 'romanticising the primitive'. Roger Sandall, former lecturer at the University of Sydney, is being lionised for saying:

> Most traditional cultures feature domestic repression, economic backwardness, endemic disease, religious fanaticism, and severe artistic constraints. If you want to live a full life and die in your bed, then civilisation – not romantic ethnicity – deserves your thoughtful vote.[282]

The new assimilationist argument has the tendency to give up on the notion of competing or even viable alternative civilisations, so we note how Sandall uses the word 'civilisation' in the singular for the place where one gets to die comfortably.

Assimilation, in any case, has the same strange logic as being modern. Either one is totally assimilated (in which case one is unrecognisable as Other) or one is not and, if not, then one has progressed part way in the process and is, therefore, in a state of lack. Identifying someone as a possible candidate for assimilation is a way of telling them, paradoxically, that they are not ready yet. The promise is held out for some unknown time in the future when the transformation will have already taken place. It is, therefore, highly appropriate to see assimilation as part and parcel of the continual process of the colonisation of any kind of Other. It is made possible by the practice of the idea of historicism, as explained by Chakrabarty as that conception of history as internally unified, unique to each period and developing over time. 'Historicism enabled European domination of the world in the nineteenth century', he says, adding that it legitimated the idea of civilisation,[283]

> Historicism was an important form that the ideology of progress or 'development' took ... [it] made modernity or capitalism look not simply global but something that became global over time, by originating in one place [Europe] and then spreading outside it ... Historicism – and even the modern, European idea of history – one might say, came to non-European peoples in the nineteenth century as somebody's way of saying 'not yet' to somebody else.[284]

Assimilationism, as an idea, is thus a late stage of colonialist historicism in that it functions to keep the not-yet assimilated in their place.[285] The project of modernity is thus conceptually equipped to maintain uneven development.

So this framework enables us to analyse the ways in which indigenous cultures were (or are) seen to be ordered in relation to other cultures in Australia. Let us say that the old order, prior to the 1970s, was one in which there was Western culture (modernised and modernist) on the one hand and, on the other, traditional (or primitive) Aboriginal culture as the only viable one, but of antiquarian interest only, 'living relics of the stone age'.[286] Any in between 'part-Aboriginal' cultures were due for assimilation, just as the traditional one was supposed to die out under the impact of modernisation.

More recently, we have seen the emergence of the category 'urban Aboriginal' rising on the basis of assertions of survival, on a liberal anthropological definition of any and every culture as constituting a whole way of life and in a context that recognised multicultural communities. Urban indigenous communities are often associated with disadvantage. To this have been added movements towards self-determination and sometimes neo-tribalism where reconstruction of culture and language are attempted.

'Indigenous modern' may seem to be an oxymoron, but it is a phrase that should be as acceptable as 'modern Australian'. We take it as an inclusive category of the contemporaneous and hence as part of an argument for implementing fully-serviced and responsibility-bearing citizenship for Aboriginal people. How can one be seen to be a fully participating citizen if one is deemed to be either from a radically incommensurable traditional culture or a perpetually disadvantaged urban one? At the very simplest, being modern means having a range of inventive responses to the contemporary world. In Europe this meant responding to rapid industrialisation and urbanisation. In Australia, for Aborigines, it meant adaptation to a highly dangerous invader, for instance, as labourers for the market-based industries. Survival has literally meant a lot of creative work, not only of a modernist sort in culture, but also in the technological, bureaucratic and economic systems that are usually associated with modernity.

So my experiment in this section – the democratisation of modernness – supports the very process of democratisation in which minorities become enfranchised and included in the polity. This process is contrary to the logic of assimilation. Democratision comes hand in hand with modernity, and with benefits as well as dangers, which have some effect in political expression. The modern has been associated with negative qualities, such as alienation, a loss of roots, a shrinking of the heroic dimension of life, including the sacred and the full expression of human passions. Some of these losses are recycled in the complex overlay of romantic nostalgia. But if we maintain that the situation we are dealing with, the inherent quarrel in a culture, is never about leaving the ancient for the open blue skies of the modern, but that modern and ancient are locked together, then this new perspective on culture may be able to shut down this romantic disenchantment mechanism that loses things to antiquity as the modern generates newness. This would be helped, for a start, by not seeing history itself as a flowing forwards, by taking the whitefella concept of history out of our calculations about culture and replacing it with the notion of the force of the ancient. To speak of force is to see events as immanent in bundles of agencies, articulations of words, concepts, bodily capacities and strengths coming from animate and inanimate beings in movement. These present events have the greatest significance and power when they are made to resonate down to the mythic layers of the past. This is not just to see events historically as unfolding, observed from a safe perspective; it is also to see one's own modest capacities as intersubjectively linked into their workings.

Let us now move to a discussion of modernist aesthetics foisted initially onto indigenous cultures without recognition of their aesthetic worth or as having its own lines of development as the aesthetic arm of an alternative modernity. The earlier strategy involved remaining with an older assimilatory aesthetics of neither–nor where we find Aboriginal artists celebrated or denigrated for something other than their artistic work. This is not just a problem for Aboriginal artists, I have argued elsewhere that the very notion of the Aboriginal bureaucrat attracts hostility from assimilatory racism.[287]

The 1950s artist Albert Namatjira, born on the Finke River, the most ancient streambed on the planet, was both modern and modernist in his artistic practice. At the beginning of his career, people who supported and promoted his work, especially the landscape painter Rex Battarbee, were happy to use the epithet 'modern Aboriginal' artist,[288] but we don't know how Namatjira responded to it. In the early stages his work was often seen as imitative of Western forms; it was 'remarkable' that he could leap out of the Stone Age and acquire artistic skills so quickly. To white observers the product was a watercolour, not, as Namatjira might have seen it, a way of moving around his country to particular sites and then doing something supplementary on canvas. It is now well established that the sites Namatjira painted were chosen for their traditional significance and power rather than simply as picturesque material.

Then, as a tall poppy, he had to fall. The narrative of failure about Namatjira dropped the 'modern' tag, so that the figure held up as an icon of assimilation (with honours and special rights given to him) was seen as suspended between two worlds and failing to make the transition to a promised assimilation that was never really desirable anyway. The story of Namatjira takes a 'tragic' turn when he was convicted of supplying liquor to his relatives, liquor that he had the right to purchase and consume alone by virtue of his exemption from the Act. His time in gaol led to his decline and early death at 57. With the overriding racist connotations of the 'clash of two worlds' or 'in between black and white' the word 'modern' simply vanishes; it has not been used about him again until now.

So while critics today might allow us to see Namatjira as a modernist there is much equivocation. In the 1950s John Cummings watched him paint and was

> surprised to see him fill his brush with a colour and return again and again to different areas of the composition with variant washes before moving on to the next colour. It is this technique that enabled Namatjira to hold all the elements of his composition in balance.[289]

In the same publication Alison French compares him to Hans Heysen, superficially similar as a painter, but dubbed a realist rather than a modernist because of his literalism; he painted to reproduce what was there.[290] French endorses Ian Burn and Ann Stephen's view that Namatjira is 'tactile' and 'diagrammatic' and exploits the 'abstract possibilities derived from the formal process of painting'.[291] He is 'motivated by the twin frames of reference – making art and being in country – he could never distort the one for the other'.[292] Making art is not about faithful representations of the observable, at the risk of making the painting wooden and detached. Namatjira achieves a different kind of real, say Burn and Stephen, through 'the self-conscious effort of pushing our eyes *up into* the landscape [which] seems to make the scene more real, suggestive of being *in* the landscape rather than *outside*, detached and contemplating it.'[293]

The immediate popular success of his painting 50 years ago and the sophisticated way we have of reading it now combine to mark his achievement as one of the most significant in the history of landscape painting in Australia. French concludes that 'Albert Namatjira both mastered and invented conventions that present an alternative to the pastoral vision.'[294] So while the European artists such as Battarbee and Heysen adapted their pastoral landscape traditions to the new material sources presented by gum trees and Central Australian country, this did not indicate the same degree of aesthetic revolution represented by Namatjira's modernism. If Namatjira met Heysen somewhere in the middle of the road the former had come further and made more adaptations than the latter. When one considers that, as the bearer of his own ancient traditions – painting on the body and on the ground contingently and impermanently for ceremony, painting as custodian or *kirda*, and so on – he must have approached the new medium with a quite different set of ideas. And yet, a painting of Haast's Bluff (c. 1956, reproduced on p.56), for instance, magnificent in its execution, captures something ineffable about that place that is continuous with its overriding importance for the Dreaming stories that subsist there. It is this revolution in continuity that also adds to Namatjira's modernist achievement and makes his role in the past a part of the Australian national present. It should, in principle, force the between-two-worlds rhetoric to disappear into irrelevance.

But no. Even in the 1980s, Vivien Johnson saw the painting of the BMW (Michael Jagamara Nelson's *BMW Art Car Project*, 1989) as a complex entanglement of Western Desert iconography and the ideals (and nostalgias) of a modern global corporation. The aboriginalised car symbolises 'the collision of ... two realities', according to Vivien Johnson.[295] And further, Margo Neale wrote recently that

> Trevor Nickolls, working in isolation, articulated themes that were typical of the time [1980s]. He described his paintings as 'a marriage of Aboriginal culture and Western culture' to form a style called *Traditional Contemporary – From Dreamtime to Machinetime*.[296]

Similarly, while 'Arone Raymond Meeks attempted to explore and strengthen the existing links between *urban* and *traditional* Aboriginal thought and culture' – and this project of linkage may be very interesting and culturally reconstructive – it set up a conceptual geography (urban/traditional) quite different from that of whitefella artists.[297] Where do *their* traditions lie? Are these artists wandering unbranded on the avant-garde frontier like lost cattle?

No one seems prepared to talk of these indigenous artists as if they were simply like Picasso, a modern artist responding in a highly creative fashion to the complications of his times by, for instance, incorporating the primitivism of African masks without the agonistics of a clash of cultures. These agonistics constitute one of the triggers for a narrative of failure, which is always on the point of emergence in the white discourses on Aborigines. Another combination of factors (grandeur of the object – the Balarinji-designed Qantas jet – popular appreciation rather than expert critique) produces a quite different effect: 'On the approach to Sydney, the chief steward may be heard to announce, proudly, that " 'you are now travelling in the world's largest modern art work." '[298]

Providing that is how you want to travel. While I have suggested that, as policy, assimilation is regressive, I am really only referring to cultural policy. To design for Balarinji (or even to travel in the plane) would only involve the notion of 'giving up', assimilating to or exchanging part of one's culture for something else if one believes there is one (Western) form of modern culture available and that we are all heading towards it. Modernity in the context of uneven development can thus have destructive effects. Carried out in the name of European modernity it has been seen as a civilising violence and criticised as involving a radical severing of the ties to community and place. People become atomised, alienated, exiled; they become captured as labour by the capitalist machine. And of course such things are the antithesis of traditionalism and nativism. Some indigenous people are explicitly hostile to the ideas of rapid change and abandonment of the past that come with modernisation and modernism.

So when Howard Morphy, in his book *Ancestral Connections*, speaks of endemic change in northern Australian artwork, he could almost use the word 'modernisation': 'The sense I got during my fieldwork was of a system in the process of continual adjustment and transformation as a consequence of both colonialism and incorporation within the Australian political and legal system'.[299] When Morphy came into the field armed with 50-year-old photographs of paintings from the area, his research associate, Narritjin, looked through the images with a deliberate lack of interest, scrutinised Morphy and said, 'I know what you are trying to do; you want to show us that our art has changed. We will show you that it has not.'[300]

This is artwork that does not normally exhibit the formal severance with tradition that would make it obviously modern, like the creation of a new genre or form. The art is contemporary, yet it is sold as traditional, thus making it a conservative element in Yolngu society. Yolngu society maintains a great degree of cultural capital and it retains a cultural core sustained thorough art and traditional ceremony, yet is modernising through participation in the mining, tourism and arts industries.

My final example begins to show us a way out of this assimilatory aesthetics of European-Australian modernism. The painter Gordon Bennett is often characterised as a postmodernist. Ian McLean says he is a 'postmodernist working in a deconstructive vein'. [301] But in his 1997 series of paintings, *Home Décor* (see p. 94), he ironically appropriates the modernist appropriator of Aboriginal iconography, Margaret Preston. 'Aboriginalist Preston was Australia's pre-eminent modernist between the wars',[302] says McLean. 'Her aesthetic, assimilationist and nationalist, and closely aligned to the Jindyworobak movement, aimed at a rare and unprecedented rapprochement between Aboriginal and Western cultures.'[303]

In *Home Decor*, Bennett brought together two modernisms, that of De Stijl's abstraction and Preston's Aboriginalism, producing 'a popular modern hybrid Australiana for the home decor of its citizens'.[304] Bennett's artistic statement could be called, in one reading, a postmodern hybrid, as he places another layer over that early modernism of Preston, allowing an historical consciousness to bloom in the temporal gap into which is inserted a critique of colonialist appropriation, even as Bennett himself is appropriating in return. Another reading is that it remains within a modernist project and reaches towards a vision of wholeness and unity rather than a postmodern fragmentation and layering. Bennett has an artistic *nom de plume* that is pointedly not a hybrid, marginal or dispossessed identity: he is John Citizen, and the Home Décor Show had paintings subtitled with a formula: [Preston + De Stijl = Citizen]. This is a contemporary way of 'being modern' and refusing the assimilatory logic which would forever make the Aboriginal aspects of his art the inheritance of tradition. This is not to say that there are no primitive emblems in his art. To the contrary, he has elsewhere and pervasively identified colonial violence as savage and sadistic: primitive barbarity but not primitivism.

Many other contemporary Aboriginal artworks, such as bark paintings produced for a rich international market, are not allowed to be modern in Bennett's sense, 'John Citizen is the euphemism Bennett has recently given himself ... a sign of modern democratic republican man.'[305] They are 'primitive postmodern'; their existence gestures towards the context of the primordial or classical. This primitivism is what the global market has wanted to see and buy ever since such items were valorised under European colonial modernism.

The definition of modernism as an aesthetic is that one's cultural work is identified as having to do with creative, adaptive life in current *milieus.* Why, then, resist seeing Aboriginal people as modern? To accept indigenous modernity is to refuse the idea of aspiration to that modernity some time in the future. There is no doubt that the severity of current social, health and economic problems in Aboriginal communities means that policy should be totally rethought, and on multiple fronts. If self-determination, with its separatist connotations, is being spoken of as a failure, then policy makers should seriously consider implementing fully serviced and responsibility-bearing citizenship for Aboriginal people, as outlined by Noel Pearson. Citizenship does not preclude cultural difference; the emphasis on modernities means treating everyone right now as if they live in the same time and place – coexisiting contemporaries – rather than as vestiges of the past or future hopefuls.

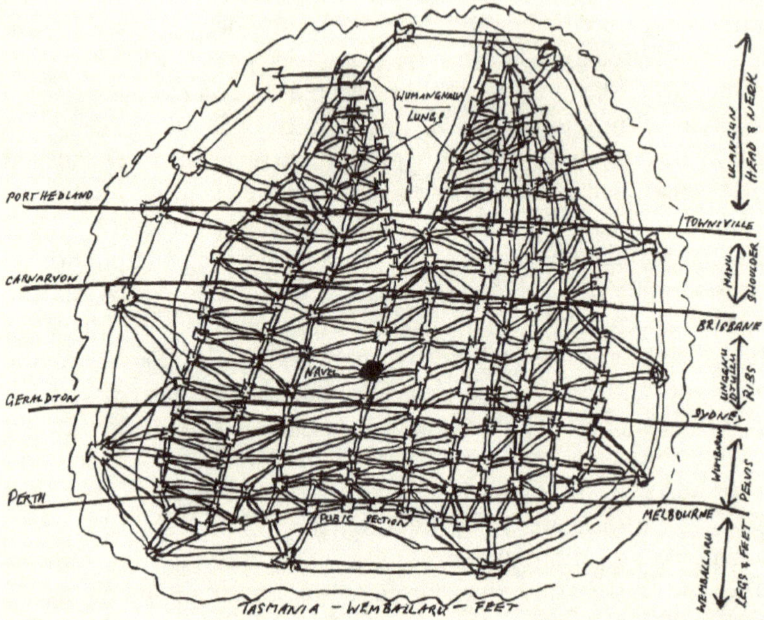

David Mowaljarlai, *Body of Australia*, from *Yorro Yorro: Everything Standing up Alive, Spirit of the Kimberley*, Magabala Books, Broome, 1993 by David Mowaljarlai and Jutta Malnic.

SECTION 4

PHILOSOPHY

1

PHILOSOPHY OF THE OTHER CONTINENT

There is no reason for Australian philosophers to write Australian philosophy because, after all, Australian philosophy does not exist and never has.

If philosophy is first of all defined by Europe, *the* continent, then one of the externals to philosophy (one of its problems, surely), would be the geography of non-philosophy. Australia, for instance, is in this non-philosophical zone, but gathering around are all sorts of connections – affective, political, territorial – that the people who live here experience, and which are also outside of philosophy, but could affect their thinking. Only placeless philosophical thinking can move from the northern continent to the southern one (under completely different conditions) and remain philosophy.

Deleuze's philosophy is part of a complex called 'continental', but its philosophical tendencies take it away from Europe, geographically, and away from Greece as an historical point of origin. Rajchman says that, thanks to Deleuze, we might

> see philosophy as having – or as having had – no intrinsic 'home' or 'land' or 'civilization,' and that we might then rethink its geographies and borders in terms of an odd potential that keeps arising in different times and places, released through many circumstances and contingencies ... instead of origins, philosophy has only a 'milieu' or 'atmosphere,' favored by certain conditions such as those provided by the 'colonizing democracy' of Athens, which brought itinerant strangers into its agora to encounter Socrates.[306]

The Australian situation, I would argue, presents one such contingency or multiplicity of forces: a decolonising tendency, coupled to a republican movement (weak, admittedly, but still a thinkable potential), a recent recasting of the duration of Australian history back into its precolonial past, a recognition of the alterity of Aboriginal thought (which presents us no longer with an image of primitivity, but with new images to think with) and, finally, a tendency, along with other countries of the region, to decentralise or provincialise Europe in our thinking.

The important thing, says Deleuze in his vitalistic philosophy, is to multiply connections and to do so outside of our academic orthodoxies. This is one procedure for a deleuzian philosophy of the political, some examples of which one finds in philosopher Paul Patton's book, *Deleuze and the Political*, for which I will do an appropriately contingent reading.[307] Deleuze himself emphasises the contingent:

> In short, there is certainly a reason for philosophy, but it is a synthetic, contingent reason – a meeting, a conjunction … Even in the concept, reason depends on the parts connecting, which could have been other ones, with other neighbourhoods. The principle of reason, such as it appears in philosophy is a principle of contingent reason, and it says: the only good reason is a contingent one, the only universal history lies in contingency.[308]

Contingency in writing lies in practices such as quotation and footnoting. It seems to me that every footnote to a European source (and I have just done it) is a reterritorialisation, therefore a recolonisation, of the philosophical text to its putative sources and away from the concept or image of a philosophy of the new continent I am trying to foster here. Such contingent acts risk bringing one's thought into line with the European ideas.

For the Old World, the New World was without history; now this part of the new world remains without philosophy, even though it has acquired History. The new history that Australia has recently acquired is still a colonising history in that it is conceived of as a dialogue between the Landed Gentry and the Noble Savages of the land. Yet so few of us actually identify with these ideal categories. We are all (even Aboriginal people) more likely, to feel foreign, thus to be in relations of exteriority to that which defines us.

Philosopher and writer Genevieve Lloyd, in a tradition of feminist philosophy and history, reflects on the exclusion of indigenous people and responsibility towards them (without making any claims for the existence of any 'Aboriginal philosophy'):

> The history of western philosophy is bound up with the formation of non-indigenous attitudes towards indigenous peoples, no less than with the formation of male-female relations. Operations of the philosophical imagination have been at work in the social practices through which indigenous peoples have been forcibly included and powerfully excluded in the ongoing enactment of the ideals of the European enlightenment. The philosophical imagination is at the nexus of theory and cultural context, the point where 'well-meant' ideas can come to amount to something 'unthought.' But it is the point too where the inherited fictions that disable our collective imaginings can be challenged.[309]

As a part of a decolonising project, which must be undertaken as a political effort in order to establish the intellectual conditions for Aboriginal philosophy and politics to work, it seems one has to step *outside* the bounds of Nation and the national politic. As Marcia Langton once said:

> Let's forget about this psychotic debate we keep having with white Australia and let's start talking to Asians and people from Eastern Europe and Africa and so on and South America and talk about something else for a change.[310]

While these connections can be multiplied, Australia also has to look to its contradictory relationship to the northern scholarly world we still consider as having the only theory that is still alive, that is, worth dialoguing with. To paraphrase Chakrabarty on India, 'European thought ... is both indispensable and inadequate in helping us to think through the various life practices that constitute the political and the historical [...].'[311]

Australia is therefore positioned in time and space and philosophically oriented in relation to these fundamental categories. Our geophilosophical position is something like that of developing countries, a subaltern position, to which the coloniser can say 'Not yet, you aren't ready', or to which its own prime minister, of colonialist mentality, can say to republicanism, 'Not yet'.

The desire to inhabit a time and place of absolute political modernity is a First World one. This is the position Patton would speak from, yet he does not subjectively occupy that position because he is an Australian committed to working out ethical strategies for Aboriginal politics. This is an incomplete, unmastered project, one carried out under the shadow of colonialism. Now, if he is committed to this project he is politically with it. He cannot be above or beyond it otherwise he is saying to his readers, 'You are not with me *yet*', which is the colonial contradiction.

2

PHILOSOPHICAL MAGIC

One of the great contradictions presented to scholars of Deleuze is how to write. Does one write masterfully, clearly, precisely and pedagogically, as does Patton, or with a poetics based on some of the philosophical principles, as does Massumi sometimes? One of those principles would involve writing with 'those hesitant gestures which accompany our encounters with the unknown'.[312] Another would be the use of the imperative voice, since, according to Deleuze, language is be made of order-words, not ordered propositions. Another would embody a dissociative logic rather than one that worked through resemblances. 'Clear' writing can risk academicism and orthodoxy to the extent that reproduces a reportage function: 'communicating what is there' (somewhere else, outside of this situation?) and thus palely reflect or react to or control response. On the other hand, writing with a Deleuzian poetic risks producing the discourse alone (crazy talk or theory babble), but not the problem or the inventive response to the problem. I have no answer.

But what I do suggest is that philosophy works a kind of magic by multiplying its registers of language. Now, you can't do this by simply dropping the Deleuzian vocabulary into the otherwise plain English text as Patton seems to here:

> the concept of aboriginal title creates a jurisprudential *smooth space* which may develop in unexpected directions. To the extent that it is able to *connect up* with other *lines* along which the sovereignty of the colonial state is under challenge, and to avoid definitive conjugation and *reterritorialisation*, native title jurisprudence as it continues to develop in Australia and Canada is a *machine* of constitutional *metamorphosis*.[313]

Similarly, cultural critic Meaghan Morris drops a bit of Deleuze and Guattari into her paper on the Pauline Hanson phenomenon (the rise of a populist New Right party in the 1990s):

> By appeasing these people, Howard in fact risked losing some of his own supporters to a movement that really looked for a while like a popular fascist as well as a nationalist 'line of flight'.[314]

Morris's use, however, is preceded by a detailed political analysis (see note 314) which, in Deleuzian fashion, articulates a multiplicity of political forces in flux, by which I mean that her range of identifiable forces includes things that might crop up in political science, or in history, or in a newspaper opinion column or everyday conversation, but that total mix of things is particular to her analysis and, perhaps more generically, to the kind of political analysis that might be written by someone who has read a heap of Deleuze. Unsurprisingly, Morris identifies this style in her writing as a mode of political address:

> It is no good talking *about* the local, the specific, the different and the heterogeneous if we do not know how to *address* constituencies other than or merely beyond our own professional and academic milieux.[315]

And the final point to note in relation to her analysis of the Hanson political moment is that it was a sympathetic analysis. Denouncing One Nation is not to understand it and failing to understand it is to play into its hands. Both negatives fall away from the more desirable position in which, as Rajchman puts it, 'the logic of multiplicity becomes inseparable from an affirmation of life'.[316] To put this simply, our affirmative interest in Australian politics (in all its aspects, because they are interconnected) should help us form images of Australia as a better place to live.

So my conclusion is that there is a case for a poetics of philosophical writing that multiplies its connections, that seeks different constituencies in the audience, that creates its own force by virtue of these multiplicities, a force that is a potential to act, like a vertiginous feeling tipping you forward. Patton himself recognises the function of magical acts in ceremonies of nationhood, but he wants to anthropologise it as belief. I would argue that these magical acts are not 'kinds of belief', but are real acts. As real as a philosophy, which inspires its reader in a way we can't quite pin down.

> In the case of modern colonialism, magical capture persists in the form of the belief that certain acts, such as the raising of flags or the reading of proclamations, are sufficient to establish sovereignty over newly discovered territories. (Patton, p. 121).

We have not left intuition and magic behind in our secular world. Insistence on the secular as a condition for thought is, in fact, as William Connolly would argue, a kind of dogma.[317] And Chakrabarty sees a parallel in our capacity to recognise different non-secular temporalities of history:

> What underlies our capacity to historicise is our capacity not to. What gives us a point of entry into the times of gods and spirits – times that are seemingly very different from the empty, secular, and homogeneous time of history – is that they are never completely alien; we inhabit them to begin with.[318]

Patton finishes his book with an appeal to novelty *and* the past, Deleuze and Guattari's philosophy is a 'legacy' that 'aims at new and creative forms of counter-actualisation of the present'.[319] This is a strange spanning of a temporal zone. The concepts used once again here are 20 or more years old. Are they still fresh and new, and does the repetition of the word 'new' in Patton's text still work the modernist magic?

3

NOMADS

I always thought the war machine chapter of *A Thousand Plateaus* was something of a joke and, accordingly, delighted in the inherent critique of anthropology and other social sciences I read into 'nomadology' – a science of failure, since it could never capture and categorise its subjects. Readers here in Australia, such as anthropologist Andrew Lattas, found it to be a romantic metaphor of liberation. But I would argue that is only so if you think such concepts to be unambiguous messages. Social scientists and other univocalists should be unnerved by a procedure that finds and advocates multiplicities in texts, murmurings in strange argots falling behind and running ahead of public pronouncements of objectivity or certainty. So in one sense I was happy to follow Deleuze and Guattari into a multiplication of the idea of government. I wrote at the time (1984):

> Nomadism has always infiltrated even the heart of government. There is, for instance, the swarming and ambiguous group of the lobby – sometimes comprised of members holding state positions, sometimes not, trading in favours and secrets, always mobilised towards specific tasks. The two groups, government and lobby, are dependent on one another for their mutual functioning ... The lobby has 'secret' workings, while government presents public positions. This points to a quite different handling, or even definition, of information. In one sense, government no longer deals in information which is dynamic and effective; it functions to display information in order to 'hold' a situation. It advertises a strict hierarchy of power positions, whereas the lobby group works with a secret solidarity, a fraternity in which each person is on the same level, and which can go underground at any time.[320]

Maybe so, but Deleuze has not had such an influence that the 'legislative assembly' has been renamed the 'legislative assemblage'.

4

SECRET ENGLISH

In revealing in these preceding pages what I thought and what I thought about what others thought, I had but one option: to write, conveying my thoughts in text. The practice of writing is the thinking. It is appropriate, therefore, to reflect on this sensitive and dynamic mode of communication. Writing is pervasive, yet only used by a small portion of the world's population, the literate. Writing is less accessible than the spoken word – being hidden away between the covers of books, or in libraries – and, on the surface, appears more permanent. The concrete fixity of written words perhaps works against its supposed permanence, for, not only can books and hard disks easily be destroyed, but they can also discourage the use of memory. The spoken word, on the other hand, may have the capacity to endure precisely through its flexibility in relation to arising situations, renewing its relevance on each occasion.

Talk is cheap, as they say, but could the deeper flow of fundamental narratives under all our talk point to a more ancient and permanent wisdom? Does this feeling lie beneath our newspaper pollsters' desire to seek out public opinion as some kind of bedrock? What of the myths and legends that are passed on by word of mouth? In other words, there are cultures of the spoken word not always displaced by the push towards universal literacy, an ideal that, in any case, is a long way from being achieved. There is a lot about these cultures too that is less accessible or even kept secret precisely with a hope that care will make it endure.

In *Ancient & Modern* I have often contrasted indigenous and non-indigenous cultures in Australia in order to reach an understanding of the relationship in terms of culture and history. So my last example and problem relates precisely to the problem of writing and sharing ideas across these cultures.

A few years ago a university in the far north of Australia sought to include indigenous cultures in the curriculum:

> in recent consultations between Northern Territory University and Yolngu elders in Arnhem land, the elders stipulated two conditions of approval for their languages and cultures to be taught within the university: first, the lecturers must agree not to teach any of the sacred/secret Yolngu knowledge with which they may have been entrusted; and second, that the university – and educators in general – accept the ongoing responsibility to teach 'secret English'.[321]

Once having grasped the importance of reciprocity in the arrangement, we can imagine the educators looking puzzled (is there really such a thing as secret English? If there is, is it sacred like Yolngu sacred/secret knowledge?), and then, maybe thinking by analogy that, if there are secret Yolngu languages, which there are, then maybe the elders are thinking of the kinds of often impenetrable 'languages' spoken by intellectuals in their research seminars. OK, fair enough.

The authors of this article about secret English, Michael J Christie and Bill Perrett go on to explore the structure of these hierarchies of languages within language. First of all, they define 'secret English' as English where 'meaning or reference claims to exceed the context of its production'.[322] This indicates that it is abstracted, generalised and perhaps not addressing anyone in particular. On the other hand they report the Yolngu view as one in which

> everyone speaks from a position with an obvious, acknowledged, linguistically marked ancestral history, and the history and location of that position necessarily saturates any assertion made through language ... Only rarely (in the secret/sacred) can we hope to have any language which transcends the positionality of the speaker and claims its meaning from some (hidden) transcendent signified. The elders' access to and familiarity with this other language contributes to their right to be trusted representatives of their people.[323]

What whitefella cultures seem to value in the elaboration of the truth as they express it is its stable functions: the object under analysis is not variable, the point of view does not shift and change, 'point of view' is not already part of the conception of the object, the addressee remains constant and the language is as far as possible devoid of emotion. These constants have the virtue of making a language of reason pervasive: it is supposed to do the same thing for all people everywhere. But while this view of language works well (and even then, only up to a point) for the scientific analysis of the physical world, specifically, the newtonian one, it really gets into trouble when it encounters the particularities of other cultures since it deliberately overlooks the specificity of context (of both production and reception).

So I have to agree with Christie and Perrett's conclusion:

> To some, formal 'enlightenment' education as we know it represents the best chance for indigenous people to recoup the losses suffered under colonialism. But in the call for a pedagogy of secret English, we find Aborigines demanding a very different kind of education, and one which entails the ongoing and situated critique of the very objectivism upon which enlightenment depends.[324]

While this addresses the flow of knowledge in only one direction, it seems that a philosophical approach is called for at any level at which cross-cultural education is set up; philosophical, since such an approach begins to explore where the threads of continuity, possible overlap and discontinuity may lie in the relationship between cultures. And since I am a non-indigenous writer I'd best begin with a careful look at the assumptions built into my approach to writing and the preparation of texts. It cannot be assumed that a single language (such as English) is the neutral and objective medium of communication, since crucial issues of the translation of phenomena from one culture to another have to be dealt with. And with these issues reside a host of considerations concerning the history of philosophy and the interpretation of experience. To call for a situated critique of enlightenment objectivism is not to abandon the pursuit of understanding altogether. It is, rather, to ask how the project of cross-cultural understanding, shadowed as it is by the influence of the Enlightenment and endeavouring to produce yet more texts in an ancient European form, best fits into new contexts such as a university's ethical engagement with indigenous knowledge. We know that academic interest in indigenous cultures is a process that has been intensely carried out since the early twentieth century in

Australia, but it has been a patchy, often one-way, conversation, often lacking humility or an acknowledgment of the shortcomings of its own position and so making for a very incomplete engagement.

The field of Aboriginal philosophy, for instance, does not exist in Australian universities, but African philosophy is a huge field in North America. Emmanuel Chukwudi Eze, the philosopher, tells us that 'within the last two decades the field of African philosophy has blossomed in North American universities and colleges. In 1995 alone over forty textbooks and scholarly monographs appeared.'[325] It could be a blessing that the 'category' of Aboriginal philosophy has not yet appeared in Australia, since the presentation of a body of knowledge describing another culture in the systematic discourses of enlightenment scientificity and certainty could be flawed from the start, producing 'packages' of indigenous knowledge in the 'right places' and in a safe 'enlightened' language.

Western disciplines that have dominated understandings of Aboriginality in Australia are anthropology, history and literature. Anthropology's interest is 100 years old, but history and literature have only engaged with indigenous knowledges for less than half that time. More recent areas are archaeology, architecture, art, cultural studies, ecological studies, medicine and tourism. Whitefella knowledge of indigenous Australia is, I will argue, very shallow. Indigenous knowledge of country, which has been built up though 60 000 years of occupation, is extensive, rich and elaborate. By elaborate I mean that knowledge is not limited to the functional or simply to that which suffices for physical survival; it builds into specifically situated and literally wonderful cultural complexes. These are embodied and situated; they sustain continuity and meaning in life and a depth of reality and attunement to interconnected relationships nourishing life in community. There are laws outlining this philosophy; those that deal with warfare and misbehaviour are part of the same system. There are many situated and interrelated ordering principles in these indigenous cultures that support the maintenance of conditions necessary to sustain continuity and keep 'everything standing up alive', as David Mowaljarlai used to say.[326] But because the approach of Enlightenment knowledge necessitates a more didactic approach, when anthropology, history and literature show up they tend to reduce their appreciation to, for instance, two important reifications: society and the word. For anthropology,

Man's activities are conceived of as socially systematic elements of community, tribe, or group (the principle activity here is the description of pre-State communities as if they were circumscribed or bounded, as if the members of that community are staying put, 'waiting' for the arrival of the observer). For history and literature the main concept is that of a temporally unfolding representation (as if the reader's main activity – among all the other things readers could be doing – is the discovery of a singular trace of 'meaning').

This philosophy would then overlap a little with cultural studies, since it links up once again with historical and anthropological methods; historical, since a contemporary field of Aboriginal philosophy cannot ignore the massive upheaval of the colonialist process (the condition and the necessity for a contemporary Aboriginal philosophy) and anthropological because primitive and sacred rituals have not been displaced by modernism or science; indeed, some have come to talk of a rearticulation in the 'modern sacred'.[327] The crucial relationship in much of Aboriginal Australian ritual, I would maintain, is between *body* and *country*, so I suggest that 'society' and 'the word' are less significant operative concepts or, rather, that they have been more recently interposed between body and country.

Added to the reduction to the social or the interpretations of texts is an attitude replete with critical judgment: things should be other than they seem. Neither of these approaches clearly 'fosters' anything, in Massumi's terms:

> Critical thinking disavows its own inventiveness as much as possible. Because it sees itself as uncovering something it claims was hidden or as debunking something it desires to abstract from the world, it clings to a basically descriptive and justificatory modus operandi. However strenuously it might debunk concepts like 'representation,' it carries on as if it mirrored something outside of itself with which it had no complicity … Prolonging the thought-path of movement … requires that techniques of negative critique be used sparingly. The balance has to shift to affirmative methods: techniques which embrace their own inventiveness and are not afraid to own up to the fact that they add (if so meagrely) to reality.[328]

So what if we think of the philosopher as a helpmeet, as someone who can help something grow? How would they do that without getting in peoples' way? They do it, I would suggest, by participating. Their helping is intransitive, they play a part in the occasions of their own becoming, they don't deliberately go out to find someone they think needs to be blessed with their help, someone they think is in a state of weakness. I have talked already about increase ceremonies among indigenous Australians. Philosophers too participate all the time in their own increase ceremonies, occasions, such as seminars, when ideas are made to grow and spread and ideas are conveyed by the special use of language.

5

LANGUAGE AS SINGULAR OR GENERAL

Patton's discussion of language makes it systemic–structural. 'Language in general may be regarded as a solution to the problem of how to communicate an infinite variety of semantic contents using a relatively small number of signifying contents'.[329]

But there is no 'language in general', there are only actual languages from which, via selective reading of data and systematic algebraic rule-writing, one can posit a general grammar. The being of language, I would argue, is geopolitical – we move from one 'textual suburb' to another[330] – and the problem it poses is not infinite generative capacity (as in the work of linguist Noam Chomsky), rather, it is how to talk to a stranger. Its problematic is a more perilous encounter with Otherness out of which meaning might be generated.

Further, Patton's privileging of semantics and content assumes the mere instrumentality of form (it would only be there to 'carry' content) and the singularity of language function. Language, after Roman Jakobson, also has phatic, conative, metalinguistic and poetic functions; it envelopes a sensorium and a more sociolinguistic exteriority.[331]

Patton's formulation of what language is sounds too much like the Idea of language (or later Society), the model from which solutions emerge, and these solutions are the actual societies we live in. But as we know, theoretical modelling is not part of the Deleuzian method that Patton is focused on here.

6

FEELINGS OF POWER

'*Something* is there,' said Stanner's unknown informant, 'like engine, like power, plenty of power, it does hard work; it *pushes*.'[332] Being in a place and feeling something is a common experience in indigenous Australia. Safety or danger are indicated by the feeling or a sense of direction. And these feelings are often located in the belly, as David Unaipon said, 'it was where all "impulses" of the body come from, where all feelings come from.'[333] The word the Ngarrindjeri from South Australia use is *miwi*, but they use it 'rarely and with reverence'[334]. This reverence does not correspond to seeing the *miwi* as soul-substance or spirituality; my feeling is that it is something much more practical than that. Tom Trevorrow, also from South Australia, describes *miwi* more fully:

> It's where we get our understanding of things and our feelings and our instincts from. And miwi we're told comes from your *pulanggi*, we call it, navel...through your *pulanggi*. Not through your ears, or your eyes, or your nose, or your mouth, or anywhere else. It's through your pulanggi. And I was told by my elders that everybody's got it ... Everybody. Blackfella, whitefella. But he said, "They gotta know what it's all about and they gotta know how to use it and they gotta know what it means." But everybody's got it, But knowing and believing in it is, you know, the secret [that is, the key] ... It's a really powerful thing and when you really feel it, you'll know what it's all about, you know.[335]

The compiler of this statement, anthropologist Diane Bell, comments that

> The notion that one could know by feeling goes against the rationalist grain. If it can't be proved or disproved, can it be

> considered knowledge? As heirs of the scientific method, westerners tend to be afraid of feelings and sentiment ... How can a body be a site of knowledge?'[336]

Indeed, body and country are the nexus of Aboriginal philosophy, and the practice of the philosophy means trusting to 'go with the feeling' that one has in the here and now. An elder is telling you a story not primarily because it is relevant to some past state of affairs, nor for future reference, but to impress something upon you now.

Patton's illuminating account of power seemed to be constructed out of a jigsaw of pieces from Foucault, Deleuze and Guattari and their intellectual antecedents, Nietzsche, in particular, fell into place.

However, in the next chapter he says:

> The history of culture provides many examples of illusory means by which individuals and groups seek a feeling of power: sacrifices to gods, cruelty to others and animals, fast cars and alcohol, to name but a few.[337]

The 'feeling of power', he says, is the mere sign of our capacity to act and in this it can be unreliable. But how can Patton be so sure that the feeling the kid gets from his fast car is not real power for him? Why are these assemblages of power (car + kid + kid's feelings) illusory while others are real? Patton's list (sacrifices to gods, cruelty to animals and others, etc.) is a list of various wayward means to power that the law and morality seek to control. Patton should know that the 'good' feeling of power that comes from, say, caring for a sick friend, is probably also illusory in the sense he uses that word. As he knows, the will to power cannot stand outside (unreal, like a fantasy) the social assemblages in which it is implicated and which it creates. And we have paused on the question of machines and power already. Where does the power of the fast car come from, when is it real and when is it illusory?

Where power comes from – in anyone's theory – remains a mystery. It is sovereign power from 'above', it can be popular resistance from 'below', it connects to the force of the state and its ultimate right physically to restrain or to hurt people, which of course takes us back to the body again. There is no doubt that power is shunted along social networks that join people up in institutions or other groups that 'give' them power. The forms power takes are changing and mobile and return us as often as not to the body and its physical and mental inventiveness.

7

THE OTHER CONTINENT

David Mowaljarlai's drawing of Australia illustrates the Other continent that I want to use as a teasing philosophical image. Here, he makes use of a principle of connectivity of all the parts of this body without organs, which is the living body of the country. The brilliance of his image is that he shows the country as a body (full, perhaps, with blood, rhizomically connected with all those lines that are nothing like the arbitrary molar aggregates of the states), in which all the parts move and are connected and interdependent, parts that cannot be annexed for different purposes. The country is not apart from life, we learn in other ceremonies, because life emerges from it and goes back in to it. But here, for the first time, I see an Aboriginal image of the nation, radically displaced onto (into?) a human being. His picture is that of a body of connected parts, just as parts of the body relate to kinship categories, just as the body is inscribed with signs (paints, cicatrices) of belonging, being married or being from a certain part of the country. The picture does not signify generally, rather, it mobilises the energy of the body. As he says in his own vitalistic philosophy, 'Everything standing up alive.'

> We get blocked by politics and politicians. We get blocked by media, by process of law. All we want to do is come out from under all of this and give you this gift. And it's the gift of pattern thinking. It's the culture that is the blood of this country, of Aboriginal groups, of the ecology, of the land itself.[338]

'Pattern thinking', as he calls it, is a principle of connectivity. It is opposed to the figure of the triangle or the hierarchy of bosses and subordinates, which, he says, characterises whitefella culture. The pattern he is referring to is related, of course, to the patterns of kinship that are a key to Aboriginal ways of being.

8

PHILOSOPHY FROM AFAR

I have been drawn towards using the word 'philosophy' in my thinking about the paradox of visiting indigenous Australia within Australia and then writing about it. As I said, making up and unmaking stories is what philosophers do in order to rethink the conventions called 'understanding'. At least my kind of philosopher. The neospiritual French philosopher Alain Badiou is really no help for me when he says: 'The conditions of philosophy are transversal. They are uniform procedures recognisable from afar, whose relation to thought is relatively invariant. The *name* of this invariance is clear: it is the name "truth".'[339]

An Australian philosopher of a more demotic bent might translate this into a colloquial English: you can recognise the truth (or bullshit) from miles away. But what if one turned and gazed in a different way, into the heart of another community, another culture? Would the uniform procedures remain relatively invariant: perhaps it is only from afar that they look the same; it is only on approaching closer that all sorts of detailed differences start to muddle the uniformity of procedure and the very institution of philosophy begins to get shaky. Let me suggest that long-sightedness is a European form of philosophical myopia and that other versions of philosophy, indigenous perhaps, have a more in-lived and intimate association with societies of people and the way they talk about themselves.

When Aboriginal people speak of truth they are most often speaking locally about country and, in their places, feel the direct effects of the cataclysmic event that has been called genocide. They want their usurpers to recognise the truth of this event, in local narrative terms often full of self-contradictions and paradoxes. This truth is not distant, 'recognisable from afar'; it is immanent in encounters that may involve procedures with words, as well as acts, feelings, hunches. Some philosophers, such as William Connolly, are willing to work with this feelingful material: 'Instincts are proto-thoughts situated in culturally formed moods, affects and situations. They are not even entirely reducible to implicit thoughts or tacit judgements ... 'And his description of Nietzsche seems to describe my own way of engaging with the complexity of how to write into or out of encounters where one is visiting with Others:

> For Nietzsche thinking bounces in magical bumps and charges across several registers. Proto-thoughts undergo significant modification and refinement when bumped into a complex linguistic network of contrasts. Moreover these visceral modes of appraisal are often invested with considerable intensity, carrying considerable energy and fervency with them into other registers of being.[340]

In AP Elkin's *Aboriginal Men of High Degree* David Mowaljarlai announces that the 'clever men' are no more.[341] The demise of the shaman, and of primitive power generally, has been an enduring motif in the literature for at least two centuries. It has accompanied the close and loving descriptions that anthropologists have made of the operations of shamanistic power. As they draw out that power, transforming it as it is shunted into the measured language of the social sciences, they consolidate another narrative about the rise of secular and scientific progress. These two narrative moments – the rise of one and the fall of the other – are more than just dialectically connected. So-called primitive societies were and always are becoming modern, just as so-called modern societies have their primitive becomings as necessary and regular occurrences.

Mowaljarlai kept up his intellectual work for 50 years. From his association with German anthropologist Andreas Lommel in 1938 to his own book in 1993, he continued to reproduce his traditions. This was the work, I will argue, of an indigenous philosopher. But what was the world of the shamans he was leaving behind? According to Mowaljarlai in Elkin's little book, *rai* (spirits) 'make' *banman* or 'medicine-men' by giving the postulants new insides, magic stones (*maban*), the 'inner' eye by which they will see what is normally invisible, and the 'aerial or astral rope' with which they will be able to travel through the air or under the ground. Elsewhere in the book, and from other parts of Australia, we learn of liquefied quartz being 'sung' all over and into initiates' bodies so they can grow feathers and fly.[342] We read of people being able to reduce their size to 7 or 8 cm or grow to 'prodigious proportions'.[343] Stories of the ability to take out and replace one's internal organs abound. All this wealth of culture was going – almost gone – yet remained condensed into Elkin's book, itself no more substantial than a hunk of bark from a paperbark tree.

Clearly, the anthropologist did not believe all this magic; he was simply recording it at face value, but as the beliefs of others (this is what we call anthropologism) while he was safely on the other side of the fence in a secular and objective world. But this other world, or something like it, was the one approached by the mature Mowaljarlai when Jutta Malnic came to record his thoughts for *Yorro Yorro: Everything Standing Up Alive*. In it, he tells us of a dream he had:

> I dreamed I went right across to Palestine country. They had those old huts and synagogues there made of mudbricks these people used to build with, flat-roofed. That's where I saw Jesus in the holy land, walking between those houses. He turned and looked at me, then kept walking and did not look back again.
>
> He never talked to me. What was he saying to my spirit? That's what I'm asking you – what am I supposed to do, what is going to happen? What is coming?
>
> This light is really live in my body, look, it's swinging me all the time. These dreams have changed my life. It's strange, but the way I see it now is that I must help not only my Aboriginal people, but all people, blacks and whites.
>
> And to come out of that darkness, we've got to try and cope with that true thing, work evenly together to represent the Christ, Jesus, not just Aboriginal-side or church-side; because this dream told me, 'This is the way you must go about it.'
>
> And I know now that God comes from the sunrise, where power comes from. Power comes from an angle, not straight above – that is my statement.[344]

This is not the confession of a Christian convert, it is a story of the accommodation of whitefella magic coming from the teachings he had heard ever since Reverend Love set up the mission in his country when he was a boy. How many readers want to bracket out this Christian material as inauthentic Aboriginality, evidence of a sullied and degraded hybrid culture? Certainly all those, possibly like Elkin, who are *fundamentally* secularists. But isn't Mowaljarlai cottoning on to some sort of magic, the most pervasive and powerful whitefella magic around, as he incorporates it into his dreaming here, making it 'live' as a light in his body, 'swinging' it almost erotically? Everything standing up alive?

And when he says 'Power comes from an angle, not straight above', I know that he is referring to several things, including the Wandjinas, Ngarrinyin 'gods' coming from 'the islands' to the northwest and the spiritual exercise, *wudu*, carried out by Ngarrinyin elders with their children every sunrise and sunset, warming their hands in the fire, touching them to parts of their body, for instance on their eyes: singing *wudu – uuu*, 'Don't look at other people's possessions, a thing might look beautiful to you and you might want it.'[345] Enlightenment, I guess he is telling is, will not come straight on, literal and obvious; the track will be vaguer, things will be hidden and progressively revealed, repeatedly revealed. A philosophy will be a way of life learnt, and, as Taussig wrote, 'Obliquity … is the name of the game.'[346]

I will argue, therefore, that indigenous philosophy is a thing of today and that its conceptualisation is a way of recasting contemporary thinking, not with a view to incorporating what the elders may have to teach us, but with showing that their teachings were and are always here and that the distinction between 'us' and 'them' is a way of talking that oversimplifies the complex cultural relations within and between cultures.

Mowaljarlai, however, had more local reasons for his seemingly millenarian tone when he said the old ways were passing. He was simply showing respect – as one must do as a young man to defer to one's elders, to acknowledge that there is plenty of secret stuff one knows not to know. But as he did so Mowaldjali handed over a lot of information about the culture of Aboriginal 'doctors' and by 1993 had published his own book, saying where the knowledge came from:

> My spirit guides have helped me with this work. At times they come and I can feel them standing next to me: my father, my grandfather or my mother or uncle. They are telling me the story, how it goes. They just pour it all out to me, telling me who they are.

It is a way of showing respect to the elders' knowledge to say that it cannot be matched, but by the time one is an elder oneself one is in a position where one has to pass something on, as Mowaljarlai has done. And in our commentary on European philosophical traditions we try to get the ideas right, not imagining for a minute that we too could one day be ancestors of some future generation; that would be far too immodest. Do we, in our modernist or postmodernist endeavours, feel any passing on responsibilities or do we want to just trade in new stuff? Mowaljarlai, it seems to me, is doing both, and it is in the gap between the traditions of his old people and his new material that a contemporary indigenous philosophy emerges. It is not entirely of the past, as if we were seeking to find an origin in a system of being once whole or complete, but it engages with the present.

If I recount a dream I had – begging your indulgence, for such ultra-subjective anecdotes are largely untellable, but I want to try to make it mean something to you – then where I had this dream is important to this project.[347] This book was written on Cadigal land. It is the usual protocol in the spirit of reconciliation, when a public event is launched, to ask the custodians of the place to welcome the participants or, in their absence, to pay homage to their land of the people one is standing on.

Now, my dream took place in a classroom in a building a couple of floors above the land. We were trying to discuss Aboriginal philosophy and there were a couple of Aboriginal students in the class who offered a presentation. Suddenly, there was a great pile of pebbles on the floor and, with her bare feet, one of the young women was tracing a path in them. This contoured path, something like a circular track, was formed by her feet working down and smoothing the little pebbles, smoothing them sideways and forwards. She was almost dancing. And then she made another track, parallel and overlapping with the first.

She was finished and suddenly I was seized with a desire to take a photograph. But it was already too late; she was smoothing over the tracks, erasing them and making her patch of stones into a smooth space.

Now, the other young woman did her thing and she was talking in a traditional language as she carried in more stones. They were like slabs of concrete. Maybe one slab and some smaller fragments piled on top. These she carried on her arms, cradled on her forearms like one might carefully place a well-ironed shirt (this analogy occurred to me at the time) and very carefully placed them one by one on the smoothed-out bed of pebbles. It was important that the smaller stones not fall off as she did this. She was repeating a text each time but I could only catch a person's name as she did this. Each slab seemed to be dedicated to a person in the class, so that we were all included by name, even myself and even an academic friend from another university who was not present.

The coda to this dream, still in the dream, is my remembering an email I had received from one of these students, Jackie was her name, before the class, asking if she could use an unusual form of presentation. I had not answered it because, I guess, it was one of those emails that presents a difficulty and so one puts it aside to think about it, and then it slips one's mind.

NOTES

1 Paul Kelly, 'I Don't Know Anything Any More', Mushroom Music, 2001, with permission.
2 Bruno Latour, 'Stenger's Shibboleth', Foreword to Isabelle Stengers, *Power and Invention, Situating Science*, Minneapolis: University of Minnesota Press, 1997, pp. xi–xii.
3 For indigenous ways that 'humans' identify with 'nature', see Fiona Magowan, 'Waves of Knowing: Polymorphism and co-substantive essences in Yolngu Sea Cosmology', in *Australian Journal of Indigenous Education*, vol. 29, no. 1 2001, pp. 22–35.
4 What makes a concept 'attractive' is not mere whimsy; it is a complex of factors: its history, its current uses, its power generated by its multiple connections.
5 *Daily Telegraph*, 22 March 2004, p. 9.
6 Dipesh Chakrabarty, *Habitations of Modernity: Essays in the Wake of Subaltern Studies*, Chicago: Chicago University Press, 2002, p. xix.
7 Isabelle Stengers reinforces this point: 'For me, as a daughter to the Western tradition, it is very important to say that we are unable to produce any conclusion from our history, because it means resisting the most obvious conclusion – we have won, we are the model for all people.' 'A "Cosmo-Politics" – Risk, Hope Change', in Mary Zournazi (ed.), *Hope: New Philosophies for Change*, Sydney: Pluto Press, 2002, p. 250.
8 John Gascoigne notes how Enlightenment ideas persisted in Australia, avoiding somewhat the 19th century Romantic Revival, that looked again at 'tangible remnants of the past … for European Australians, ignorant or contemptuous of the long Aboriginal past, theirs was an entirely new land with nothing to mark past ages. As a consequence the late-eighteenth century impulses of the Enlightenment took a particularly secure hold in Australia …', *The Enlightenment and the Origins of European Australia*, Cambridge: Cambridge University Press, 2002, p. xii; see also Michel Serres, *The Troubadour of Knowledge*, trans. Sheila Fiona Glaser, Ann Arbor: University of Michigan Press, 1997.
9 Michel Serres with Bruno Latour, *Conversations on Science, Culture and Time* (hereafter cited as *CSCT*), trans. Roxanne Lapidus, Ann Arbor: University of Michigan Press, 1995, p. 60.
10 Mary Graham says, in a rich account, that 'Aboriginal law is "grown" not "made" – and this is what also makes it a system of natural law', 'Some thoughts about the philosophical underpinnings of Aboriginal worldviews', in *Worldviews: Environment, Culture, Religion*, vol. 3, no. 2, 1999, p. 116.
11 Pierre Hadot (ed.), Arnold Davidson, trans. Michael Chase, *Philosophy As a Way of Life: Spiritual exercises from Socrates to Foucault*, Oxford: Blackwell, 1995.
12 Michel Serres with Bruno Latour, *CSCT*, trans. Roxanne Lapidus, Ann Arbor: University of Michigan Press, p. 103.
13 Mary Graham: 'Aboriginal logic maintains that there is no division between the observing mind and anything else: there is no "external world" to inhabit.' 'Some thoughts about the philosophical Underpinnings of Aboriginal Worldviews', in *Worldviews: Environment, Culture, Religion*, vol. 3, no. 2, 1999, p. 113.
14 Greg Dening, 'Deep narratives in cultural encounters', in Emma Greenwood, Klaus Neumann and Andrew Sartori (eds), *Work in Flux*, Melbourne: University of Melbourne History Department, 1995, p. 73.
15 Jean Starobinski, 'Les Cheminées et les Clochers', *Magazine Littéraire*, 280, September 1990, quoted in Marc Augé, *Non-Places: Introduction to an Anthropology of Supermodernity* trans. John Howe, London: Verso, 1995, p. 75.
16 Gaston Bachelard, *The Poetics of Space*, trans. Maria Jolas, Boston: Beacon Press, 1964.

17 Bruno Latour, *War of the Worlds: What About Peace?*, trans. Charlotte Bigg, Chicago: Prickly Paradigm Press, 2002, p. 13.
18 Tony Swain, *A Place for Strangers: Towards a history of Australian Aboriginal being* (hereafter cited as *APS*), Cambridge: Cambridge University Press, 1993, p. 27; see also p. 49.
19 ——, *APS*, pp. 42–43.
20 ——, *APS*, p. 32.
21 Krim Benterrak et al., *Reading the Country: Introduction to nomadology*, 2nd edn, Fremantle: Fremantle Arts Centre Press, 1996.
22 Tony Swain, *APS*, p. 32.
23 ——, *APS*, 33.
24 Deborah Bird Rose, 'To Dance with Time: A Victoria River Aboriginal Study', *Australian Journal of Anthropology*, 2000, 11:3, p. 295.
25 Swain, *APS*, p. 20.
26 Deborah Bird Rose, 'Exploring an Aboriginal Land Ethic', *Meanjin* 3/1988, p. 378.
27 Tony Swain, *APS*, p. 51.
28 ——, *APS*, p. 54.
29 ——, *APS*, p. 282.
30 ——, *APS*, p. 284.
31 Stephen Greenblatt, *Marvellous Possessions: The wonder of the New World*, Chicago: Chicago University Press, 1991, p. 9.
32 Tony Swain, *APS*, p. 256.
33 ——, *APS*, p. 254–55.
34 '... the mimetic faculty carries out its honest labor suturing nature to artifice and bringing sensuousness to sense by means of what was once called sympathetic magic, granting the copy the character and power of the original, the representation the power of the represented.' Michael Taussig, 'A Report to the Academy', from *Mimesis and Alterity: A particular history of the senses* (hereafter cited as *MA*), New York: Routledge, 1993, p. xviii.
35 Tony Swain, *APS*, p. 256.
36 See, for instance, the work of polemicist Keith Windschuttle, *The Fabrication of Aboriginal History. Vol. 1, Van Diemans Land 1803–1847* (hereafter cited as *TFAH*), Sydney: Macleay Press, 2002.
37 Ross Gibson, *Seven Versions of an Australian Badland*, St Lucia: University of Queensland Press, 2002, pp. 58–59.
38 Named after Eddie Mabo from the Torres Strait Islands, this High Court decision (*Mabo and others v. the State of Queensland* (1982)) recognised for the first time that the people of Murray Island retained a title to their land that was not extinguished by the annexation of their island to the state of Queensland, thereby effectively cancelling the legalistic fiction of *terra nullius* (empty land).
39 Keith Windschuttle, *TFAH*.
40 Giorgio Agamben, *Infancy and History: The destruction of experience*, trans. Liz Heron, London: Verso, 1993, p. 91.
41 Marc Augé, *Non-Places: Introduction to an anthropology of supermodernity*, trans. John Howe, London : Verso, 1995, pp. 24–25.
42 Dipesh Chakrabarty, *Provincializing Europe* (hereafter cited *PE*), p. 27.
43 Jane Bennett, *The Enchantment of Modern Life: Attachments, crossings and ethics* (hereafter cited as *TEML*), Princeton: Princeton University Press, 2001, p. 97.
44 Chakrabarty, *PE*, p. 26.
45 TGH Strehlow, *Aranda Traditions* (hereafter cited as *AT*), Melbourne: Melbourne University Press, pp. 125–26.
46 Chris Healy, *From the Ruins of Colonialism: History as social memory*, Melbourne: Cambridge University Press, 1997.
47 Lloyd Robson, *A History of Tasmania*, Melbourne: Oxford University Press, 1991.
48 Taussig, *MA*, p. 45.
49 'The Hobart Carnival', National Film and Sound Archive.
50 *Tasmanian Mail*, 26 February 1910, p. 14.
51 David Glassberg, *American Historical Pageantry: The uses of tradition in the early twentieth century*, Chapel Hill: University of North Carolina Press, 1990, p. 43.

52 David Glassberg, *American Historical Pageantry*, p. 283.
53 Graham Jenkin, *Conquest of the Ngarrindjeri: The story of the Lower Murray Lakes tribes*, Point McLeay: Raukkan Publishers, 1995 (1979), p. 228.
54 *Tasmanian Mail*, 26 February 1910, p. 14.
55 Graham Jenkin, *Conquest of the Ngarrindjeri*, pp. 225–26.
56 Jenkin has used the spelling of David's father James's name.
57 Graham Jenkin, *Conquest of the Ngarrindjeri*, pp. 226–27.
58 *Hobart Mercury*, 3 March 1910, p. 2.
59 Paul Carter, *The Road to Botany Bay*, London: Faber and Faber, p. xv.
60 Cited in David Glassberg, *American Historical Pageantry*, p. 69.
61 ——, *American Historical Pageantry*, p. 286.
62 Michael Taussig, *MA*, New York: Routledge, 1993, p. 44.
63 Charles Darwin, quoted in Michael Taussig, *MA*, p. 75.
64 Joyce Morris, interview with the author.
65 David Unaipon, *Native Legends*, Adelaide: Hunkin, Ellius and King, c. 1929.
66 Taussig, *MA*, p. 176.
67 ——, *MA*, p. 176.
68 ——, *MA*, p. 44.
69 ——, *MA*, p. 250.
70 ——, *MA*, p. 255.
71 Marcia Langton, 'The Valley of the Dolls: Black humour in the art of Destiny Deacon', in *Art and Australia*, 35/1, 1998, p. 106.
72 Taussig, *MA*, p. 251.
73 'A descriptive analysis of bank notes is needed. The unlimited satirical force of such a book would be equalled only by its objectivity. For nowhere more naively than in these documents does capitalism display itself in solemn earnest.' Walter Benjamin, 'Tax Advice', in *One Way Street and other writings*, trans. E. Jephcott & K. Shorter, Verso, London, 1979.
74 *West Australian*, 26 September 1997, p. 4.
75 Gustave Flaubert, cited in Walter Benjamin, 'Theses on the Philosophy of History', *Illuminations*, London: Fontana, 1992, p. 248. Benjamin is critical of the empathy with periods of history and their struggles that this 'medieval' *acedia* implies.
76 BH Warmington, *Carthage*, London: Robert Hale, 1960, p. 208.
77 John Albert Jansen, writer and director of *John Berger: A Kind of Grace*, prod. Manja Wilkinson, *Humanistische Omroep Stichting*, 1996.
78 'There still survived many thousands of people of Phoenician race in North Africa ...' Warmington, p. 208. 'The Romans, like most people in antiquity, attached little importance to the idea of race, and the destruction of Carthage did not mean that there was any attempt to root out Carthaginian civilisation.' Warmington, p. 209.
79 Bruno Latour, *War of the Worlds: What about peace?*, trans. Charlotte Bigg, Chicago: Prickly Paradigm Press, 2002, p. 25–26.
80 Tony Hewett, 'Mansell to lobby Libya over trade', *Sydney Morning Herald*, 30 March 1988, p. 10.
81 'Mansell wants Libya to Help Put Case to UN', *Age*, 14 May 1987, reprinted in Bain Attwood and Andrew Marcus (eds), *The Struggle for Aboriginal Rights: A documentary history*, Sydney: Allen & Unwin, 1999, p. 308.
82 Susan Buck-Morss, *The Dialectics of Seeing: Walter Benjamin and the Arcades project* (hereafter cited as *TDS*), Cambridge: Massachusetts Institute of Technology Press, 1997, p. 212.
83 Indigenous modernism could be defined as the inventive adaptations – aesthetic, social or technological – to the rapid changes brought by colonisation.
84 CP Mountford, *The Art of Albert Namatjira*, Melbourne: Bread and Cheese Club, 1944, p. 26.
85 Susan Buck-Morss, *TDS*, p. 164.
86 Deborah Bird Rose, *Dingo Makes Us Human* (hereafter *DMUH*), Melbourne: Cambridge University Press, 1992, p. 218. Rose writes: 'In saying that life is good, Yarralin people are asserting that every kind of living thing has its own place, its own origins, its own right to exist. They place no species at the centre of creation.'
87 Edward S Casey, *The Fate of Place: A philosophical history*, Berkeley: University of California

Press, 1997, p. 199.

88 Cited in Casey, *The Fate of Place*, p. 199.

89 Deborah Bird Rose, *Nourishing Terrains: Australian Aboriginal views of landscape and wilderness*, Canberra: Australian Heritage Commission, 1996.

90 Marcia Langton, *Burning Questions*, Darwin: Northern Territory University Press, 1998.

91 Asa Wahlquist, 'Land Management needs both cultures', *Australian*, 27 January 1999, p. 27.

92 Lesley Instone, Lines Across the Land, PhD thesis, Melbourne: Monash University, 2001, p. 115.

93 At the rate of 309 000 hectares per year according to C Miller in 'Bleak forecast for Life on the land', *Age*, 29 May 1999, p. 13; quoted in Instone, p. 89.

94 George Seddon, *Landprints: Reflections on place and landscape*, Melbourne: Cambridge University Press, 1997, p. 70.

95 WJT Mitchell, 'Imperial landscape', in WJT Mitchell (ed.), *Landscape and Power* (hereafter cited as *LP*), Chicago: Chicago University Press, 1994, p. 10.

96 Deborah Bird Rose, personal communication, 2003.

97 David Halperin, 'Out of Australia', in Gay Hawkins and Stephen Muecke (eds), *Culture and Waste: The creation and destruction of value*, Lanham, Maryland: Rowman & Littlefield, 2002, pp. 4–7.

98 Paddy Roe, quoted in Stephen Muecke, *Textual Spaces: Aboriginality and cultural studies*, Sydney: UNSW Press, 1992, p. 115.

99 Gaston Bachelard, *The Poetics of Space*, trans. Maria Jolas, Boston: Beacon Press, 1964.

100 Paul Carter, *The Lie of the Land*, London: Faber and Faber, 1996.

101 *Wedgetail Eagle Dreaming* (Arrernte and English), CAAMA, 1991, presented by Rosalie Riley, narrated by Harold (Ross) Ellis.

102 Helen Ross et al., 'Aboriginal Issues in Land Use', unpublished paper, Centre for Resource and Environmental Studies, ANU, October 1993.

103 David Unaipon, 'Narroondarie Wives', in *Paperbark: A collection of Black Australian writings*, p. 26.

104 ——, 'Narroondarie Wives', p. 26.

105 Deborah Bird Rose, *DMUH*, p. 73.

106 Marie Reay, 'A Decision as Narrative', in RM Berndt (ed.), *Australian Aboriginal Anthropology: Modern studies in the social anthropology of the Australian Aborigines*, Nedlands: University of Western Australia Press, 1970, p. 168.

107 Reay, 'A Decision as Narrative', p. 169.

108 Stephen Muecke, *No Road (bitumen all the way)* (hereafter cited as *NR*), Fremantle: Fremantle Arts Centre Press, 1996.

109 See Philip Morrissey, 'Aborigines and Corporatism', in Michele Grossman (ed.), *Blacklines: Contemporary critical writing by Indigenous Australians*, Melbourne: Melbourne University Press, 2003.

110 Ghassan Hage, *White Nation: Fantasies of white supremacy in a multicultural society*, Sydney: Pluto Press, 1998.

111 In *The Law of the Land*, Henry Reynolds uses the notion of 'terra nullius' in the history of colonisation, but this concept was not actually in place in the eighteenth century. Concepts of savagery and civilisation no doubt had a similar function for colonising purposes, but 'terra nullius' itself emerged only much later.

112 Jacques Derrida, *The Other Heading: Reflections on today's Europe*, trans. Pascale-Anne Brault & Michael B Naas, Introduction by Michael B Naas, Indiana University Press, 1992. p. xxii; Derrida's emphasis.

113 Jacques Derrida, 'Faxitexture', in Cynthia C Davidson (ed.), *Anywhere*, New York: Rizzoli, 1992.

114 Noel Pearson, 'Mabo: towards respecting equality and difference', in G Cowlishaw (ed.), *Race Matters*, Canberra: Aboriginal Studies Press, 1997, p. 218.

115 Swain, *APS*, p. 288.

116 Address to Aboriginal Philosophy seminar, University of Technology, Sydney, 2 September 1997.

117 Mary Graham, in 'Some thoughts about the philosophical underpinnings of Aboriginal

worldviews', *Worldviews: Environment, Culture, Religion*, vol. 3, no. 2, 1999, pp. 108–09, in which she says that, in Aboriginal philosophy, 'the custodial ethic is achieved through repetitive action' and speaks also of a 'modern rites of passage program'.

118 Deborah Bird Rose 'Taking Notice', *Worldviews: Environment, Culture, Religion,* vol. 3, no. 2, 1999.

119 ——, *DMUH*, pp. 218. Rose writes: 'In saying that life is good, Yarralin people are asserting that every kind of living thing has its own place, its own origins, its own right to exist. They place no species at the centre of creation.'

120 ——, *DMUH*, pp. 226

121 WJT Mitchell, 'Imperial landscape', in WJT Mitchell (ed.), *LP*, Chicago: University of Chicago Press, 1994 p. 5. This is the second of his 'Theses on Landscape'.

122 John Berger, *Ways of Seeing* (hereafter cited as *WS*), Harmondsworth: Penguin, 1972, pp. 106–08

123 For example, Kenneth Clark, *Landscape into Art*, 1949, quoted by Mitchell, p. 6.

124 Berger, *WS*, p. 108.

125 William Robinson, quoted in the exhibition *The Revelation of Landscape*, S. H. Ervin Gallery, Sydney, 11th January to 2nd March, 2003.

126 In Lynn Seear (ed.), *Darkness and Light*, p. 53, as quoted in Robert Dixon, 'Two Versions of Australian Pastoral: Les Murray and William Robinson', in Chris Wallace-Crabbe and Judith Ryan (eds), *Imagining Australia*, forthcoming, 2005, Cambridge: Harvard University Press.

127 ——, *Darkness and Light*, p. 52, as quoted in Dixon.

128 Lou Klepac (ed.), *William Robinson*, Sydney: Beagle Press, 2001.

129 Dixon, 'Two Versions of Australian Pastoral', p. 8.

130 —— 'Two Versions of Australian Pastoral', p. 11.

131 Bernice Murphy, 'Extending old traditions and creating new ones: The multiple strands of contemporary Aboriginal and Torres Strait Islander Art', in Margie West (ed.), exhibition catalogue for Telstra Presents the 18th National Aboriginal and Torres Strait Islander Art Award, 2001 Darwin: Museum and Art Gallery of the Northern Territory, p. 16.

132 Ross Gibson, *South of the West: Postcolonialism and the narrative construction of Australia*, Bloomington: Indiana University Press, 1992, p. 63.

133 ——, 'Enchanted Country', *World Literature Today*, Summer 1993, p. 475.

134 ——, 'Enchanted Country', p. 476.

135 Mitchell, 'Imperial landscape', p. 15.

136 Marc Treib, 'Reduction, elaboration and Yügen: The Garden of Saiho-ji', *Journal of Garden History*, 2 [9], 1989.

137 Joseph Mallard, 'Terra Nullius', *Law, Text, Culture*, Autumn 1998, p. 49.

138 Michel Foucault, *The Order of Things: An Archaeology of the Human Sciences*, New York: Vintage, 1994, p. xvii–xviii; Foucault's emphasis.

139 Louise Pelletier and Alberto Perez-Gomez (eds), *Architecture, Ethics and Technology*, Montreal: McGill–Queens University Press, 1994, p. 4.

140 John Rajchman, *Constructions*, Cambridge, Mass: MIT Press, 1998, p. 18.

141 Bernard Cache, in Michael Speaks (ed.), trans. Anne Boyman, *Earth Moves: The furnishing of territories* (hereafter cited as *EM*), Cambridge, Mass: MIT Press, 1995, p. 23.

142 ——, *EM*, p. 29.

143 Gilles Deleuze, *Cinema 1: The Movement Image*, trans. Hugh Tomlinson & Robert Galetta, Minneapolis: University of Minnesota Press, 1989.

144 Cache, *EM*, p. 3.

145 ——, *EM*, p. 23.

146 Translator's preface to Cache, *EM*, p. ix.

147 Susan Dermody and Liz Jacka, *The Screening of Australia* (hereafter cited as *TSA*), Sydney: Currency Press, 1987, vol. 1, p. 188.

148 ——, *TSA*, vol 2. p. 115

149 Phil Noyce, interviewed by Michael Carlton, Sydney: Australian Film, Television and Radio School, 1978.

150 PP McGuinness's 1977 review in the *National Times* seems to indicate Noyce's success: 'Noyce manages to avoid sentimentality and cliché, to produce performances from his

actors of an extraordinary degree of naturalness and to say almost everything that needs to be said by implication.' He goes on to endorse an anarchist line on the film, which will remind Australian readers of his current journalism that indicates how political sympathies can change: 'It is not surprising that the articulate activists among the Aborigines, especially those who have come to the cities, should tend to a hostile attitude to whites and that there should be a temptation to total and violent rejection of the so often duplicitous governments which pretend to be concerned for their welfare.'

151 See Gary Foley's *Koori History* website at <http://oliv.com.au/foley/ backroads/reviews /rvwindex.html>. Note that the Black Panther Party is seriously documented in Bain Attwood and Andrew Markus (eds), *The Struggle for Aboriginal Rights: A documentary history*, Sydney: Allen & Unwin, 1999, pp. 252–26.

152 ——, *Koori History* website.

153 John Emery, 'The First Day of Spring', in *Summer Ends Now*, St Lucia: University of Queensland Press, 1980, pp. 66–73.

154 Dermody and Jacka, *TSA*, vol. 2. p. 42.

155 ——, *TSA*, vol. 2. p. 115.

156 Another ending of the film was proposed but never made. In this rejected version, instead of one being killed and the other arrested by the police, the mates would make it all the way to Sydney Harbour Bridge, only to get the Parisienne stuck in a traffic jam. At this point the mates would leave the car on the bridge and continue on foot.

157 John Rajchman, *Constructions*, pp. 3–4.

158 Dougie Young, 'They Say it's a Crime', *The Songs of Dougie Young*, Canberra: Australian Institute of Aboriginal and Torres Strait Islander Studies, 1994.

159 See Mark Jackson, unpublished paper presented to a Colloquium for the Departments of Architecture and English Literature, University of Florida, Gainsville, May 1996, and 'Technology and Time: Key Notions for an Ethics of Architecture', *Constructing Identity: Proceedings of the 86th ACSA Annual Meeting and Technology Conference*, Washington, DC: ACSA Press, 1998, pp. 36–41.

160 Gaston Bachelard, *The Poetics of Space*, Boston: Beacon Press, 1969, p. xiii.

161 ——, *The Poetics of Space*, p. xix.

162 Jane Bennett, *TEML: Attachments, crossings and ethics*, Princeton: Princeton University Press, 2001, pp. 27–28.

163 James Corner, 'A Discourse on Theory II: Three Tyrannies of Contemporary Theory and the Alternative of Hermeneutics,' *Landscape Journal*, (Fall 1991) p. 131.

164 John Rajchman, *Constructions*, p. 67.

165 ——, *Constructions*, p. 9.

166 Strehlow, *AT*, pp. 7–8.

167 Marcia Langton, 'Certainty and Uncertainty: Aboriginal studies as the fulcrum of national self-consciousness', in Terry Smith (ed.), *First Peoples: Second chance*, Canberra: Australian Academy of the Humanities, 1999, p. 39.

168 Donald Stuart, *Yaralie*, Melbourne: Georgian House, 1962, p. 9.

169 ——, *Yaralie*, p. 10.

170 ——, *Yaralie*, p. 11.

171 ——, *Yaralie*, p. 11.

172 <http://www.capeyorkpartnerships.com>.

173 <http://www.abc.net.au/rn/talks/bbing/stories/s226372.htm>.

174 Paul Barclay, <http://www.abc.net.au/rn/talks/bbing/stories/s226372.htm>.

175 'You've always got to be worried when you hear the world "practical" from this government. It's like an anti-matter particle which obliterates the noun it's meant to describe.' Paul Keating, 'The Centenary of Federation: Beyond the Celebrations', paper presented at a public address, 1 December 2000, Sydney: University of Technology.

176 Robert Blackley, <http://www.abc.net.au/rn/talks/bbing/stories/s226372.htm>.

177 As quoted by Deborah Cassrels, 'Evolution of Manne', *Australian*, 29 December 2002, p. 16.

178 Noel Pearson, <http://www.abc.net.au/rn/talks/bbing/stories/s226372.htm>.

179 <http://www.capeyorkpartnerships.com>.

180 Jackie Huggins, 'Always was, always will be', *Australian Historical Studies*, vol. 25, no. 100,

1993, p. 459.

181 Quoted by Philip Morrissey, 'Moving, remembering, singing our place', in Michele Grossman (ed.), *Blacklines: Contemporary critical writing by Indigenous Australians*, Melbourne: Melbourne University Press, 2003, p. 193.

182 Strehlow, *AT*, pp. 143–44.

183 Stephen Garton, *The Cost of War*, Melbourne: Oxford University Press, 1996, p. 8.

184 Greg Dening, 'Anzac Day', in *Performances*, Melbourne: Melbourne University Press, 1996, p. 225.

185 Michael Taussig, *The Magic of the State*, New York: Routledge, 1996, p. 3.

186 ——, *The Magic of the State*, p. 195.

187 In 1997 a major report was published on the forced separation of Aboriginal families by government agencies for most of this century. Prime Minister John Howard created controversy by refusing to apologise for this injustice. See *Bringing Them Home: Report of the National Inquiry into the Separation of Aboriginal and Torres Strait Islander Children from their Families* (Commissioner: Ronald Wilson), Sydney: Human Rights and Equal Opportunity Commission, 1997. For a more interpretive history, see Anna Haebich, *Broken Circles*, Fremantle: Fremantle Arts Centre Press, 2000.

188 WEH Stanner, *After the Dreaming*, Sydney: Australian Broadcasting Commission, 1969.

189 Georges Bataille, 'The Sacred', in *Visions of Excess, Selected Writings 1927–1939*, trans. Alan Stoekl, Minneapolis: University of Minnesota Press, 1985, p. 242. 'The sacred is only a privileged moment of communal unity, a moment of the convulsive communication of what is ordinarily stifled.'

190 Stanner, 'Religion, Totemism and Symbolism' [1965] (hereafter cited as 'RTS'), in Max Charlesworth et al. (eds), *Religion in Aboriginal Australia: An Anthology*, St Lucia: University of Queesnland Press, 1984, p. 149.

191 ——, 'RTS', p. 149.

192 ——, 'RTS', pp. 167–68.

193 Brian Massumi, *A User's Guide to Capitalism and Schizophrenia*, 1994, p. 10.

194 'The initiatory rites all rose to a tense crisis that brought about ... a physical–moral–spiritual change in the initiates ... Rites of initiation existed as *disciplines*. They both *fashioned* the uncompleted man and *transformed* him into a being of higher worth.' WEH Stanner, 'RTS', p. 151.

195 Stanner, 'RTS', p. 168.

196 ——, 'RTS', p. 168.

197 ——, 'RTS', p. 168.

198 ——, 'RTS', p. 151.

199 José Gil, *Metamorphoses of the Body*, trans. S. Muecke, Minneapolis: Minnesota University Press, 1998, p. xii

200 Michael Taussig, *Shamanism, Colonialism and the Wild Man: A study in terror and healing*, Chicago: Chicago University Press, 1987, p. 328.

201 José Gil, *Metamorphoses*, 1998, p. xii.

202 Stanner, 'RTS', p. 165–66.

203 Ian Keen, *Knowledge and Secrecy in an Aboriginal Religion,* Oxford: Clarendon Press, 1994, p. 42.

204 ——, *Knowledge and Secrecy*, p. 42; Keen's emphasis.

205 Stanner, 'RTS', p. 152.

206 ——, 'RTS', p. 145.

207 ——, 'RTS', p. 155.

208 'A comparable difficulty affects our ability to grasp their jurisprudence, economy and polity. The categories and concepts are fatally pre-arranged. They are quite unsuited to the facts.' Stanner, 'RTS', p. 155.

209 ——, 'RTS', p. 155.

210 José Gil, *Metamorphoses*, pp. 126–27. Gil also notes: 'In certain stories, characters are petrified by a magic spell because they did not know how to translate the codes, for example they have not been able to go through an initiation procedure.' p. 318.

211 ——, *Metamorphoses*, p. 232.

212 Krim Benterrak, Stephen Muecke & Paddy Roe, *Reading the Country: Introduction to*

nomadology, Liverpool: University of Liverpool Press, 1996, p. 141.

213 José Gil, *Metamorphoses*, pp. 52–3.

214 Jacques Derrida, *Specters of Marx: The state of the debt, the work of mourning, and the new international* (hereafter cited as *SOM*), trans. Peggy Kamuf, New York: Routledge, 1994.

215 For Kierkegaard, according to Zizek, '*religion is eminently modern*: the traditional universe is ethical, while the Religious involves a radical disruption of the Old Ways – true religion is a crazy wager on the Impossible we have to make once we lose support in the tradition', Zizek's emphasis, Slavoj Zizek, *The Ticklish Subject: An Essay in political ontology*, New York: Verso, 1999, p. 115.

216 Tony Swain, *APS*, p. 233.

217 Mary Durack & Elizabeth Durack, *All-About: The Story of a Black Community on Argyle Station, Kimberley* (hereafter cited as *AA*), Sydney: *Bulletin* monograph, 1935.

218 Bruno Latour, *We have never been modern*, trans. Catherine Porter, Cambridge, Mass: Harvard University Press, 1993.

219 Keith Windschuttle, *The Killing of History: How a discipline is being murdered by literary critics and social theorists*, Sydney: Macleay Press, 1996, p. 24.

220 Elizabeth A Wilson, *Neural Geographies: Feminism and the Microstructure of Cognition*, London: Routledge, 1998, p. 22.

221 Tim Rowse, ' "Were You Ever Savages?" Aboriginal Insiders and Pastoralists' Patronage' (hereafter cited as 'WYES'), *Oceania*, vol 58, no. 2, p. 93.

222 ——, 'WYES', p. 94.

223 ——, 'WYES', p. 88; my emphasis.

224 ——, 'WYES', p. 89; my emphasis.

225 See Neville Green, *The Forrest Rivers Massacres*, Fremantle, Fremantle Arts Centre Press, 1995 and subsequent debate.

226 Bulla, in Bruce Shaw, *Countrymen: The life histories of four Aboriginal men as told to Bruce Shaw*, Canberra: Australian Institute of Aboriginal Studies, 1986, p. 181.

227 Ann McGrath, *'Born in the cattle': Aborigines in Cattle Country*, Sydney: Allen & Unwin, 1987, p. x.

228 Rowse, 'WYES', p. 97

229 Robert Smith, who worked closely with Elizabeth Durack during her Burrup period, speaks of her 'possession' by Burrup and of how he was the 'synthesis of several Aboriginal men I have known – there is a great deal of Argyle Boxer'. 'The Incarnations of Eddie Burrup', *Art Monthly Australia*, February–March 1997, p. 5.

230 Rowse, 'WYES', pp. 81–82.

231 Mary Durack & Elizabeth Durack, *AA*, p. 14.

232 ——, *AA*, p. 13, the dating puts Boxer's birth date in 1880.

233 Mary Durack, *Sons in the Saddle*, London: Constable, 1983, p. 379.

234 Bulla, in Shaw, *Countrymen*, p. 170.

235 'You wanna come down see'm corroboree to-night?' Nubbandah asks the white community. 'Im properly good one, all right.'
'Different kind?' we ask sceptically, being fully acquainted with the usual somewhat monotonous procedure. Mary Durack and Elizabeth Durack, *AA*, p. 60.

236 Bulla, in Shaw, *Countrymen*, p. 180.

237 Lommel, 1950, p. 23, cited in Rowse, 'WYES', p. 96.

238 Swain, *APS*, pp. 238–39.

239 ——, *APS*, p. 236.

240 ——, *APS*, p. 240.

241 ——, *APS*, p. 238.

242 Michel Serres with Bruno Latour, *CSCT*, trans. Roxanne Lapidus, Ann Arbor: University of Michigan Press, p. 45.

243 Bulla, in Bruce Shaw, *Countrymen, The Life Histories of four Aboriginal Men as told to Bruce Shaw*, Canberra: Australian Institute of Aboriginal Studies, 1986, p. 181.

244 Rowse, 'WYES', p. 82.

245 ——, 'WYES', p. 89.

246 Mary Durack writes that Boxer was usually MP Durack's travelling companion because, 'unlike the Kimberley-born Aborigines, he did not mind how far afield he rode, or among

what potentially hostile tribespeople. It could hardly be said that he was without fear, or had no reason for it, but he prided himself on being alert to every native wile and strategy, sleeping at all times "with one eye open" and a hand on the revolver on his belt.' *Sons in the Saddle*, p. 63.

247 Bulla, in Shaw, *Countrymen*, p. 181–82 (see note in Shaw).

248 Paddy Roe, 'Mirdinan', in *Gularabulu: Stories of the West Kimberley*, Fremantle: Fremantle Arts Centre Press, 1983, pp. 1–17.

249 'He'd open his guts just to show a trick and they'd all go back the same way again, with all the guts sewed up again ... That fella was wide open like when you kill a killer. You could see his guts hanging right down to the ground, his heart, liver, and everything.' Shaw, *Countrymen*, pp. 180–81.

'At Ivanhoe they'd say, "Ah, look out look out, emu comin through the ration camp", the old people's camp, "sendim up dog" '. There was no more emu, only Boxer. The next minute when they went out along a little bit you saw him. Well, where's that emu gone? ... Same as the white man doctor the blackfellers are just the same. Who's the powerful? Who's the strongest? The white man or the blackfeller, see, out of those two? To tell the truth the white man doctor didn't know what to say. I saw this done, you know, and I knew that. That's fair dinkum.' Shaw, *Countrymen*, p. 181.

250 Mandi, in Shaw, *Countrymen*, p. 39.

251 Durack, *Sons in the Saddle*, pp. 158–66.

252 Shaw, *Countrymen*, p. 183.

253 Rowse, 'WYES', p. 93.

254 Bulla, in Shaw, *Countrymen*, p. 80.

255 Deborah Bird Rose says that Boxer may not have been born; a story she has from the Yaralin says that he came out of a hole in the Pinkerton Ranges. Personal communication, 2000.

256 Derrida, *SOM*, p. 48.

257 Peter J Taylor, *Modernities: A Geohistorical Interpretation*, Minneapolis: University of Minnesota Press, 1999, p. 5.

258 Renato Rosaldo makes the same point: 'In the United States [in contrast to Latin America] questions of modernization do not enter the public realm of grappling with vital social issues. Such social issues as poverty and the shameful infant mortality rates among African Americans and the poor, for example are treated as neither signs of underdevelopment nor as failures of uneven modernization ... ', Renato Rosaldo, 'Foreword', Néstor García Canclini, *Hybrid Cultures: Strategies for Entering and leaving Modernity*, Minneapolis: University of Minnesota Press, 1995, p. xv.

259 Taussig, *MA*, p. 20.

260 Jane Bennett, *TEML*, p. 65.

261 ——, *TEML*, p. 64.

262 'Whatever position one takes up in the debate on the presence or absence of history (or of "historicity") in tribal societies, one thing is certain: tribal peoples only conceive their institutions according to a single pattern, finding any way they can to assimilate all innovations into the traditional frameworks of their inherited practices. This contrasts starkly with our modern societies, which, oriented towards the future, always stalked by change, construct project after project to resolve new problems that are always cropping up. And these problems result from the effects of free forces, that is, unmastered ones, that haven't been through the mill of technique and habitualisation. Thus, in a certain way, the answer that tribal peoples bring to the sudden appearance of novelty, could perhaps be exemplary for the study of our own societies, even if the nature of this innovation is not the same in both cases. But nor is it entirely different. Whatever the field of power, where tribal peoples have only a single model of thought, we are always looking for answers by multiplying the alternatives. This applies to the fields of economy, law, politics, education, psychiatry and culture.' José Gil, *Metamorphoses of the Body*, trans. S Muecke, Minneapolis: University of Minnesota Press, 1998, p. x.

263 Charles Taylor, 'Two Theories of Modernity', in Dilip Parameshwar Gaonkar (ed.), *Alternative Modernities*, Durham: Duke University Press, 2001.

264 Charles Taylor, 'Two Theories of Modernity', p. 173.

265 Dilip Parameshwar Gaonkar (ed.), *Alternative Modernities*, Durham: Duke University Press, 2001.

266 Susan Buck-Morss, *TDS*, Cambridge: MIT Press, 1997, p. 212.

267 See my entry 'Indigenous', in Tony Bennett (ed.), *New Key Words*, Oxford: Blackwell (forthcoming, 2005).

268 Christopher Norris, *Deconstruction and the 'unfinished project of modernity'*, London: Athlone, 2000, p. 7.

269 Norris, *Deconstruction*, p. 8.

270 André Gunder Frank, *ReOrient: Global economy in the Asian age*, Berkeley: University of California Press, 1998.

271 Robert JC Young, *Colonial Desire: Hybridity in theory, culture and race*, London: Routledge, p. 36.

272 Chakrabarty's gloss, *Habitations*, p. 156.

273 Charles Taylor, 'Two Theories of Modernity', p. 176.

274 David F. Noble, *The Religion of Technology: The Divinity of Man and the Spirit of Invention*, New York: Penguin, 1997, p. 9.

275 Michel Serres says: 'Our god is the machine, the technical object, which stresses our mastery of our surroundings, which regulates certain group relations or certain viscous psychological relations, but which suddenly plummets, like a lead weight, into the depths of a formidable anthropology', in *CSCT*, p. 141.

276 See the ABC television series *Bush Mechanics* (2001) for a fascinating fictocritical treatment of indigenous bricolage of automobile technology in relation to the social use of cars.

277 R Chandarasekaran, 'Australia's "Stolen generation" seeks payback: Aborigines want apology for kidnappings', *Washington Post*, 6 July 2000, p. A01.

278 6 October 2000, <http://www.abc.net.au/news/2000/10/item 20001005173505_1.htm>. 'Mr Ruddock has told two foreign newspapers that one of the reasons Aborigines are disadvantaged is their relatively recent contact with developed civilisations.' See also 4 October 2000, <http://www.abc.net.au/news/2000/10/item20001003180316_1.htm>. Thanks to Naomi Wolfe for bringing this information to my attention.

279 Peter Sutton quotes statistics to show that the government's claims to have made progress for indigenous social conditions are unfounded, 'The Politics of Suffering: Indigenous Policy in Australia Since the Seventies', n.d.

280 Bruno David, Marcia Langton & Ian J McNiven, 'Re-inventing the Wheel: Indigenous peoples and the Master Race in Ruddock's "wheel" Comments', *Philosophy, Activism, Nature*, no. 2, 2002, p. 36.

281 <http://www.abc.net.au/news/2000/10/item20001005173505 _1.htm>, 6 October 2000.

282 Bettina Arndt, 'A Culture of Denial', *Sydney Morning Herald*, 26 April 2001, p. 11.

283 Chakrabarty, *PE*, Princeton: Princeton University Press, 2000, p. 7.

284 ——, *PE*, p. 8.

285 It can be claimed that, independently of any assimilation policy, there is an unforced assimilation process in which difference is incorporated without anyone thinking much about it. For this to be true it depends on the validity of some general model of socialisation in which societies are becoming more and more homogenised towards a desirable norm. There is no sign that they are. Another problem with this position is that it unproblematically assumes the hegemonic power, or the attractiveness, of the 'norm' to which one would assimilate.

286 Francesca Merlan has noted that commentaries on Aboriginal claims about Coronation Hill are usually framed within a binary of 'tradition' and 'modern-ness', a binary that tends to separate the two from each other as if each component is entirely distinct and autonomous. Aboriginal modern-ness is thus understood here as involving either a loss of traditions or an invention of traditions, or both. For Merlan, however, traditional belief and modern contexts fold into each other in dynamic ways. Ken Gelder and Jane Jacobs, *Uncanny Australia: Sacredness and Identity in a postcolonial Nation*, Melbourne: Melbourne University Press, 1998, p. 71.

287 Stephen Muecke, *Textual Spaces*, p. 17: 'Aboriginal bureaucrat' becomes a monstrous term for both the Left radical consensus and the Right, for the former because of anti-institutional libertarian tendencies, for the latter because they want their natives pure.

288 Rex Battarbee, *Modern Aboriginal Paintings*, Adelaide: Rigby, 1971.
289 Alison French, *Seeing the Centre: The Art of Albert Namatjira 1902–1959* (hereafter cited as *STC*), Canberra: National Gallery of Australia, 2002, p. 131.
290 ——, *STC*, p. 133.
291 ——, *STC*, p. 133.
292 ——, *STC*, p. 133.
293 ——, *STC*, p. 134.
294 ——, *STC*, p. 134.
295 Quoted by Ken Gelder, 'Aborigines and Cars', in Sylvia Kleinert and Margo Neale (eds), *The Oxford Companion to Aboriginal Art and Culture*, Melbourne: Oxford University Press, 2000, p. 449.
296 Margo Neale, 'United in the Struggle: Indigenous Art from Urban Areas', in *The Oxford Companion to Aboriginal Art and Culture* (hereafter cited as UIS), p. 270.
297 ——, UIS, p. 270; my emphasis.
298 Cited by Margo Neale, UIS, p. 277.
299 Howard Morphy, *Ancestral Connections*, p. 304.
300 Morphy, *Ancestral Connections*, p. 182.
301 Ian McLean, 'Gordon Bennett's Home Decor: The Joker in the Pack', in Colin Perrin (ed.), *In the Wake of Terra Nullius*, Autumn, *Law • Text • Culture* (hereafter cited as 'GBHD'), vol. 4, no. 1, 1998, p. 288.
302 ——, 'GBHD', p. 290.
303 ——, 'GBHD', p. 289.
304 ——, 'GBHD', p. 291.
305 ——, 'GBHD', p. 191.
306 John Rajchman, *The Deleuze Connections* (hereafter cited as *TDC*), Cambridge: MIT Press, 2000, p. 40; Rajchman's emphasis.
307 Paul Patton, *Deleuze and the Political*, London: Routledge, 2000.
308 Gilles Deleuze, *Qu'est-ce que la philosophie?*, trans. S Muecke, Paris: Minuit, 1991, p. 90.
309 Genevieve Lloyd, 'No One's land: Australia and the Philosophical Imagination', *Hypatia*, vol. 15, no. 2 (Spring 2000), p. 37.
310 Cited in S Muecke, 'Cultural Activism, Indigenous Australia, 1972–1994' in Kuan-Hsing Chen (ed.), *Trajectories: Inter-Asia Cultural Studies*, London: Routledge, 1998, pp. 308–309.
311 Chakrabarty, *PE*, p. 6.
312 Patton, *Deleuze and the Political*, p. 19.
313 ——, *Deleuze and the Political*, p. 131; my emphases.
314 Meaghan Morris, ' "Please explain?" Ignorance, poverty and the past', *Inter-Asia Cultural Studies*, vol. 1, no. 2, 2000, p. 220. What follows is Morris's properly political analysis of the One Nation phenomenon: 'In reality most of One Nation's policies were antithetical to Howard's, especially their economic protectionism. However, by attacking Hanson's critics Howard hoped to secure for himself the votes of her admirers – a volatile mix of some committed racists, survivalists, flat-tax utopians and "gun lobby" extremists with a large and diverse constituency of "losers" from economic globalisation. The latter included some rural communities, residents of dying towns enduring bank closures and high youth suicide rates along with deeply entrenched unemployment, the no-longer mobile middle classes in outer suburban regions, and working families convinced that immigration increases job insecurity; all melded with a wide range of people feeling culturally disaffected by two decades of governmental feminism and multiculturalism.'
315 ——, 'Please explain?' p. 229; Morris's emphases.
316 Rajchman, *TDC*, p. 76.
317 William E Connolly, *Why I am not a Secularist*, Minneapolis: University of Minnesota Press, 1999.
318 Chakrabarty, *Provincialising History*, p. 113.
319 Patton, *Deleuze and the Political*, p. 137.
320 Benterrak et al., p. 245.
321 Michael J Christie & Bill Perrett, 'Language, Knowledge and the Search for "Secret English" in Northeast Arnhem Land', in Richard Howitt et al. (eds), *Resources, Nations*

and Indigenous Peoples, Melbourne: Oxford University Press, 1996, p. 57.

322 ——, 'Secret English', p. 62

323 ——, 'Secret English', p. 63

324 ——, 'Secret English', p. 63

325 Emmanuel Chukwudi Eze, *Postcolonial African Philosophy: A Critical Reader*, Cambridge, Mass.: Blackwell, 1997, p. 1.

326 David Mowaljarlai, with Jutta Malnic, *Yorro Yorro: Everything Standing up Alive: Spirit of the Kimberley*, Broome: Magabala Books, 1993.

327 Ken Gelder & Jane Jacobs, *Uncanny Australia: Sacredness and identity in a postcolonial nation*, Melbourne: Melbourne University Press, 1998.

328 Brian Massumi, *Parables for the Virtual: Movement, Affect, Sensation*, Durham: Duke University Press, 2002, pp. 12–13.

329 *Deleuze and the Political*, p. 41.

330 Stephen Muecke, *NR*, Fremantle: Fremantle Arts Centre Press, 1996, pp. 20–23.

331 Roman Jakobson, 'Closing Statement: Linguistics and poetics', in Thomas A. Sebeck (ed.), *Style in Language*, Cambridge, Mass.: MIT Press, 1960.

332 WEH Stanner, p. xx; Stanner's emphases.

333 As paraphrased and quoted by Diane Bell, *Ngarrindjeri Wurruwarrin, A World that Is, Was and Will Be*, Melbourne: Spinifex Press. 1998, p. 218.

334 Bell, *Ngarrindjeri Wurruwarrin*, p. 218.

335 Quoted in Bell, *Ngarrindjeri Wurruwarrin*, p. 219.

336 Bell, *Ngarrindjeri Wurruwarrin*, pp. 224–5.

337 Patton, p. 75.

338 <http://www.abc.net.au/rn/talks/8.30/lawrpt/lstories/lr311001.htm>

339 Badiou, *Manifesto for Philosophy*, p 33; Badiou's emphasis.

340 William E Connolly, *Why I am not a Secularist*, Minneapolis: University of Minnesota Press, 1999, p. 27.

341 AP Elkin, *Aboriginal Men of High Degree*, St Lucia: University of Queensland Press, 1977, p. 148.

342 ——, pp. 84–85.

343 ——, p. 87.

344 David Mowaljarlai and Jutta Malnic, *Yorro Yorro: Everything standing up alive*, Broome: Magabala Books, 1993, pp. 37–38.

345 ——, *Yorro Yorro*, p. 105.

346 Taussig, *Defacement*, p. 187.

347 *Sunday*, 12 February 2000.

SELECTED BIBLIOGRAPHY

Agamben, Giorgio (1993) *Infancy and History: The destruction of experience*, trans. Liz Heron, Verso, London.

Augé, Marc (1995) *Non-Places: Introduction to an anthropology of supermodernity*, trans. John Howe, Verso, London.

Bachelard, Gaston (1964) *The Poetics of Space*, trans. Maria Jolas, Beacon Press, Boston.

Battarbee, Rex (1971) *Modern Aboriginal Paintings*, Rigby, Adelaide.

Benjamin, Walter (1979) *One Way Street and other writings*, trans. E. Jephcott & K. Shorter, Verso, London.

Bennett, Jane (2001) *The Enchantment of Modern Life: Attachments, Crossings and Ethics*, Princeton University Press, Princeton.

Benterrak, Krim et al. (1996) *Reading the Country: Introduction to nomadology*, 2nd edn, Fremantle Arts Centre Press, Fremantle.

Berger, John (1972) *Ways of Seeing*, Penguin, Harmondsworth.

Bringing Them Home: Report of the National Inquiry into the Separation of Aboriginal and Torres Strait Islander Children from their Families (1997) Human Rights and Equal Opportunity Commission, Sydney.

Cache, Bernard (1995) trans. Anne Boyman, *Earth Moves: The furnishing of territories*, MIT Press, Cambridge, Mass.

Canclini, Néstor García (1995) *Hybrid Cultures: Strategies for Entering and leaving Modernity*, University of Minnesota Press, Minneapolis.

Carter, Paul (1987) *The Road to Botany Bay*, Faber and Faber, London.

—— (1996) *The Lie of the Land*, Faber and Faber, London.

Casey, Edward S (1997) *The Fate of Place: A philosophical history*, University of California Press, Berkeley.

Chakrabarty, Dipesh (2002) *Habitations of Modernity: Essays in the Wake of Subaltern Studies*, Chicago University Press, Chicago.

—— (2000) *Provincializing Europe*, Princeton University Press, Princeton.

Christie, Michael J & Bill Perrett (1996) 'Language, Knowledge and the Search for "Secret English" in Northeast Arnhem Land', in Richard Howitt et al. (eds), *Resources, Nations and Indigenous Peoples*, Oxford University Press, Melbourne.

Connolly, William E (1999) *Why I am not a Secularist*, University of Minnesota Press, Minneapolis.

David, Bruno, Marcia Langton & Ian J McNiven (2002) 'Re-inventing the Wheel: Indigenous peoples and the Master Race in Ruddock's "wheel" Comments', *Philosophy, Activism, Nature*, no. 2.

Deleuze, Gilles (1991) *Qu'est-ce que la philosophie?*, Minuit, Paris.

—— (1989) *Cinema 1: The Movement Image*, trans. Hugh Tomlinson & Robert Galetta, University of Minnesota Press, Minneapolis.

Dening, Greg (1996) 'Anzac Day', in *Performances*, Melbourne University Press, Melbourne.

Derrida, Jacques (1994) *Specters of Marx: The state of the debt, the work of mourning, and the new international* trans. Peggy Kamuf, Routledge, New York.

Donald, Stuart (1962) *Yaralie*, Georgian House, Melbourne.

Durack, Mary & Elizabeth (1935) 'All-About: The Story of a Black Community on Argyle

Station, Kimberley', *Bulletin*, Sydney

Eze, Emmanuel Chukwudi (1997) *Postcolonial African Philosophy: A Critical Reader*, Blackwell, Cambridge, Mass.

French, Alison (2002) *Seeing the Centre: The Art of Albert Namatjira 1902–1959*, National Gallery of Australia, Canberra.

Gaonkar, Dilip Parameshwar (ed.) (2001) *Alternative Modernities*, Duke University Press, Durham.

Gascoigne, John (2002) *The Enlightenment and the Origins of European Australia*, Cambridge University Press, Cambridge.

Gelder, Ken & Jane Jacobs (1998) *Uncanny Australia: Sacredness and Identity in a Postcolonial Nation*, Melbourne University Press, Melbourne.

Gibson, Ross (1992) *South of the West: Postcolonialism and the narrative construction of Australia*, Indiana University Press, Bloomington.

—— (2002) *Seven Versions of an Australian Badland*, University of Queensland Press, St Lucia.

Gil, José, *Metamorphoses of the Body* (1998) trans. S Muecke, University of Minnesota Press, Minneapolis.

Graham, Mary (1999) 'Some thoughts about the philosophical underpinnings of Aboriginal worldviews', *Worldviews: Environment, Culture*, Religion, vol. 3, no. 2.

Grossman, Michele (ed.) (2003) *Blacklines: Contemporary critical writing by Indigenous Australians*, Melbourne University Press, Melbourne.

Hadot, Pierre (ed.) (1995) Arnold Davidson, trans. Michael Chase, *Philosophy As a Way of Life: Spiritual exercises from Socrates to Foucault*, Blackwell, Oxford.

Haebich, Anna (2000) *Broken Circles*, Fremantle Arts Centre Press, Fremantle.

Hage, Ghassan (1998) *White Nation: Fantasies of white supremacy in a multicultural society*, Pluto Press, Sydney.

Healy, Chris (1997) *From the Ruins of Colonialism: History as social memory*, Cambridge University Press, Melbourne.

Huggins, Jackie (1993) 'Always was, always will be', *Australian Historical Studies*, vol. 25, no. 100.

Keen, Ian (1994) *Knowledge and Secrecy in an Aboriginal Religion*, Clarendon Press, Oxford.

Langton, Marcia (1999) 'Certainty and Uncertainty: Aboriginal studies as the fulcrum of national self-consciousness', in Terry Smith (ed.), *First Peoples: Second chance*, Australian Academy of the Humanities, Canberra.

—— (1998) *Burning Questions*, Northern Territory University Press, Darwin.

Latour, Bruno (1993) *We Have Never Been Modern*, trans. Catherine Porter, Harvard University Press, Cambridge, Mass.

—— (1997) 'Stenger's Shibboleth', Foreword to Isabelle Stengers, *Power and Invention, Situating Science*, University of Minnesota Press, Minneapolis.

—— (2002) *War of the Worlds: What about Peace?*, trans. Charlotte Bigg, Prickly Paradigm Press, Chicago.

Lloyd, Genevieve (2000) 'No One's land: Australia and the philosophical imagination', *Hypatia*, vol. 15, no. 2.

Magowan, Fiona (2001) 'Waves of Knowing: Polymorphism and co-substantive essences in Yolngu Sea Cosmology', in *Australian Journal of Indigenous Education*, vol. 29, no. 1.

Massumi, Brian (1992) *A User's Guide to Capitalism and Schizophrenia, Deviations From Deleuze And Guattari*, MIT Press, Cambridge, Mass.

—— (2002) *Parables for the Virtual: Movement, Affect, Sensation*, Duke University Press, Durham.

McLean, Ian (1998) 'Gordon Bennett's Home Decor: The Joker in the Pack', in Colin Perrin (ed.), *Law • Text • Culture In the Wake of Terra Nullius*, vol. 4, no. 1.

Mitchell, WJT (1994) 'Imperial landscape', in WJT Mitchell (ed.) Chicago University Press, Chicago.

Morphy, Howard (1991) *Ancestral Connections*, University of Chicago Press, Chicago.

Morris, Meaghan (2000) '"Please explain?" Ignorance, poverty and the past,' *Inter-Asia*

Cultural Studies, vol. 1, no. 2.

Morrissey, Philip (2003) 'Moving, remembering, singing our place', in Michele Grossman ed., *Blacklines: Contemporary critical writing by Indigenous Australians*, Melbourne University Press, Melbourne.

Mowaljarlai, David, with Jutta Malnic (1993) *Yorro Yorro: Everything Standing up Alive: Spirit of the Kimberley*, Magabala Books, Broome.

Muecke, Stephen (1998) 'Cultural Activism, Indigenous Australia, 1972–1994' in Kuan-Hsing Chen (ed.), *Trajectories: Inter-Asia Cultural Studies*, Routledge, London.

—— (1996) *No Road (bitumen all the way)*, Fremantle Arts Centre Press, Fremantle.

—— (1992) *Textual Spaces: Aboriginality and cultural studies*, UNSW Press, Sydney.

Noble, David F (1997) *The Religion of Technology: The Divinity of Man and the Spirit of Invention*, Penguin, New York.

Patton, Paul (2000) *Deleuze and the Political*, Routledge, London.

Pearson, Noel (1997) 'Mabo: towards respecting equality and difference', in G Cowlishaw (ed.), *Race Matters*, Aboriginal Studies Press, Canberra.

Rajchman, John (1998) *Constructions*, MIT Press, Cambridge, Mass.

—— (2000) *The Deleuze Connections*, MIT Press, Cambridge, Mass.

Robson, Lloyd, (1991) *A History of Tasmania*, Oxford University Press, Melbourne.

Roe, Paddy (1983) 'Mirdinan', in Stephen Muecke (ed.), *Gularabulu: Stories of the West Kimberley*, Fremantle Arts Centre Press, Fremantle.

Rose, Deborah Bird (1992) *Dingo Makes Us Human*, Cambridge University Press, Melbourne.

Rowse, Tim (1987) "'Were You Ever Savages?" Aboriginal Insiders and Pastoralists' Patronage', *Oceania*, Vol. 58, no. 2.

Seddon, George (1997) *Landprints: Reflections on place and landscape*, Cambridge University Press, Melbourne.

Serres, Michel with Bruno Latour (1995) *Conversations on Science, Culture and Time*, trans. Roxanne Lapidus, University of Michigan Press, Ann Arbor.

Shaw, Bruce (1986) *Countrymen: The life histories of four Aboriginal men as told to Bruce Shaw*, Australian Institute of Aboriginal Studies, Canberra.

Stanner, WEH [1965] 'Religion, Totemism and Symbolism', in Max Charlesworth et al., (eds), *Religion in Aboriginal Australia: An Anthology*, University of Queensland Press, St Lucia, 1984.

—— (1969) *After the Dreaming*, Australian Broadcasting Commission, Sydney.

Strehlow, TGH (1947) *Aranda Traditions* Melbourne University Press, Melbourne.

Swain, Tony (1993) *A Place for Strangers: Towards a history of Australian Aboriginal being*, Cambridge University Press, Melbourne.

Taussig, Michael (1996) *The Magic of the State*, Routledge, New York.

—— (1993) *Mimesis and Alterity: A particular history of the senses*, Routledge, New York.

—— (1987) *Shamanism, Colonialism and the Wild Man: A study in terror and healing*, Chicago University Press, Chicago.

Taylor, Charles (2001) 'Two Theories of Modernity', in Dilip Parameshwar Gaonkar (ed.), *Alternative Modernities*, Duke University Press, Durham.

Taylor, Peter J (1999) *Modernities: A Geohistorical Interpretation*, University of Minnesota Press, Minneapolis.

Unaipon, David (1929) *Native Legends*, Hunkin, Ellius and King, Adelaide.

—— (1990) 'Narroondarie Wives', in Jack Davis, et al. (eds), *Paperbark: A collection of Black Australian writings* University of QLD Press, St. Lucia.

Wilson, Elizabeth A (1998) *Neural Geographies: Feminism and the Microstructure of Cognition*, Routledge, London.

Young, Robert JC (1993) *Colonial Desire: Hybridity in theory, culture and race*, Routledge, London.

INDEX

activism, Aboriginal 83
Agamben, Giorgio 24
Ah Mat, Richard 104
Alice Springs 67
ancestors 16–17
ancients and moderns, quarrel 9, 25
anthropologism 175
anthropology 109–15, 162, 166, 174–75
ANZAC 29
Arrernte (Aranda) 16, 27, 97–98, 106
assimilation 143–45, 150

Bachelard, Gaston 13, 55, 91
Backroads 82–88, 91
Badiou, Alain 173
baiami 18
Balarinji 149
Battarbee, Rex 146
Battle Mountain 19
Bell, Diane 170–71
Bengal 26
Benjamin, Walter 9, 36, 134–35
Bennett, Gordon 94, 150–51
Bennett, Jane 26, 92, 133–34
Berger, John 43–44, 71–72
Berman, Marshall 138
Bhabha, Homi K ix
bodies 22, 50, 115–17, 152, 172
Bohemia, Jack 123
book, as artefact 37, 105
Boxer (*warramungu*) 120–31
Brennan, Gloria 62–63
Buck-Morss, Susan 47–48
Burn, Ian 147
Burrup, Eddie 124
Bush Mechanics 191n

Cache, Bernard 80
cannibalism 19
Cape York Partnerships 102–103
capitalism 102–104
Carter, Paul 33, 36, 55
Carthage, sacking of 43–44, 46–47
Casey, Edward 13, 50
Chakrabarty, Dipesh 8, 25–26, 137, 139, 144, 157, 161
children 16, 60, 69–70
  spirit children [*rai*] 54–55
Christie, Michael J 164–65
cinema 81
citizenship 150–51
Clark, Kenneth 72–73
coexistence 63
Coffie, Essie 85, 91
Colbung, Ken 41
commentary 27
compassion 43–44
connectivity 172
Connolly, William 174
contingency 4, 36, 79, 156
contradiction 79
Cook, James 5–6, 24, 46
cosmology 17, 70
country 16–17, 50, 167
culture, definition 10, 18
  as surplus 64–65
Cummings, John 147

David, Bruno 143
death 15, 16, 48, 59, 60, 64–65, 107–108, 118, 131
deconstruction 120–23, 130–31
defamiliarisation 61
Deleuze, Gilles 10, 79, 81, 155–56, 159–62
democracy, Indian 26
democratisation and modernity 145–46
Dening, Greg 11–12, 107
Derrida, Jacques 65–66, 120–22, 253
detachment *see* distance
distance, critical or reflective 18, 36, 61–62, 74, 111, 173
Dixon, Robert 73–74
djanba 124–27
djuluru 19–20, 131
Drysdale, Russell 72
Durack, Mary 120–31
Durham, Jimmie ix, 77

ecocriticism 53
ecofascism 50
Edwards, Coral Oomera 69, 75, 90
Elkin, A P 174–75
emotions 43–44
English, secret 131, 163–65
enlightenment 3, 9, 72, 165, 176
ethics 11, 88–90
exfoliation 115–17
Eze, Emmanuel Chukwudi 166

Flaubert, Gustave 43
Foley, Gary 83
force 146
Foucault, Michel 78, 89
Frank, André Gunder 138
French, Alison 147

Gaddafi, Colonel 46
Garadjeri 99–101
genius loci 80–81
Gibson, Ross 23, 77
Gil, José 112–18
Glassberg, David 30
Godard, Jean-Luc 85
Gomez, Alberto Perez xx
Graham, Mary 179n, 180n
Greenblatt, Stephen 18
Guattari, Félix 10
gurra [bandicoot] dreaming 27, 97–98

Haase, Barry 143
Haast's Bluff 56, 148
Habermas, Jürgen 137
Halperin, David 53–54
Hammond, Victoria 73
Hanson, Pauline 160
Healy, Ryan 89–90
heterotopia 78, 89
Heysen, Hans 147–48
historicism 144
historiography 39–40
history, indigenous 25, 33
  cross-cultural 27
  experimental 130
  Tasmanian 29–35, 46
Hobart Carnival 29
Honeymoon Gap 59
Howard, John 108
Huggins, Jackie 104–05
humanism 14
Hunter, Bill 84
hybridity 26, 106, 150

increase ceremonies 168
Instone, Leslie 52
interdisciplinary method 49
interval 78, 80–81, 88
invention, scientific 33
Isaacs, Clarrie 41–42

Jackson, Mark 90
Jakobson, Roman 169
Jenkin, Graham 32–33
Johnson, Vivienne 148

Kalkatungu 19
Keen, Ian 114
Kelly, Paul 3
kinship 16, 63, 70, 79, 121, 172
kirda 16
Kropinyeri, Harold 29
kurdungurlu 16

Lake Mungo 25
landscape architecture 80, 89
landscape function 77, 91
Langdon, William Chauncy 34
Langton, Marcia 38, 52, 98, 156
language 169
Last Post 106–108
Latour, Bruno 3, 26, 45–46, 121
Lattas, Andrew 162
Lausanne 81
Leopold, Aldo 17
literature, Australian 98–101
Lloyd, Genevieve 156–57
logic, alternative 79, 92
logocentrism 51
Lommel, Andreas 126, 174
wudu 176
Lurridjarra trail 50

Mabo 65
Macassans 18
magic
  in cultural studies 47, 49, 65, 108, 133
  in philosophy 159
  in writing 35
Mallard, Joseph 78
Mansell, Mick 46
Marxism 120
Massumi, Brian 110–11, 167
Meeks, Arone Raymond 148
Merlan, Francesca 192n
metamorphosis 116–17
milieu 10, 11, 105, 151
millenarianism 19, 176
mimesis 20, 27, 36–38, 40, 110, 133
Mirdinan 130
Mitchell, W J T 53, 71–72, 77
miwi 170
morality 104
Morgan, Sally 105

morphing 26
Morphy, Howard 149
Morris, Meaghan 160
Mountford, C P 46, 55
movement 4, 81, 110–11, 117, 146
Mowaljarlai, David 152, 166, 172, 174–77
multiplicities 4, 48. 160, 162
mulunga 19, 127
Munn, Nancy 15–16
Murphie, Bernice 74–75

Namatjira, Albert 47, 56, 146–47
Napangardi, Dorothy 74–76
Narritjin 149
native police 23
Neale, Margot 148
Nelson, Michael Jagamarra 148
Nickolls, Trevor 148
Noble, David 140–41
nomadology 162
Norris, Christopher 137
Noyce, Phil 82–84

O'Donohue, Lowitja 38
Old Bulla 123–25, 131
Olympics, Sydney 2000 64
ontology 17

pageantry, historical 30–34
Papunya painting 72, 75
Patton, Paul 156–61, 169, 171
Pearson, Noel 66, 67, 102, 151
performance 29–40, 131
Perkins, Rachel 3
Perrett, Bill 164–65
philosophy
  Australian 155
  African 166
posthumanism 89–90
power, Aboriginal 120, 128–29
  feelings of 170–71
pragmatics 11
primitivity 37–40, 133–34
  primitive postmodern 151
protocols, cultural 59
purity 25, 50, 100, 128, 139

race relations 83–90
Rajchman, John 79, 85, 155, 160
Reay, Marie 61–62
reconciliation 142
religion 109–15
representation, power of 18, 36
  critique of 110–12
responsibility 102, 145, 151
revolution 25
Reynolds, Henry 22, 40, 65

Rimbaud, Arthur 132
ritual 20–21, 26–28, 106–108, 111, 117–18
Robinson, William 72–75
Robson, Lloyd 29–30
Roe, Paddy 44, 49–50, 54–55, 68, 130
Romanticism 53, 76–77, 146
Rosaldo, Renato ix
Rose, Deborah Bird 17, 51, 53, 70
Rottnest Island 41, 80, 89
Rowse, Tim 121–29
rubbish 49–51, 53
Ruddock, Philip 142–43
ruins 135–36

sacred 109
Sandall, Roger 143–44
Santal people 26
Scott, Kim 105
Serres, Michel 10
sexuality, queer 61–63
Shoemaker, Adam 29
sovereignty 66
  and currency 38–39
Stanner, W E H 109–15, 170
Starobinski, Jean 12
Stephen, Ann 147
Strehlow, T G H 27, 98, 106
Stuart, Donald 98–101
sublime 50
Sullivan, Jack 124–25, 130
Swain, Tony 15–21, 67, 126–28
symbol 103, 111

Tasmania, *see* history
Taussig, Michael 20, 29, 37, 38, 107–108, 133
Taylor, Charles 135–36, 139
technology
  spatial 14
  as religion 140–41
terra nullius 13, 65
Third World 132–33
Todd, Frank Morton 34
Tonkinson, Bob 128
Torres Strait Islands 18
transformation 78, 89, 100, 108, 111, 130
translation 114, 138
Trevorrow, Tom 170
two-up 39

Uluru 9
Unaipon, David 29–40, 60, 170
universals 67–68

value 53–54
variability 79
verticality (versus horizontality) 81

violence 122–23, 150
vitalism 108, 117, 172

war 17
  Aboriginal wars 118–19
Wartpiyarri, Hector 60
waste 53
wilderness 48, 74, 51–53

Williams, Fred 72
Wilson, Elisabeth A 122
Windschuttle, Keith 121–22
writing 35–36, 61–62, 163

Yagan 39, 41–42
Yaralie 98–101
Yolngu 150, 164

Also published by UNSW Press

LOOKING FOR BLACKFELLAS' POINT

Mark McKenna

Winner of

Book of the Year NSW Premier's Literary Awards 2003

Douglas Stewart Non-Fiction Prize NSW Premier's Awards 2003

Australian Cultural Studies Award 2002

Blackfellas' Point, once an Aboriginal camping ground and meeting place on the Towamba river in south-eastern New South Wales, is the starting point for this poignant exploration of Australian cultural identity and history. From the familiar vantage point of Blackfellas' Point McKenna unravels his history of Australian identity: a history that resonates with a sense of place.

Through intimate, descriptive prose McKenna unveils the politics of injustice and oppression intrinsic to our cultural history and identity. In doing so he expresses the desire of both Indigenous and non-Indigenous Australians to reconcile this history through political and social change in the 20th century and beyond.

'A powerful meditation, in local and national terms, on the continuing meaning of dispossession . . . McKenna's book burns with a fierce and loving commitment to the place, its history and all its people.'
PETER READ, *The Age*

'McKenna's ambition is . . . amply fulfilled. To hear the silences, to see the absences, to be hopeful in awful circumstances takes a special sort of sensitivity. McKenna tells his true stories with gentle grace.'
GREG DENNING, *The London Review of Books*

ISBN 0 86840 644 9

FSC
www.fsc.org
MIX
Papier | Fördert
gute Waldnutzung
FSC® C083411

Zeitfracht Medien GmbH
Ferdinand-Jühlke-Straße 7
99095 Erfurt, Deutschland
produktsicherheit@kolibri360.de